ENEMIES AND FRIENDS

The United Front in Chinese Communist History

ENEMIES AND FRIENDS

The United Front in Chinese Communist History

Lyman P. Van Slyke

1967
STANFORD UNIVERSITY PRESS
STANFORD, CALIFORNIA

Stanford University Press
Stanford, California

Printed in the United States of America
L.C. 67-26531

To Barbara

Preface

THE PAST HALF-CENTURY of Chinese history is a vast revolutionary panorama, which presents peculiar difficulties to those who study it. The Chinese themselves, obviously the ones best able to order the contemporary record, have often found it difficult to do so because of their own intimate and overwhelming involvement in these very events. Others must work out a basic description of what happened before they can proceed to problems of interpretation. Thus, inevitably, interpretation and analysis must go hand in hand with the most elementary spadework, and often it is only at the end of a study that one has learned enough to know what questions should have been asked at the beginning. Moreover, the sources for the study of modern China are scattered, often difficult of access, and frequently uncatalogued.

But the very things that make the study of modern China difficult also account for its challenge and its fascination. One is aware of fresh and vital problems, unknown areas awaiting exploration. If we lament the fact that our knowledge of China during the past fifty years is fragmentary, we can also feel that we are adding materially to that knowledge.

During the years I have been working on this book, I have felt both the frustrations and the rewards of the study of modern China. That the latter so far outweigh the former is largely the result of the generous assistance and encouragement I have received from many individuals and institutions, both here and abroad. I owe a very special debt to my teachers at the University of California, especially to Joseph R. Levenson, Franz Schurmann, and Shih-hsiang Ch'en. Without access to the archives of the Bureau of Investigation under the Ministry of Justice, Republic of China, this study could hardly have been completed. Their willingness to allow me to use these priceless documents on the history of the Chinese Communist movement is an outstanding example of international intellectual cooperation. My thanks also go to Eugene Wu and John Ma, who aided me at the Hoover Institution, where most of the remainder of the research for this book was done.

Many colleagues have helped me in one way or another, and I trust they know how much I value their friendship, support, and assistance. I must record, however, my special and various gratitude to Dennis J. Doolin, John Israel, Carl Leban, Donald J. Munro, and Michel C. Oksenberg. I wish to thank the Ford Foundation, the Center for Chinese Studies at the University of California, and Stanford's East Asian Studies Committee. At various stages in this study, each provided generous financial and institutional support. I am indebted to Chuang Yin for the Chinese characters that grace the dust jacket. Finally, to my family, above all to my wife and to my mother, for their patience and for their faith in me, I am profoundly appreciative.

All views expressed herein are entirely my own, and for any deficiencies that remain, either in interpretation or in spadework, I am solely responsible.

L.P.V.S.

Stanford University
August 1967

Contents

Abbreviations Used in the Text

APD	China Association for the Promotion of Democracy
BDP	Bourgeois-Democratic Parties
CC	Central Committee
CCP	Chinese Communist Party
CEC	Central Executive Committee
Comintern	The Third (Communist) International
CPPCC	Chinese People's Political Consultative Conference
CY	Communist Youth
DL	China Democratic League
ECCI	Executive Committee of the Communist International
KMT	Kuomintang (Nationalist Party)
NCA	National Construction Association
PCC	Political Consultative Conference
PWDP	Peasants' and Workers' Democratic Party
RCKMT	Revolutionary Committee of the Kuomintang
UFWD	United Front Work Department
UNCL	United National Construction League

Introduction

> Who are our enemies? Who are our friends? He who does not know how to distinguish his enemies from his friends cannot be a revolutionary, yet at the same time it is no easy task to distinguish them. If the Chinese revolution . . . has shown such meager results, it is not the goal but the tactics which have been wrong. The tactical error committed is precisely the inability to rally one's true friends in order to strike at one's true enemies.
>
> Mao Tse-tung, *Analysis of the Classes in Chinese Society,* 1926

THESE WORDS, taken from the first sentences of the first essay in Mao's *Selected Works,* touch on a problem of cardinal importance to any elite group: how to deal with the vast majority of the population that lies outside the elite. This problem is particularly acute for a revolutionary elite attempting to overthrow an established order, and many such movements have never found a satisfactory solution to it. To be too exclusive is to risk isolation and impotence; to be too inclusive is to risk losing discipline and singleness of purpose.

On one level, this is a problem of tactics and organization. How can the elite group influence outside groups and individuals with a minimum of alienation among the outsiders and a minimum of compromise by the elite? How can the enthusiasms and abilities of outsiders be employed in the revolutionary cause? How should such work be organized? But on a more fundamental level, the problem involves the elite's conception of its role in society. It involves, ultimately, the elite's view of society itself. This is particularly true for a Communist party, since Marxism requires that all matters of policy at some point be justified, or at least accounted for, in theoretical terms. In the Chinese Communist movement, one of the ways of seeking a solution to this problem over the years has been one form or another of the united front.

In Western writings on China, the united front is usually given only passing attention. To many, the term refers only to the two uneasy alliances between the Chinese Communist Party (CCP) and the Kuomintang (KMT): the first from 1924 to 1927, when the youthful forces of Chinese nationalism were attempting to unify China; and the second during the late 1930's and early 1940's, when Japanese aggression temporarily forced all Chinese to unite. Few appreciate the role played by the united front in the civil war (1945–49) and in the CCP's exercise of power after 1949. Most people assume that during the civil war the united-front policy was of little consequence because so many Chinese had already lost faith in the KMT. As for the united front after 1949, it has meant mainly the window dressing that small puppet parties and a few aging public figures can provide. Running through these views is the assumption that the united front was a temporary—though perhaps useful—political tactic, but not an integral part of the Communist movement in China.

When we turn to the Chinese Communists themselves, however, and above all to Mao Tse-tung, we find a very different assessment of the united front. In 1939, Mao wrote, "The united front, armed struggle, and Party building are the three fundamental problems of our Party in the Chinese revolution."[1] He sounded the same theme ten years later, on the eve of the founding of the People's Republic, when he spoke of the united front, the Red Army, and Marxism-Leninism as the three principal weapons of the Party.[2]

Which view more accurately describes Chinese Communist history? I am convinced that Mao's view is much nearer the truth. I have chosen, therefore, to deal with the united front as a protean theme that runs through most of the history of the CCP and illustrates, I believe, some of its unique characteristics. I am not attempting a general history of the CCP, nor am I asserting that the united front is the most important aspect of that vast revolutionary movement. In tracing the development of the united front, I shall concentrate on the years from 1935 on, since it was in this period that the policy took definitive shape. The pre-Maoist period will be treated in much more summary fashion.

[1] Numbers refer to the Notes, pp. 279–98. Notes at the foot of the page are keyed to the text by letters. For complete authors' names, titles, and publication data on books cited in both kinds of notes, see the Bibliography, pp. 299–311.

Like some of the border regions established by the CCP, spanning the boundary between two provinces but not fully controlling either, this study straddles the boundary between two provinces of historical writing. Insofar as it deals with an ideological theme, it enters the province of intellectual history. But because the united front was first of all a matter of practical politics, there is no avoiding the province of the straight historical monograph—that is, the actual conditions and events out of which Mao's conception grew. Squarely on the boundary is an attempt to show that once particular events had led Mao to generalize his ideas on the united front, the generalizations gradually became an inseparable part of his thought and in turn influenced his handling of other specific problems.

In this last sense, the study approximates a case history in the dialectical generation of Chinese Communist thought: from practice to ideology and back to practice, which is surely part of what is meant by "From the masses, to the masses." But this process is not necessarily inevitable. In trying to understand what has happened, I am not suggesting that it had to happen in precisely this way. Some of the CCP's border regions, after all, could not be defended.

In the 1920's, united-front tactics were involved in the nearly disastrous defeats the Party suffered; but during the 1930's, as Mao gradually developed and refined his revolutionary strategy, a new concept of the united front emerged. Developed essentially on Chinese initiative, the united front derived from real needs and actual experience more than from theoretical considerations. Gradually, as I have suggested, it became an integral part of Chinese Communist thought and practice. What Mao has said, in essence, is that the united front isolates the enemy by winning the vast majority to the side of the revolution; then, through struggle, the isolated and now vulnerable enemy is destroyed. At all times the integrity of the Party ensures a correct revolutionary line, whatever the difficulties or setbacks encountered.

This vision of unity and struggle under the leadership of the Party makes up much of the content of Chinese Communist experience. And it is largely on the basis of this experience that the CCP has thus far exercised the power it won in 1949. One has only to look, for example, at Lin Piao's famous speech on wars of national liberation, in which he used precisely the categories Mao had so often invoked—armed struggle, a bolshevized Party, and a united front: "In order to win a people's war it is imperative to build the broadest possible united front. . . . A Communist Party must hold aloft the national banner and, using the weapon of the united front, rally around itself the masses and the patriotic and anti-imperialist people who form more than 90 per cent of a country's population."[3]

Yet the world changes, both inside and outside China. In recent years, particularly since the Hundred Flowers period in 1957, one senses that the united front has become more formalized and less directly relevant to the enormous problems facing the Party. When Mao linked the united front with the theory of contradictions within the people, he was in fact emptying it of much of its specific content by making it essentially abstract.

Internationally, the united front makes little sense, despite Lin Piao's metaphor concerning the "countryside" and the "cities" of the world. In so complex an arena the analysis is hard to make and even harder to apply. The inducements and threats that are so much a part of the united front are difficult for China to exercise internationally; perhaps more important, there is as yet no worldwide common goal to which the Chinese Communists can claim exclusive rights, as they once succeeded in doing with nationalism inside China. On the international level the united front has its principal significance as a part of the technique of wars of national liberation in undeveloped nations, which draw upon Chinese experience but may have no direct link with Peking.

I have suggested that the techniques of the united front grew out of efforts to solve particular problems; and that once these techniques were raised to a certain level of generality, they influenced the perception and handling of other problems. It seems that there is yet another step in the direction of increased abstraction. The greater the success of an ideological formula in handling the problems of an earlier period, the greater the tendency to apply it to the perhaps different problems of a later period. Once credit for success has been publicly accorded a formula, the prestige of its inventor is bound up with it. After this point has been reached, failure of the formula may not result in its abandonment, because renunciation might indict the leadership that had espoused it. This is what has happened with the united front.

At first, until about 1936, the concrete situation was the independent variable, and the united front was a dependent variable, a tactical effort to cope with events over which the Party had little control. Then came a period, roughly the war years, during which the real needs of the Party and a revamped united-front strategy existed in a dialectical relationship, affecting each other mutually. Even after 1949, the united front was still very useful as an analytic and operational approach so long as major sectors of Chinese society required transformation. It was consciously used in the land-reform movement, the "three-anti" and "five-anti" movements, and the socialization of commerce and industry. But after these changes were successfully completed, and after the traumatic failure of the Hundred Flowers experiment in 1957, the reversal of the relationship was complete, and the united front became a wholly independent variable. Domestically, it was no longer a tactic, no longer a strategy, but an element of "thought." The united front became one of the prescriptive lenses through which Chinese society was viewed, even though it no longer conformed closely to the realities of that society. In short, the united front underwent a process of ideological escalation that in recent years has rendered it increasingly formal and increasingly irrelevant to action.

This process of ideological escalation is also a process of integration, making the united front an essential part of the "thought of Mao Tse-tung." But there is a more personal sense in which the united front has become a permanent part of the Maoist outlook. Psychologically, it is a way for Mao to convince *himself* that he really is the leader of the vast majority of the Chinese people; that whatever the points of difference among the Chinese people, he has within him the moral force that can make the Party's goals—his goals—the genuine and enthusiastic goals of the masses. Given this view of himself, of Chinese history, and of the revolutionary process, Mao cannot terminate the united front without seriously compromising his legitimacy in his own eyes.

Chapter 1

The Legacy of Lenin

In the intellectual and political turmoil that followed the Revolution of 1911 and World War I, China seemed indeed an old world unable to die, a new world powerless to be born. Among the cross-currents of old sanctions and new theories, regional governments and venal parliaments, attempted restorations and student demonstrations, Marxism as a theory attracted only scant attention; but the forcible birth of a new world in backward Russia under the revolutionary surgery of Lenin and the Bolsheviks was another matter. The Russian Revolution was at first only dimly understood in China, but within a few years it was seen to contain two great lessons: Bolshevik party organization and Lenin's theory of imperialism. As interpreted for the Chinese by representatives of the Communist International, both concepts had important implications for the united front.[1]

Imperialism and the World Revolution

Lenin's theory of imperialism was the ideological link between Asian nationalism and international Communism. By the late nineteenth century, Lenin argued, capitalism in the most advanced nations of Europe and America had moved beyond the stage of more or less free competition among a large number of firms. In the interests of more efficient production and the elimination of rivals, enterprises tended to become larger in size and fewer in number. The result was a strong tendency toward monopoly and the formation of combines and cartels. (Lenin stressed this process particularly with respect to banks and other financial institutions, which, he believed, had assumed a dominant position because they controlled huge capital resources in the form of deposits, investments, and loans.) These enormous enterprises were able to accumulate capital on a scale so vast that a single country could no longer absorb all the money available for investment. The outlet for surplus funds was imperialistic colonization of the backward or unoccupied portions of the earth, particularly in Africa and Asia. This imperialism might or might not involve direct political domination, but it always meant the economic subordination of the colony or sphere of interest to the source of the capital invested there.

These conditions, Lenin believed, had profound implications for the international proletariat and the Socialist movement. With the "super-profits" drawn from its colonies finance capitalism could bribe parts of the Western working class, raising the standard of living in order to lower their revolutionary ardor. Hence, the labor aristocracy in England, the United States, Germany, and other industrial countries became, in a sense, shareholders in imperialism.

Lenin's solution to this problem was to call for national liberation movements in the colonial areas. If enough colonies could gain their independence, the position of the great capitalist powers would be much weaker. Without colonial super-profits, the ruling class would have to shut off the dole that had eased the misery of the proletariat, and the onset of the revolution would be brought nearer. Thus, for Lenin, the rise of nationalism in the East was one step in the destruction of the national state in the West.

In backward areas, national liberation movements could not be truly proletarian because of the relative absence of industrial capitalism. But they would have as their enemies imperialism and feudalism, the enemies of the proletariat everywhere. Whenever a native bourgeoisie existed in a backward area, foreign imperialism and domestic feudalism were *its* enemies too, for neither would willingly permit a native bourgeoisie to threaten its economic interests. In short, it was the common oppression of both the Eastern bourgeoisie and the Western proletariat by international capitalism that made an alliance between them possible.

Lenin believed that after bourgeois-nationalist uprisings in Asia had weakened the ruling classes of the major Western powers and thus accelerated the coming of the socialist revolution, the European proletariat would be in a position to help the Eastern peoples achieve their final liberation, a liberation that the undeveloped Eastern proletariat could not soon attain unaided. With European aid, some backward areas might even be able to bypass the capitalist stage of development almost entirely. In short, Lenin envisioned a spiraling revolutionary feedback, from Asia to Europe and back to Asia.

Yet at the same time, Lenin was a Bolshevik revolutionary, and as such he wanted the Eastern peoples to develop local Communist parties, parties with organizational integrity, a revolutionary platform, and freedom of action. To Lenin, the party always came first. He viewed alliances as a temporary expedient, to be avoided if possible, and if unavoidable, to be contracted on explicit and maximum Bolshevik terms. Certainly, no alliance was permissible if it limited his party's strength or freedom of action.

What, then, were the priorities in China? Was it the first task of the Comintern to build a solid Chinese Communist Party, capable of standing on its own feet and defending itself against present and future enemies? Or was it more important to strike a blow at the imperialists by strengthening and supporting the Kuomintang? The nature of the alliance between the CCP and the KMT would depend very heavily on which alternative was taken.

In the end, the Comintern tried to eat its cake and have it too, to develop a viable Chinese Communist Party *and* to strengthen the Kuomintang. It was argued that the CCP would eventually grow strong enough to take over the nationalist movement from the inside, ousting the "bourgeois" elements whom it no longer needed.

Early Comintern Views

In the West, the Comintern took a generally leftist and revolutionary line until the clear decline of European radicalism in 1921. A turn to the right was proclaimed at the Third Comintern Congress in the early summer of 1921, coinciding with the suppression of the Kronstadt Revolt and the start of the New Economic Policy in Russia. The European sections of the Comintern were directed to avoid putsches and to win over the masses by patient attention to such matters as wages and working conditions. Previously, Communist parties had attempted to gain power by splitting the labor movement and leading the proletariat directly into revolution. Now these parties were ordered to move more cautiously, and to consolidate their gains in preparation for a future revolutionary upsurge. Much of this activity was an appeal to the workers to abandon their Socialist leaders and follow the Communists in what was termed a "united front from below." But some room was left for a "united front from above," a conditional alliance with the Socialist leadership, provided the Socialists would accept the conditions imposed by the Communists—which in general they would not.

During 1922, some ultimately abortive efforts were made to erect such an alliance under the ambiguous rubric of "workers' government"—for example, the conference of the "three Internationals," the Second, Second-and-a-half (Vienna), and Third. Borkenau identifies Lenin, Trotsky, Radek, and Bukharin as tending to the right in problems of united-front tactics, while Zinoviev "saw the danger of right opportunism as the greater menace."[2] In any case, the Comintern was shot through with contradictory views about united-front tactics. It was out of these contradictions, differences of opinion, and shifts in the Comintern line that the first united front in China took shape.

As Allen S. Whiting has shown, early Soviet interest in China was reflected not in a single policy, but in a great variety of sometimes conflicting attitudes and policies. The two Soviet agencies most concerned with China were the Comintern and the People's Commissariat of Foreign Affairs (Narkomindel). In general, the Comintern was concerned with China's revolutionary potential and with the strategies that should be employed to realize this potential. The Narkomindel, on the other hand, sought "to win recognition from the Chinese Republic while reasserting Russian influence in the sensitive border areas of Outer Mongolia and North Manchuria."[a] This difference in policy orientation was paralleled by differences in geographical emphasis: the Comintern operated mainly in central and southern China (above all in Shanghai and Canton), while the Narkomindel dealt with the warlord governments in Peking. By 1924, when the Sino-Soviet Treaty was signed and Comintern strategy had taken shape, the differences between the two agencies were narrowing and they were working more nearly in concert. Since we are primarily concerned in this book with the evolution of the CCP's united-front policy, we shall focus our attention on the activities of the Comintern.

It is sometimes forgotten that when the Comintern first formulated its strategy for the non-Western world, the specific question of China was a relatively minor issue, and the Chinese Communist Party had not yet been organized. Even so, the question of priorities suggested above was raised very sharply at the Second Comintern Congress, held in Moscow in the summer of 1920. Two sets of theses on the colonial areas were presented: one by Lenin, the other by the young Indian Communist M. N. Roy. Lenin stressed the need for conditional alliances with "bourgeois-democratic" movements in the colonies. But Roy, who deeply mistrusted the Asian bourgeoisie, was opposed to such alliances: "Two distinct movements which grow farther apart every day are to be found in the dependent countries. One is the bourgeois-democratic nationalist movement, with a program of political independence under the bourgeois order. The other is the mass struggle of the poor and ignorant peasants and workers for their liberation from various forms of exploitation. . . . The foremost and immediate task is to form Communist parties which will organize the peasants and workers and lead them to the revolution."[3] After prolonged debate, the committee on colonial matters, which was anxious to pass on to other business, retained most of Lenin's conception, but appended

[a] Whiting, p. 6. A third agency that had some interest in China was the Red International of Trade Unions (Profintern). But its role was much less important than that of the Comintern and the Narkomindel.

Roy's alternative theses, glossing over the difference by describing colonial movements as "national-revolutionary" rather than "bourgeois-democratic." Lenin explained: "The meaning of the above change is that we, as Communists, should support the bourgeois movements of liberation in the colonies only if these are really revolutionary, when those who represent these movements would not oppose us in our efforts to educate and organize the peasantry and the masses of exploited people in general in the revolutionary spirit. When this is impossible, the Communists must oppose the reformist bourgeoisie."[4]

Thus the final draft of the theses incorporated, but failed to resolve, precisely the difficulty we have just sketched:

> All Communist parties must support by action the revolutionary liberation movements in these [colonial] countries. The form which this support shall take should be discussed with the Communist party of the country in question, if there is one. . . . A resolute struggle must be waged against the attempt to clothe the revolutionary liberation movements in the backward countries which are not genuinely Communist in Communist colors. The Communist International has the duty of supporting the revolutionary movement in the colonies and backward countries only with the object of rallying the constituent elements of the future proletarian parties—which will be truly Communist and not only in name—in all the backward countries and educating them to a consciousness of their special task, namely that of fighting against the bourgeois-democratic trend in their own nation. The Communist International should collaborate provisionally with the revolutionary movement of the colonies and backward countries, and even form an alliance with it, but it must not amalgamate with it; it must unconditionally maintain the independence of the proletarian movement, even if it is only in an embryonic stage.[5]

Roy's misgivings about collaboration with the bourgeoisie were shared by many Comintern members far more eminent than he. Zinoviev, Safarov, and others were consistently more anti-bourgeois in their statements than Lenin's 1920 theses. They had no theoretical objections to the theses; they simply had no love for "bourgeois-nationalists" in the flesh. This became evident at the Congress of the Toilers of the Far East, held in Moscow in January 1922.[b]

The Congress, designed as a counter to the 1921–22 Washington Conference on Naval Disarmament and Far Eastern Affairs, was attended by 144 delegates, most of them from the Far East. Among these delegates were representatives from the KMT and the CCP—the latter then very much in an "embryonic stage." So far as China was concerned, Zinoviev set the tone: he criticized the KMT and Sun Yat-sen for harboring hopes of support from America, and warned the young Chinese nationalists against any attempt to urge China's claims on Outer Mongolia. The CCP representatives did not even mention Sun or the KMT. The KMT representative, who called himself Tao, was allowed to make a "supplementary report" only after a special request and a floor vote. Tao attempted a rebuttal: the KMT had little interest in the United States, he said, and did not seek the return of Outer Mongolia. He maintained that the revolutionary programs of the KMT and the Comintern "on the whole . . . fully coincide."[6] But the Comintern delegates, especially Safarov, were annoyed by Tao's presumption in suggesting that the KMT and the Comintern were somehow equivalent. "We are not so naïve," Safarov informed Tao, "as to imagine this Party [the KMT] is a revolutionary Communist party."[7] Safarov also spelled out, in terms much closer to Roy's than to Lenin's, the proper relation between the working class and the Chinese bourgeoisie: "The Chinese workers must go independently on their own way, not linking their fate with any democratic party or with any bourgeois elements. We know perfectly well that in the immediate future there can be no sharp conflicts between us

[b] We note in passing two other meetings of this period, the Baku Congress of the Peoples of the East, held in September 1920, and the Third Comintern Congress, held in June 1921. China received only cursory attention at both, but it was at the Third Congress that the Comintern first analyzed the more advanced sections of Chinese society as being composed of four distinct social classes: workers, peasants, petty bourgeoisie, and bourgeoisie. This formula was later adapted by Maring to apply, not to Chinese society as a whole, but specifically to the KMT (see below, p. 16).

and these bourgeois-democratic organizations . . . but if they should limit the development of proletarian class-consciousness, we shall oppose them completely."[8]

Near the end of the Congress, Safarov summarized the Comintern position: "We give our support to this movement [the national democratic movement in the colonial and semi-colonial countries], as such, to the extent that it is directed against imperialism . . . and will do so in the future, but, on the other hand, we cannot recognise this struggle as our struggle, as the struggle for the proletarian revolution."[9] Safarov did not consider what should be done in China if anti-imperialism and the Communist-led revolution should prove incompatible.

Although the Comintern in Moscow, with KMT representatives in attendance, was thus endorsing a conditional alliance of equals on Bolshevik terms, events in China were about to move in the other direction. There, where debates were less significant than events, the situation tended to evolve in ways that Comintern headquarters and the CCP could only imperfectly control.

The United Front Takes Shape

In July 1921, the CCP was formally organized in Shanghai. This First Congress, attended by 12 delegates, issued no public statements, but drew up a rather simple organizational program and a series of decisions about "the objects of the Communist Party of China."[10] These documents make it clear that at this early date the CCP had a very "closed-door" attitude: its members were ordered to "sever relations with any party or group which opposes our program."[11] Furthermore, "toward the existing political parties, an attitude of independence, aggression, and exclusion should be adopted . . . and [we] should allow no relationship with the other parties or groups."[12] Indeed, the desirability of overthrowing Sun Yat-sen and the southern government was hotly argued, with a majority of delegates in favor and a minority opposed on the ground that the KMT, despite its errors, "more or less represented the new tendency for the time being."[13]

It is probably true, as Ch'en Kung-po affirms, that at this time the CCP decided to join the Comintern and to send a monthly report to the Comintern's Far Eastern Secretariat in Irkutsk. Two Comintern representatives were in Shanghai at the time, but their influence on the First Congress was probably not extensive.[c]

A year later, at its Second Congress (early summer 1922), the CCP issued its first public statements.[14] These documents show considerably more organizational maturity and understanding of Bolshevik Marxism than those of the First Congress. They also quite clearly reflect the attitude toward the KMT that had been expressed a few months earlier at the Congress of the Toilers of the Far East (Chang Kuo-t'ao, one of the CCP delegates to that congress, had presented a detailed report to the Central Committee of the CCP). The CCP was interested primarily in the labor movement, and was willing to form only a conditional united front with the Kuomintang. One statement read: "The proletariat's urgent task is to act jointly with the democratic party to establish a united front of democratic revolution to struggle for the overthrow of the military and for the organization of a real democratic government." It called for a conference, including "revolutionary elements of the KMT and revolutionary Socialists, to discuss the question of creating a united front against warlords of the feudal type and against all relics of feudalism."[15] There was no suggestion that the two parties be in any way amalgamated.

In the end, however, the CCP joined the KMT not as an equal ally but by way of dual party membership for individual Communists. The chief architect of this policy was Maring (Hendricus Sneevliet), a Dutch Comintern agent who had recently worked out a similar united-front tactic in Indonesia.[d] This may have inclined

[c] G. N. Voitinsky and Maring were present, but according to Chang Kuo-t'ao did not attend any of the meetings. The rather naïve simplicity of the organizational program would tend to confirm Chang. See Ch'en Kung-po, Introduction, pp. 18, 27–28.

[d] Isaacs, pp. 58–59. Maring had helped found the Left-Wing Social Democrats, a proto-Communist party. Individual members of this group had joined the Saraket Islam, a loose religio-nationalist movement in opposition to Dutch rule. As a result of this tactic, the Left-Wing Social Democrats gained a considerable mass following.

him toward greater reliance on the bloc-within approach than would have been the case with a Communist whose experience had been entirely European. At the Second Comintern Congress he had attempted to adjust Roy's views to those of Lenin, saying that while there might be some theoretical problems in formulating the precise relationship to be adopted between the Communist and nationalist movements, the two had no choice but to work together. To follow any other course was to play the "dogmatic Marxist."[16] Like Lenin, he advocated a closer collaboration than his Comintern colleagues, Roy, Zinoviev, and Safarov.[17]

Maring was in Shanghai in early August 1922 when Sun Yat-sen arrived there in defeat after his expulsion from Canton by Ch'en Ch'iung-ming, formerly his main military supporter. Shortly thereafter, Dalin, a representative of the Young Communist International, met with Sun and sounded him out about a two-party alliance. Sun rejected such an arrangement, but said, possibly with an eye to Russian aid, that he would permit individual members of the CCP and the Youth Corps to enter the KMT.[18]

Armed with this knowledge, and perhaps feeling that the demoralized KMT would never be easier to infiltrate and dominate, Maring called a meeting at Hangchow, apparently on his own authority,[e] to persuade the CCP to accept Sun's terms for the creation of a united front. Ch'en Tu-hsiu later claimed that most of the Central Committee opposed this suggestion. It is said that Maring had to invoke Comintern discipline to push the proposal through, but it is more likely that he invoked his personal prestige as Comintern representative, hoping he would be supported in Moscow.

Maring had earlier expressed his impatience with theoretical hairsplitting. Now he must have been equally impatient with the dogmatic arguments of these naïve and inexperienced converts. In an effort to give the proposed alliance, which he deemed necessary on pragmatic grounds, some doctrinal sanction, he applied the four-class alliance of the Third Comintern Congress (see above, note *b*). But instead of using it to describe Chinese society as a whole, he

[e] Isaacs, p. 59n. Maring told Isaacs years later that he "had no specific instructions," nor "any document in my hand."

applied it specifically to the Kuomintang: the KMT was not a class party in the Marxist sense, but a loose coalition of four classes—workers, peasants, petty bourgeoisie, and bourgeoisie.[f] Hence it was perfectly proper for the representatives of one class, the workers, to enter the KMT and ultimately gain control of it.

Under other circumstances, Maring might conceivably have been overruled by Comintern headquarters, since the alliance seemingly violated Lenin's order that Communist parties remain separate. But the temporizing attitude of the Third Comintern Congress was even more apparent at the Fourth Congress (Moscow, November 1922). Workers of many countries continued to look to Socialist rather than Communist leadership. As a consequence, the Comintern advised its Asian sections that they could ill afford to be so fastidious about their allies. It was more important to get access to the masses and win them over, even if this required apparent compromises. Even Roy had moved much closer to the position of Lenin's original theses, though he was still very wary of possible collaboration between the colonial bourgeoisie and the imperialists.

The leader of the CCP, Ch'en Tu-hsiu, was present at this Comintern congress, but he left the official statements to Liu Jen-ch'ing. Liu's remarks are wholly pragmatic:

> Starting from the premise that in order to exterminate imperialism in China an anti-imperialistic united front will have to be erected, our party has decided to form a united front with the national-revolutionary party, the Kuomintang. The nature of this united front will be expressed in the fact that we, under our own names and as single individuals, will join the party. The reason for it is twofold. In the first place, we want to propagandize many organized workers in the national-revolutionary party and win them over for us. In the second place, we can only fight imperialism if we combine our forces, the forces of the petty bourgeoisie and the proletariat. We intend to compete with this

[f] Earlier formulations had identified the KMT as a bourgeois political group, not a multi-class alliance. Maring's explanation goes against the Marxist dictum that a party is the political extension of a particular economic class.

> party in regard to the winning of the masses by means of organization and propaganda. If we do not join this party we shall remain isolated, and we shall preach a Communism which holds great and noble ideas, but one which the masses do not follow. The masses would rather follow the bourgeois party, and this party would use the masses for its own purposes. If we join the party, we shall be able to show the masses that we too are for revolutionary democracy, but that for us revolutionary democracy is only a means to an end. Furthermore, we shall be able to point out that although we are for this distant goal, we nevertheless do not forget the daily needs of the masses. We shall be able to gather the masses around us and split the Kuomintang.[19]

Thus, whatever the reluctance of the CCP to accept this decision might have been three months earlier at the Hangchow conference, it is clear that by the time of the Fourth Comintern Congress Maring's policy had been accepted.

Even so, it was not until January 1923, according to Pavel Mif, that the first formal instructions "to coordinate the activities of the Kuomintang and the young Chinese Communist Party" were issued by the Executive Committee of the Communist International (ECCI).[20] By this time, Li Ta-chao, and perhaps a few others, had already entered the KMT. Their action was almost simultaneous with the further improvement of USSR-KMT relations as a result of the conversations between Sun Yat-sen and Soviet representative A. A. Joffe in Shanghai in January 1923. At its Third Congress (June 1923), the CCP finally gave full and official recognition to the policy. The united front had taken the form it was to retain until the split in 1927.

Meanwhile, in Moscow, Lenin lay mortally ill; and the problem of priorities in China remained hidden to torment his successors.

Chapter 2

The Bloc Within

WHEN THE CCP DECIDED in 1922–23 to enter the Kuomintang and form a "bloc within," the KMT was at one of the lowest points in a history that had known many moments of desperate weakness. As a party, the KMT was a congeries of politicians and intellectuals united mainly by personal loyalty to Sun Yat-sen, the center of a series of highly unstable alliances with various regional militarists, and above all, a tradition. As a symbol of modern nationalism, it had promise that far outran its actual influence. Meanwhile, the nature of the party, plus Sun's apparent willingness to accept Russian aid and advice, made it seem quite likely that a combination of the CCP and the Russians working together would be able to reorganize and direct the KMT successfully.

Once the KMT-CCP alliance was formally sealed, the Comintern, besides developing the CCP, had to concern itself with the direct strengthening of the Kuomintang through reorganization, material and financial aid, and the use of Russian political and military advisers. This was done in the hope that the revitalized Kuomintang would become an effective anti-imperialist force, helping to drive the Western nations from their dominant positions in Asia. Of course, the Russian advisers would meanwhile be directing the KMT toward the left. At the same time, the Communists would be taking over the KMT from the inside, and would be using it as a base from which to organize the masses—not only for nationalism, but also for Communism. Thus the defeat of the foreign imperialists and the overthrow of the domestic "bourgeoisie" could be accomplished more or less simultaneously.

This plausible analysis soon led to the dilemma that nearly destroyed the Chinese Communist Party. If a growth in the power of the Kuomintang meant a corresponding growth in the influence and strength of the Russians and the CCP, then the Kuomintang should be made as strong and unified as possible. But an increase in its power increased its independence and its ability to suppress any attempt to subvert it. Therefore—and this was what made the dilemma so agonizing—the CCP became more vulnerable even as it became stronger. Critics of the bloc-within policy easily saw the risks, but were unable to show that a shift in policy could preserve the gains already made, or even materially reduce the danger. Defenders of the bloc within stressed its positive features, but were uneasily aware of the difficulty of consolidating and protecting the CCP's position.

By the time the contradictions of the bloc within became apparent, the KMT-CCP-Comintern alliance had developed a momentum and a logic of its own, and it seemed best to Stalin to continue along the same general lines. By this time, he had already committed his personal prestige to supporting the policy, and the attacks of his opponents, especially Trotsky, made it unlikely that he would change.

In the bitter atmosphere of charge and countercharge that followed the nearly total destruction of the Chinese Communist movement in the spring and summer of 1927, no one wanted to be identified with the unsuccessful united-front policy. Trotsky denounced Stalin for forcing the CCP into a lethal entanglement with the KMT. Stalin claimed he had always taken an aggressive and revolutionary line ("squeeze them out like lemons"), but had been sabotaged by a despicably weak-kneed Chinese leadership. Ch'en Tu-hsiu insisted that he had always opposed such close cooperation, but had been constrained by Comintern representatives and Comintern discipline and was now being made a scapegoat. All parties could with some justice defend themselves. No one had viewed the alliance with the Kuomintang as anything but a tactical move. But there were differences in emphasis, ranging from Roy's hostility to Maring's enthusiasm. Such differences, when translated into action, frequently appear afterward as wide differences in principle. Yet no one in Russia, apparently, had foreseen the denouement until it was too late to avert it.[a]

Nevertheless, it can be argued that the disaster of 1927 hid the successes that preceded it. The extent of the defeat may well have been a measure of how much was attempted. Other policies might have lost less by risking less. An earlier split with the KMT might have meant only that something like the defeat of 1927 might have taken place earlier than it did. The CCP's rapid growth from a membership numbering a few dozen intellectuals to a mass party seriously competing for national power was an impressive accomplishment. Perhaps no set of policies could have achieved complete success in so short a time.

The Early Weakness of the CCP

In February 1923, an event took place that did much to reconcile Ch'en Tu-hsiu and other laggards to the Comintern policy they had so reluctantly accepted. This was the February Seventh Incident, the bloody but almost unopposed suppression of a strike by the CCP-dominated Hankow Railway Workers' Union. The troops of Wu P'ei-fu, in control of the area through which the rail line ran, had little trouble in breaking the strike and smashing the union. They smashed more than the union—they also destroyed Ch'en's

[a] Brandt has shown that even Trotsky, who is often represented as more foresighted than Stalin, was far from certain about what should be done (Brandt, pp. 154–78). It is interesting to speculate on the course Lenin might have followed in China, had he lived. Brandt has suggested (pp. 15–16) that Lenin's Turkish policy in 1921 gives us some reason to think that he might have favored close collaboration between the CCP and the KMT. In need of an ally to the South, Lenin supported the nationalist leader Mustafa Kemal even after he became aware that Kemal was suppressing the Turkish Communist movement. Borkenau confirms this tendency: "But in practice, as certainly as the Mufti of Jerusalem and Abd-el-Krim, the chieftain of the Rifi tribes in Morocco, are not progressive bourgeois, equally certainly the Comintern allied itself with all anti-French and anti-English forces, of whatever social description." Borkenau, pp. 291–92.

hopes for a Communist-led proletarian upsurge of the classic Marxist type.[b]

The weakness exposed by Wu's warlord army was not simply that of the proletariat. The CCP, during the first four years of its existence, was microscopic in size. Manifestos pictured the Party as a gigantic figure at the head of a broad and endlessly forward-moving stream of humanity, but the facts lagged behind. In 1922, the CCP and the Youth Corps (later "Communist Youth" or CY) together counted between 200 and 300 members.[1] By the spring of 1925, the Party had only some 1,000 members.[2]

The CCP expanded phenomenally during and after the May Thirtieth movement. During 1925–26, the combined membership of the CCP and the CY reached 30,000 (by this time the CCP was considerably larger than the CY).[3] Growth slowed but did not stop in the months up to April 1927. Yet throughout these years the mass movement was growing at a rate beyond the CCP's capacity to control or even encompass it. Prior to the February Seventh Incident, when CCP membership was numbered in the hundreds, an estimated 125,000 to 150,000 workers in Shanghai, Ch'angsha, Hankow, Tientsin, and Canton were under Communist "guidance." By early 1925, these numbers had increased to some 540,000 workers and 400,000 peasants.[4] The task of expanding the CCP to keep up with such rapid developments was almost impossible. This was particularly true as CCP agitators and organizers fanned out ahead of the advancing forces during the Northern Expedition in 1926. Mao claimed 2 million members of peasant associations in Hunan alone in January 1927.[5] They were, he made it clear, taking things into their own hands. Other sources put the total labor movement at 1.2 million in mid-1926.[6]

Schwartz writes: "Trotsky and Isaacs, in all their attacks against the Stalinist line, tacitly assume that the Chinese Communist Party

[b] Schwartz, pp. 47–48. CCP influence in this area was in part the legacy of an earlier brief liaison between Wu and the Russians. See also Wilbur and How, p. 45. "Most of the labor unions," wrote Teng Chung-hsia, "so carefully built up during the previous two years—except for certain unions in Canton and Hunan—were crushed, and the Chinese labor movement entered into a period of decline." Wilbur and How, p. 47.

had achieved effective control of the mass movement."[7] This was not the case. The CCP was able to initiate and strongly influence the mass movement, but it was unable to create an independent force capable either of unified action or of withstanding determined military attempts to break it up and suppress it. Stalin had this fact in mind when he countered Pavel Mif's demand that soviets be established in the countryside by observing, "It would be ridiculous to think that there are sufficient revolutionaries in China for this task. . . . Anyone who thinks that some tens of thousands of Chinese revolutionaries can cover this ocean of peasants is making a mistake."[8]

The CCP suffered from two other weaknesses during these early years. The first was inexperience. Initially, of course, no one in China was a full-time, professional revolutionary. The CCP learned rapidly, but membership remained small until mid-1925. By the time of the split in 1927, the vast majority of Chinese Communists had been Party members for less than two years. In the summer of 1926, the CCP's greatest organizational defect was said to be the weakness of its cells and fractions at the mass level. The Central Committee observed that "although Party membership has increased in quantity, its quality has actually deteriorated," and cited lack of a revolutionary philosophy of life, lack of a spirit of hard work, and a tendency toward corruption as the most common signs of this decline.[9] Furthermore, the great expansion in membership took place just when it would most excite the suspicion and hostility of the KMT—perhaps inviting a counterstroke before the new members could be trained and hardened.

The CCP's other weakness was the absence of independent Communist military and political power. Until Chiang Kai-shek's coup on March 20, 1926, this did not seem to be a serious defect.[c] The

[c] In Canton, on the morning of March 20th, Chiang suddenly arrested, detained, or deposed a number of his rivals. Most, but not all, were Communists. Chiang justified his action as a counterstroke necessitated by the threatening action of the gunboat *Chungshan*, commanded by a Communist. A detailed account, written from a position very hostile to Chiang, will be found in Isaacs, pp. 89–110. Chiang's own version is contained in his *Soviet Russia in China*, pp. 37–40.

KMT's chief Russian adviser, Michael Borodin, had reorganized that party along Bolshevik lines, and continued to have tremendous influence. At the First Kuomintang Congress (January 1924), where the reorganization was approved, three Communists were elected to the KMT Central Executive Committee (CEC), and six others were alternate members. Furthermore, Borodin saw to it that a revolutionary platform was adopted and backed by Sun Yat-sen's prestige, despite the opposition of conservative KMT members who opposed the entry of the Communists.

At the Second KMT Congress (January 1926), the Communists improved their position: seven Communists were members of the CEC (one-fifth of the total), and 24 were alternate members. Ch'en Tu-hsiu and others, probably suspecting that Chiang Kai-shek was using the KMT Left–CCP coalition to oust his own rightist opponents, attempted to maintain as much independence of action as possible, particularly in the mass movement. But none could deny the powerful position that the CCP and the Russians had achieved. Communists held important posts in both the government and the KMT: they headed the Organization and Peasant Departments, and acted as secretaries or deputies in the Propaganda, Labor, Youth, Overseas, Merchant, and Women's Departments. Chou En-lai was the political officer at Chiang's Whampoa Academy, the military school charged with training a politically reliable officer corps. Chou and others were political commissars in the First Army, the KMT's most effective military force. Other military elements were also subject to Communist influence. Russian advisers held extremely important positions, sometimes virtually exercising command functions.

But after the coup of March 20, 1926, this situation changed drastically: Russian influence was curtailed, Communists were barred from the post of political commissar, and high CCP officials who held concurrent posts in the KMT were subject to dismissal. The dangers created by these moves were well understood by both the CCP and the Russians on the scene:

> There are two different conclusions. One is that Chiang intends to sincerely temper the incident of March Twentieth and to co-

> operate with the Left for the cause of the National Revolution. If this should be the case, it would be very profitable to us.
>
> The second conclusion is that Chiang's actions are intended to deceive his opponents for a second move. . . . *Should we adopt the second conclusion, we would have to be prepared to fight him.*
>
> Whichever conclusion we adopt, our basic policy is to cooperate with Chiang to the very end possible. We should not, however, overlook the second conclusion even if we adopt the first.
>
> The Chinese Communist Party is in agreement with this view and completely approves this basic policy.[10]

In fact, the CCP had no independent military force with which to oppose Chiang, and therefore had little choice but to placate him. Russian military aid and advice continued to go to the KMT because there was nowhere else it could go.

These hard facts—a small and inexperienced Party, absence of military strength, and a mass movement partly out of control—limited the alternatives available to the CCP.

The Changing Nature of the Alliance

Prior to Chiang's March Twentieth stroke, there were plenty of misgivings, but the bloc-within policy seemed to be working reasonably well. The year 1925 had been especially successful for the Russians and the CCP. True, the May Thirtieth strike wave had receded, the bourgeoisie had vacillated, and the troops of Chang Tso-lin had tried to suppress the General Labor Union (GLU) in Shanghai. But the very existence of the GLU—and its brilliant handling of the Shanghai strikes—was encouraging. The revolutionary base in Kwangtung had been made quite secure. CCP membership was growing rapidly. Chiang Kai-shek, though it was widely suspected that he was acting as much out of personal ambition as principle, had nevertheless reduced the influence of the right-wing Western Hills Faction (which was a challenge to his leadership as well as a potential threat to the CCP).

But CCP cooperation with the KMT was primarily a matter of individual relationships with no firm organizational structure. It was, therefore, dependent upon the good will of individuals, notably Wang Ching-wei and Chiang Kai-shek. When Chiang made his move, and after Wang went abroad in virtual exile, the KMT Left was, as the Russian adviser Nilov put it, completely empty—it had neither leaders nor masses.[11]

In the months following the March Twentieth affair, the official policy of the CCP Central Committee, backed by the ECCI, was: (1) to help create a distinct organizational and doctrinal left wing in the KMT, and to ally with it against the KMT Center and Right; (2) to expand the mass movement as aggressively as was compatible with continued cooperation with the KMT Left. There was strong dissent from various quarters, especially the Kwangtung Regional Committee of the CCP. The KMT Left, these critics said, was and would remain nonexistent; the mass movement should be fully unleashed, whatever the consequences. The Central Committee, though not certain how far it could trust the KMT Left, replied that if one assumed that there was no such thing, then only capitulation or split and struggle were possible.[12] The Committee also realized that to encourage the masses prematurely was both irresponsible and ineffective. Therefore, the core of Communist policy was to remain in alliance with the KMT Left and help it take over the KMT, to expand the CCP, and to gain a firm control over the mass movement. Because of the further concentration of power in the hands of Chiang Kai-shek with the start of the Northern Expedition, this policy did not appear particularly promising at first. But between July and October 1926, with Chiang busy at the front, the CCP was able to exploit the many rivalries within the KMT, and to make considerable progress in forming a coalition opposed to Chiang.[d] All this was in agreement with the line laid down by the Seventh Enlarged Plenum of the ECCI (November 22–December 16, 1926), namely, that the tasks of the CCP were to struggle

[d] Wilbur and How, pp. 392–93. It was at this time that the CCP began to refer for the first time to the "Three Great Policies" as the criterion of membership in the KMT Left. Earlier, neither Sun nor other KMT figures had singled these out for special attention. The "Three Great Policies" were alliance with Soviet Russia, alliance with the Communist Party, and support of the workers and peasants. In this form they are a CCP invention.

against the KMT Right, to help form a KMT Left and cooperate with it, and to criticize the KMT Center.

Apparent progress was made in limiting Chiang's influence among the military.[e] This was paralleled during the early months of 1927 by political action, climaxed by the Third KMT CEC Plenum, held from March 10 to 17, at which the Left-CCP coalition won a clear victory.[13] Chiang was still an important leader, and his actual military command was not touched; but his power in the KMT was greatly curtailed. Wang Ching-wei, on his way back to China, was now more important in the party structure than Chiang. Simultaneously, five new ministries were added to the National Government; two of these, the Ministries of Labor and Agriculture, were headed by the Communists Su Chao-cheng and T'an P'ing-shan. The Plenum also began preparations for the convocation of a joint KMT-CCP conference to iron out the differences between the two groups. Thus it appeared that the program of the ECCI and the CCP was justified by the successes won from October 1926 to March 1927. But the ground was shifting: it was now not so much a matter of conciliating Chiang Kai-shek as of adjusting to those who seemed to have the best chance of controlling him.

If these apparent gains had definitely increased the CCP's independent strength, perhaps the mass movement could have been pushed at the same time. But just at the moment when it was so important to cultivate the strength of the Left as a check against the military power of the Right, agrarian radicalism and the labor movement appeared to jeopardize both the position of the KMT Left and the CCP's relation to it. The agrarian revolution endangered the land tax and alienated the officer corps of the armed

[e] A military alliance designed to isolate Chiang was moving forward under T'ang Sheng-chih, whose Alumni Association of Four Military Academies (led by the Paoting Clique) was a counterweight to Chiang's Whampoa Alumni Association. When Chiang began his move against Shanghai, his position was less secure than previously. T'ang reportedly had commitments from Chang Fa-k'uei's Fourth Army, Ch'en Ming-shu's Eleventh Army, Chu P'ei-te's Third Army, the Ninth and Tenth Armies, and Li Tsung-jen. The First and Sixth Armies were still loyal to Chiang, but there was some question even there, particularly in the First Army's First Division, commanded by Hsüeh Yüeh.

forces, many of whom came from rural landowning backgrounds. Labor agitation in the larger cities—e.g., strikes in industries such as transport, communications, and armaments—frequently had a disruptive effect on the economy, which was inimical to the goals of the CCP. Economic conditions were particularly bad in Wuhan.[f] As the Central Committee put it, "The greatest danger is that the mass movement is developing toward the Left, while the political and military authorities, seeing the swift growth of the mass movement, are seized with panic and begin to incline to the Right. Should these extreme tendencies continue to develop in the future, the cleavage between the masses and the government will deepen, and in the end the Red united front will be demolished, and the whole national government will be endangered."[14] This was exactly the thought behind Stalin's telegram of October 1926, which directed the CCP to hold back the peasant movement so as not to lose the support of military leaders.[15]

Nevertheless, most theoretical pronouncements ignored the requirements of practical politics and retained a consistently radical tone. The Theses of the Seventh ECCI Plenum, for example, included the following declaration:

> The fear that the aggravation of the class struggle in the countryside will weaken the united anti-imperialist front is baseless. . . . Not to approach the agrarian question boldly by supporting all the economic demands of the peasant masses is positively dangerous for the revolution. To refuse to assign to the agrarian revolution a prominent place in the national-liberation movement, for fear of alienating the dubious and disloyal cooperation of a section of the capitalist class, is wrong. This is not the revolutionary policy of the proletariat. The Communist Party must be free of such mistakes.[16]

Thus the call to step up the peasant movement was combined with a demand for continued collaboration with groups that wanted to slow it down. One policy overrated the CCP's ability to control

[f] Isaacs, p. 123. Isaacs here notes that 535 strikes were recorded in 1926, with the trend continuing in early 1927.

the action of the masses and thereby create independent strength. The other policy exaggerated the CCP's ability to dominate and direct its bourgeois political and military allies. T'an P'ing-shan remarked ruefully, "We must safeguard the interests of the peasantry, but on the other hand we must maintain and solidify the united front of the national-revolutionary movement. In so contradictory a situation, it is far from easy to maintain a correct tactical line."[17]

It was indeed difficult. In this period, the united-front policy of the Comintern could give no consistent guidelines because it was, in fact, self-contradictory. It proclaimed two enemies—foreign imperialism and domestic non-Communist rivals—but the demands of one struggle were inconsistent with those of the other. This meant the establishment of priorities. In an initial effort to achieve its anti-imperialist goals, the Comintern in effect assigned second priority to the CCP, yet it was unable or unwilling to recognize the consequences this entailed. The inconsistency might be disguised by equivocal statement, but this did not change the harsh realities of the situation. So great was the momentum of this policy, and apparently so limited were the alternatives to it, that even after Chiang began his "purification movement" the same contradictory arguments were used to continue the alliance with the KMT Left in Wuhan—with very similar ultimate results.

One last indirect but important consequence of these indecisive policies was that they seriously compromised the CCP's appeal to nationalism. If the liberation movements in the colonies were to be based on an alliance of the international proletariat with local nationalists, then the colonial Communist parties were obviously a part of the international component and could only appeal to nationalism by associating themselves with "bourgeois" nationalists. Yet the Comintern demanded a secondary attack on these same nationalists. As long as the KMT appeared to be unifying China and improving her position in the world, the Communist charge that the KMT was really selling out to the imperialists did not ring true for many Chinese. And the Kuomintang could countercharge that on Comintern orders the CCP was dedicated to the overthrow of the KMT, and not to the achievement of China's national objectives.

Ironically, the Chinese Communist leaders were condemned in China as anti-nationalist subversives at the same time that they were condemned by Moscow for capitulating to the Kuomintang. In a sense, both charges were true. Although the CCP won impressive victories, it had no real chance of attaining its goals as long as it acted in accord with the Comintern conception of a tactical, international, and revolutionary united front. The bloc within, a united front from above, was essentially a Russian formulation accepted by a weak and unarmed Chinese Communist Party. Obviously, a new approach was necessary.

Chapter 3

The United Front from Below

The General Nature of the United Front from Below

In Comintern practice the united front from below usually implied a long-term struggle to win the masses—especially the workers—away from their non-Communist leaders to the Communist side. In time, the workers would realize that only the Communists were prepared to fight for the immediate interests of the proletariat—wages, working conditions, length of working day, etc. Understanding this, they would repudiate false leaders who presumed to speak in their interests but actually served the exploiting classes. The Communists would then gradually organize and steel this mass base as a prelude to the revolution. Until this happened, however, economic strikes were to replace purely political strikes, and rash, adventurist actions—above all, putsches—were to be carefully avoided.

The ideal time for a united front from below was thus a period of acute economic distress, when the proletariat would despair of any betterment of its condition through conventional, non-Communist organizations. Yet the revolution had to appear to be still some distance in the future. If the working classes seemed to be in an immediately revolutionary mood, then obviously a protracted united front from below would be neither necessary nor desirable. As Schwartz points out, "In a period of 'revolutionary upsurge,' one does not confine one's attention to economic demands."[1]

In the West, the united front from below was aimed against the Socialist leadership of the labor movement. The Socialists were viewed as nothing more than the left wing of the bourgeoisie, while the fascists constituted its right wing. Thus the Socialists were simultaneously betrayers of the proletariat and obedient servants of the fascists. Socialism, in short, was social-fascism. The onset of the depression reinforced the Kremlin's belief that the undeniably suffering workers of many countries would become increasingly leftist and revolutionary. If capitalism was moribund, as the Comintern claimed, then obviously nothing was to be gained by cooperating with those who were allied to the dying order. Instead, Communists were directed to expose Socialists as the disguised fascists they really were. Non-Communist unions were not to be shunned as reactionary, but infiltrated, in order to win the workers away from their present leaders. Economic demands were the immediate tactic, but political organization was the goal.

In worldwide terms, the Comintern's shift toward united fronts from below took place between the fall of 1927 and the summer of 1929. Factional struggles in Russia played a very important part in this shift: having silenced or removed the remaining Trotskyite opposition, Stalin then ousted the Right Opposition (led by Bukharin, the head of the Comintern) by this move to the Left, and hence gained complete control over the Russian Party, the Comintern, and the national Comintern sections. When the Sixth Comintern Congress met in the summer of 1928, the Stalinist faction took final and definitive control of the Comintern machinery and increased its control of the national Communist parties. But at this time there was still "a certain balance between Right and Left, between Bukharin and Stalin . . . though the issue could not be doubtful."[2] Therefore, the adoption of the united front from below was not so clear-cut as it later became.[a] At the Sixth Congress, the Stalinists held that the period of capitalist stabilization was coming to an end, and that a new round of imperialist wars was approaching. The revolution, too, was drawing nearer, but was not really imminent. This formulation was perfectly suited to the exclusive use of a united front from below.

[a] In the Tenth ECCI Plenum (July 1929), the Eleventh Plenum (March–April 1931), and the Twelfth Plenum (September 1932). See Degras, III, *passim*.

Summary of Events in China, 1927–1935

Prior to the debacle of 1927, Trotsky had argued that the workers and peasants in China were ready to rise, and had demanded that Stalin issue the call for radical action and the formation of soviets. Stalin retorted that the time was not yet ripe, and insisted that the CCP preserve its alliance with the KMT. By late 1927, however, the two men had changed roles. Trotsky now charged that the revolutionary tide in China was ebbing because of Stalin's criminal errors. Stalin, on the other hand, claimed that the situation was more promising than ever.

The task of exploiting the rising tide fell initially to Ch'ü Ch'iu-pai, a young, sensitively introspective Communist who had joined the Party in 1922 in Russia, where he had been sent as a newspaper correspondent. Near the end of 1926 and early in 1927, he had been openly critical of Ch'en Tu-hsiu's handling of the alliance with the KMT. With the support of the new Comintern representative, Besso Lominadze, Ch'ü and other members of the so-called "left opposition" deposed Ch'en in August 1927, and Ch'ü was moved into a position of leadership for which he was not particularly well fitted. He then began implementing a Comintern policy that called for urban insurrections,[b] to be coordinated with agrarian uprisings and supported by Communist military units (orders for the formation of such units had now, belatedly, been issued). In such a "revolutionary" situation, there was, of course, little time or inclination to carry out a united front from below; nor is there evidence that Ch'ü was directed to do so.

The stories of the abysmal and bloody failures that ensued—at Nanch'ang, at Swatow, and above all at Canton—are well-known.

[b] Schwartz has shown that although both Comintern and CCP manifestos stressed the importance of the agrarian question and (after September) the formation of rural soviets, the main thrust of the insurrections was to be through the cities and under the leadership of the proletariat. (Schwartz, pp. 94–96.) Further evidence of the urban orientation of Comintern–CCP policy in this period is to be found in the reaction to Mao's Autumn Harvest Uprisings, which were condemned as purely peasant in nature. See Schwartz, pp. 100–102, and Rue, pp. 73–81.

Ch'ü's failure to succeed where success was impossible resulted in his ouster shortly after the beginning of 1928. Meanwhile, Stalin had somehow to account for these failures. He accomplished this considerable feat by removing those he could not convince; his argument (prefiguring the position of the Sixth Comintern Congress) was that in China a general upsurge had encountered a temporary but not decisive setback, a momentary trough between two revolutionary waves. This was a somewhat less optimistic view of prospects in China than had been held during the second half of 1927; but it provided Stalin with an all-purpose metaphor. He would be right whatever happened: if the Chinese revolution developed, the new upsurge was approaching; if it did not, China was still momentarily becalmed. In either case, failure could be attributed only to errors in implementation, not to the overall theory. The problem with this line was that it did not indicate what should be done, and when.

If Ch'ü Ch'iu-pai had been wiped out on the crest of the wave, his successor, Li Li-san, was swamped in the trough. Li, who took over from Ch'ü in mid-1928, was a tough and resourceful, but autocratic, Communist leader who had been prominent in the organization of the labor movement. One of the heroes of the May Thirtieth movement in Shanghai, he too had been opposed to the policies that had been forced on Ch'en Tu-hsiu. With his rise to power, Li was directed to avoid putsches; to organize the urban proletariat carefully but rapidly; and to promote, under working-class leadership, the kind of rural soviets and Red Army that Mao Tse-tung and Chu Teh were creating in Kiangsi. As before, the cities were to be the focus and the countryside an important auxiliary. When sufficient progress had been made—and when the revolutionary high tide had arrived—the CCP would have the strength to achieve "initial successes in one or several provinces."[c] These successes would be

[c] This was the language of the Sixth CCP Congress, held in Moscow simultaneously with the Sixth Comintern Congress. The phraseology reflected the realization that China was very greatly fragmented, and that nationwide success could not be expected all at once.

gained by simultaneous rural (Red Army) and urban uprisings. Rural forces were to converge on key cities to assist the revolutionary workers; then the democratic dictatorship of workers and peasants would extend its influence throughout the province.

It was Li Li-san's abortive attempt to implement this policy that jeopardized his Comintern support and enabled his many enemies in the CCP to engineer his downfall. In late July 1930, when Chiang Kai-shek was heavily engaged in the north against the warlord alliance of Feng Yü-hsiang and Yen Hsi-shan, Li ordered the seizure of Ch'angsha, the capital of Hunan province. The city was occupied for a scant five days, and was then retaken by White forces. Li managed to keep his position until the end of November, when he resigned from the Political Bureau and departed for Moscow.

During the four years between Li Li-san's downfall and the rise of Mao Tse-tung, the Central Committee (as distinct from the soviet areas, where Mao and Chu Teh had their principal strength) was dominated by the so-called "Returned Students," or "Twenty-eight Bolsheviks." These young Communists had spent most of the years since 1926 at Sun Yat-sen University in Moscow. They owed their position in the Party largely, if not entirely, to the backing of their mentor, Pavel Mif. They were viewed as having a scholastic understanding of Marxism but very little practical revolutionary experience; and they were bitterly resented by those who had been on the firing line in China during the previous years. Their leader was Ch'en Shao-yü (Wang Ming), only 23 years old when he took charge of the Party. Until 1932, Ch'en was Secretary-General of the CCP; then he left for Moscow, where he became one of the Comintern's principal spokesmen on the colonial areas. Ch'in Pang-hsien (Po Ku), another of the group, succeeded Ch'en as Secretary-General. Other important members of the Returned Students were Chang Wen-t'ien (Lo Fu), Wang Chia-hsiang, and Shen Tse-min.

The Returned Students, who retained the urban orientation of their predecessors, were at constant odds with the policies and growing power of Mao and the leaders of the Kiangsi Soviet. They recognized the legitimacy of Mao's activity, up to a point; but they denied its ultimate primacy and remained more attuned to Comintern directives than to Chinese realities. Under their leadership, the Central Committee had its headquarters in Shanghai, until the risks of continued operation there were simply too great. In the fall of 1932, they were forced to move the Central Committee to Juichin, the capital of the Soviet regime. An uneven decline in their actual influence can probably be dated from this time, though it was not until the Tsun-yi Conference of January 1935, after the beginning of the Long March, that Mao was able to assume the chairmanship of the Central Committee and the Politburo. It was even longer before he was able to fully consolidate his control of the Party.

The Futility of the United Front from Below

Probably never in the history of Comintern operations in China was a policy less appropriately named than the "united front from below," for neither in theory nor in practice was it a united front. Instead, the CCP, on Comintern orders, was making a last effort to cling to and revive an urban revolutionary movement based on the proletariat. That the revolution could succeed without this movement was deemed impossible, and it was considered absolutely essential to match the growth of Communist power in the rural areas with equal or greater growth in the cities. The united front from below was to be a part of this effort.

In China, of course, there was nothing corresponding to the European Socialist movement, nor did the CCP after 1927 have the legal status of most Western Communist parties. After the split of 1927, the Chinese urban labor movement was crushed as an independent force.[3] When the Fourth All-China Labor Congress met in Hankow in June 1927, it claimed representation of 2.8 million organized workers (not all, of course, were in Communist-controlled unions). By the Fifth Congress, held secretly in Shanghai in November 1929, the total had sunk to 70,000, of whom 60 per cent were in the soviet areas. Of the remaining 40 per cent, an insignificant total of 5,748 Red trade-union members were located in Shanghai, Hong Kong, Hankow, Tientsin, Wusih, and Amoy.[4]

In public, Communists attributed this decline to savage repression by the Kuomintang and the various regional militarists; privately, they admitted that their own errors had contributed to the losses.[d] There can be no doubting the ferocity with which the movement was suppressed: thousands of Communists, leftists, and ordinary workers were executed; many more were fired for union activity.[e] The insurrections promoted by Ch'ü Ch'iu-pai had brought the workers into the streets, and the CCP had proved unable to protect them. It is little wonder that under these circumstances the workers became unresponsive to Communist efforts in their behalf. This was far less a matter of lacking grievances than it was of lacking confidence in the Communists.

But it was not by violent repression alone that the independent labor movement was destroyed. The Nanking government also carried out an extensive reorganization and supervision of legal unions. The workers in a given firm or industry were often required to join these "yellow unions," where they could be watched.[f] In 1928, official figures showed a total of 1,117 registered unions, with a membership of 1,773,998.[5] There is probably some padding here, through the inclusion of guilds and other "quasi-unions," but even so, the contrast with the Red unions is striking. Another technique used by employers was to dismiss adult male workers and replace them with women and children—who not only drew lower wages, but were easier to control. Thus, according to statistics on Chinese-owned firms at the end of 1928, there were 122,632 men, 163,792 women, and 48,147 children under 16 in the factories of

[d] These "admissions" were often intended as criticisms of Party leaders who had been denounced and removed. They therefore have a partisan quality, and are not necessarily to be taken at face value.

[e] A 1928 report on Red trade unions noted: "Within the factories, if one worker is caught in connection with our Red trade-union work, then five or ten other workers in the same factory, picked at random, are also punished publicly to terrify the whole body of workers and make them afraid of any contact with us." Quoted in Helen F. Snow, p. 72.

[f] Liu Shao-ch'i claimed that there were seven big "yellow" unions in Shanghai, including the Commercial Press and the postal workers. Railway workers and others were similarly organized. Helen F. Snow, pp. 64–65.

Shanghai, Hankow, Tientsin, and Wusih.[g] Finally, there was a certain amount of paternal reformism, in the yellow unions and elsewhere. The workers were also propagandized by liberals not affiliated with either the CCP or the KMT (such as Teng Yen-ta's Third Party, which had crystallized out of the KMT Left) and by ex-Communists (such as Ch'en Tu-hsiu, who lost few opportunities for condemning the labor policy of the current CCP leadership).

The date of the earliest call for the united front from below in China is still a matter of some uncertainty, though Hsiao Tso-liang is incorrect to place it as late as February 1931.[h] In July 1929, the ECCI directed its affiliated parties "to intensify their work of mobilizing the broadest working masses by employing the new form of the tactics of the united workers' front from below."[6] When Li Li-san was being repudiated, however, one of the charges against him was that he had failed to carry out this policy. During the last months of 1930, he confessed—perhaps under duress—that one of his errors had been the rejection of a united front from below.[7] Presumably this referred to the refusal of the CCP to join the yellow unions until late in 1929, on the grounds that these unions were hopelessly reactionary. "Because of this," said Liu Shao-ch'i, "the Red labor unions not only could not cooperate with the Yellow unions but also came into conflict with them, and the Red labor unions could not win over part of the workers who were misled by their leaders into joining these unions."[8]

At the Eleventh ECCI Plenum (March–April 1931), which set the seal on Li's ouster, he was denounced by A. Lozovsky in the following terms: "It was decided to dissolve the trade unions, and in their place committees of action were established, which were in reality committees of inaction. This left deviation cost the Chinese trade-union movement very dear. It was in any case in a very diffi-

[g] Tyau, pp. 420–25. I have been unable to find comparable statistics for earlier years. The best study of the labor movement in the earlier period is Jean Chesneaux, *Le Mouvement ouvrier chinois de 1919 à 1927* (Paris: Mouton, 1962). But his data cover different industries and include many foreign-owned firms.

[h] "Comintern strategy of a united front from below was first mentioned... by Li Li-san and Ch'ü Ch'iu-pai in their confessions... of February 15, 1931." Hsiao Tso-liang, p. 154.

cult situation because of the frightful terror, and this self-liquidation isolated our party even more from the masses."[9] In place of this, the Chinese were told:

> Proletarian hegemony and the victorious development of the revolution can be ensured only if the CCP becomes a proletarian party not merely in virtue of its political line, but also in its composition and in the part played by industrial workers in all its leading bodies. Fearless, methodical, and vigorous recruiting of the best workers into the party must become the main political task of all its cells and committees. The CCP must infiltrate its basic organizations into all large industrial undertakings. Party organizations must be reestablished and strengthened in all the important centers of the country. It must in the shortest possible time reestablish the broken links with the groups of party members in industrial undertakings, who have for some years struggled on without the guidance of and contact with party organizations. . . . Greater activity by the red unions, in particular in the leadership of strikes, will create favorable conditions for setting up a mass opposition movement in the yellow unions and carrying out the tactics of the united front from below.[10]

That the united front from below was being discussed in China at least as early as November 1930 is clear from a short article written by an unknown Communist who used the name Lao Tun.[i] Lao Tun asserted that one was either revolutionary or reactionary; non-Communists could not long remain independent, and would soon have to choose sides. Collaboration with the authorities was tantamount to betrayal of the working class. Instead, the rank and file in non-Communist groups must come under direct CCP control, after first repudiating their own leaders. Stress was placed on meeting the "pressing needs" and "vital interests" of the masses. The particular organization to which a person belonged was not crucial, since all were oppressed and made to suffer. This declaration was meant to correct the view that the members of yellow or-

[i] Lao Tun, "Hsia-ts'eng t'ung-i chan-hsien." The writer assumes general familiarity with the meaning of the policy, thus suggesting that it had already received formal sanction.

ganizations were unworthy of attention. Lao Tun called for more attention to specific issues than to general propaganda.

Thus the Returned Student leadership, under Ch'en Shao-yü and his colleagues, assumed power with explicit orders to carry out the united front from below. But in a formulation almost identical to that of the deposed Li Li-san, Ch'en promised, "We shall be able to prepare uprisings in large urban industrial centers, and by coordinating the uprisings of the workers in the cities with the action of the Red Army [based in the rural soviets] we shall be able to take those cities."[11] Yet in January 1931, Ch'en and his faction purged two of the most important labor leaders still in the Party, Ho Meng-hsiung and Lo Ch'ang-lung.

Although the united front from below had now become an explicit task of the CCP, the Party wrote only now and then of its concrete efforts to carry out this task in the cities of China; and the documents produced on the subject betray an almost pathetic awareness that an unrealistic policy was up against an overwhelming reality. One Party member discussed various ways of discrediting the existing leadership of labor unions and strike committees.[12] Some held, he wrote, that when counterrevolutionary elements had influence with the working masses, a few of them should be included on the strike committee so that their schemes and betrayals would be shown up. Others argued that it was confusing and dangerous to have these elements serve on strike committees with the apparent sanction of genuine proletarians. Instead, ordinary workers should organize the strikes. This actual participation in struggle would emphasize the contradiction between the workers and their leaders and bring the workers to the Communist side. The author does not say which method is the more effective.

Hung Ch'i (*Red Flag*) recounts an instance of the use of the united front from below in an unnamed "important center in the country."[13] After the firing of certain telephone workers, a meeting of over 100 employees was held, at which a committee of 17 was nominated. This was "doubtless a fighting committee, an organizational form of the united front from below." But it was broken up because many workers thought it was a red labor cell and refused to submit to its leadership. Then some of the committee members, "in Li-san fashion," took direct individual action, adding to the consternation of the ordinary workers. As a crowning blow, members of the rival yellow union managed to mix phony propaganda leaflets in with the genuine ones the workers were handing out. This misled many people, the author notes plaintively, and soon there was, in fact, nothing left but a red cell. The article concludes that work in the yellow unions must be made more effective.

Students were also approached—but not reached—by the united front from below. In his study of the student movement, John Israel writes of this policy:

> In the schools, this exclusive policy emphasized the distinction between "capitalist counterrevolutionary" and impoverished "proletarian" students. Another technique of the party line was to soft-pedal political slogans so as to transfer agitation from the anti-Japanese issue to the "vital demands" of the students. Thus, young cadres instigated campaigns to oust "reactionary" chancellors, to abolish or lower tuition, to strengthen school facilities, to improve the cuisine, to oppose inspection of student mail and dormitories, and to protest expulsions. In these ways the party sought to weaken and discredit KMT educational policies.[14]

Israel concludes that the policy did little to change the almost total loss of contact between Party and students.

Although imperialism was always viewed as the ultimate enemy of the Chinese people, nationalism was not at first given a place of importance in the united front from below. Instead, CCP policy aimed at the overthrow of the KMT as a prior condition for the struggle against imperialism. In any case, the external threat had to take second priority to the problem of survival in the face of the KMT's white terror in the cities and extermination campaigns against CCP base areas.

Japan resumed her active aggression against China in September 1931, when the Mukden Incident led to the loss of Manchuria. As a result of the anti-Japanese boycotts and demonstrations that followed, heavy fighting broke out in Shanghai during January and February of 1932; Chinese resistance, led by Ts'ai T'ing-k'ai and the Nineteenth Route Army, proved surprisingly stubborn. These events produced an increase in the CCP's anti-Japanese propaganda, but had little effect on Communist policy or action. Russia and the Comintern, however, were very concerned about Japanese action in the Far East, where they saw the establishment of Manchukuo as harmful to Russian interests and the prelude to possible further encroachments. This concern was clearly reflected in the resolutions of the Twelfth ECCI Plenum (September 1932): "The imperialist powers, and first of all, the imperialists of France and Japan, are exerting every effort to extend and strengthen the anti-Soviet bloc in order to deliver a decisive blow at the basis of the world proletarian revolution—the USSR."[15] The tasks of the Communist parties of the world included the mobilization of "the masses for the active defence of the USSR, China, and the Chinese Soviet Revolution."[16] The following instructions were sent to the CCP:

> The CP of China must continue to exert every effort to guarantee the hegemony of the proletariat in the mass anti-imperialist movement in Kuomintang China. For this purpose the CP of China must set itself the task of further developing and deepening the soviet movement, strengthening the Red Army of the Chinese soviets, linking up the soviet movement with the mass anti-imperialist struggle in Kuomintang China, widely and consistently using the tactic of the united front from below in the anti-imperialist struggle of the masses, organizing the masses under the slogan of a revolutionary national liberation war for the independence, unity, and territorial integrity of China, against all imperialists, for the overthrow of the agent of imperialism—the Kuomintang.[17]

This policy did not prevent the Russian Government from attempting to protect its flank by recognizing Nanking and signing a Sino-Soviet nonaggression treaty in June 1932.

Both the Comintern and the CCP asserted that resistance to Japan was impossible as long as the "fascist regime" of Chiang

Kai-shek still functioned as the agent of domestic feudalism and foreign aggression. The Chinese people faced a two-headed enemy. Shortly after the Mukden Incident, on September 30, 1931, the CCP Central Committee issued the following statement, ironic in view of later developments: "The Kuomintang recently has begun to spread amusing, absurd, and lying rumors that in Kiangsi the Communists and the leaders of the workers'-peasants' Red Army, Chu Teh and Mao Tse-tung, are ready to fight for a 'united front against the external enemy' and go over to the side of the Kuomintang. The Chinese Communist Party is the eternal enemy of the imperialists and the Kuomintang."[j]

The Chinese Soviet Republic, with its capital at Juichin, Kiangsi, declared war against Japan in April 1932, a full six months after the Mukden Incident and over a month after hostilities had ceased in Shanghai. True, this declaration was largely symbolic, since the Soviet forces were hundreds of miles from the nearest Japanese. But if it was meant to symbolize Communist leadership of opposition to Japan, it was poorly timed. The Juichin leaders asserted, "In order to wage war actively against Japanese imperialism, it is necessary first of all to destroy the reactionary rule of the Kuomintang, which is assisting the imperialists to strangle the national-revolutionary movement."[18] Thus, through 1932, the CCP remained committed to the united front from below in all its aspects.

In January 1933, two important elements of the CCP, the Provisional Government of the Chinese Soviet Republic and the Revolutionary Military Council of the Red Army, for the first time indicated a willingness to make alliances with non-Communist military units, but the real object of this maneuver was probably an armistice with the troops attacking the soviet areas, not a meaningful alliance against Japan. The proposal, signed by Mao, Chu Teh, Hsiang Ying, and Chang Kuo-t'ao, set forth three conditions for the alliance: immediate cessation of the offensive against the soviet

[j] Quoted in McLane, p. 267. Is it possible that some such sentiment might have existed in Kiangsi and been blocked, as it was here, by the Central Committee in Shanghai? Note that the statement is issued by the Central Committee but is applied specifically to the Kiangsi Soviet and its leaders.

areas; an immediate guarantee of popular democratic rights, such as freedom of assembly, association, speech, strike, and publication; the immediate arming of the people and the formation of armed volunteer troops for the defense of China's independence, unity, and territorial integrity.[19] The proposed alliance was to be directed against both the KMT and the Japanese, fusing the two struggles into one revolutionary war.

It was on the basis of this program that a fragile and short-lived alliance was struck with the leaders of the Fukien People's Revolutionary Government.[k] Apparently the Fukien side took the initiative, sending one Hsü Ming-hung to the Communists in Kiangsi. An "Anti-Japanese, Anti-Chiang Preliminary Agreement" was signed on October 26, about a month before the proclamation of the People's Revolutionary Government. All the concessions were on the Fukien side: they were to eliminate all KMT forces on their side of an agreed armistice line; to release all political prisoners; to approve in advance all organizational activity of a revolutionary nature; to grant freedom of speech, publication, and association and the right to strike; and to make active preparations for military action against Chiang. The CCP, in return, agreed not to attack across the armistice line, and to restore commercial relations. The agreement stipulated that when all this had been done, a specific military agreement would be worked out.[20]

This alliance did not mean, however, that the CCP would permit its ally to exercise complete autonomy. On December 5, a statement by the Central Committee urged the Fukienese masses to organize

[k] The Fukien "regime," which lasted only from November 20, 1933, to January 13, 1934, was composed of various non-Communist elements. Some, like Chang Po-chün, Huang Ch'i-hsiang, and P'eng Tse-hsiang, had been associated with the leftist, but non-Communist, Third Party. The Third Party had originated in the anti-Chiang section of the KMT Left and had been outlawed. Its first leader, Teng Yen-ta, was executed in 1930. More important in Fukien were Kwangtung-Kwangsi militarists who had been connected with the Fourth Army. Ch'en Ming-shu, in particular, seems to have been one of the principal architects of the CCP alliance. Also involved were Ch'en's longtime associates Ch'en Chi-t'ang and Li Chi-shen. The principal military forces, those of the Nineteenth Route Army, were under the command of Ts'ai T'ing-k'ai, who had led the spirited defense of Shanghai in January–February 1932. The provincial governor, Chiang Kuang-nai, also cooperated.

and arm themselves, stage strikes, and overthrow landlords. They were also instructed to "bring pressure to bear upon the rebels and to present an effective united front with the Communists." The statement went on to accuse the Fukien leaders of reformism, of suppressing the mass movement, and of resembling "just another group of old KMT politicians."[21] Immediately after the fall of the Fukien regime, the Central Committee refused to waste any sympathy on these erstwhile allies, and instead condemned them for failing to fight the KMT and Japan, encourage strikes, arm the masses, and push the agrarian revolution. Apparently the CCP supported the Fukien rebels with little more than gratuitous advice and criticism.

We have no certain evidence of who argued for what policy within the CCP. Apparently the Central Committee wired Moscow for instructions and was directed to form a strictly military alliance with the Fukien group.[22] Since the Preliminary Agreement was signed by both the Soviet Central Government *and* the Red Army, Mao may have taken a somewhat more positive attitude toward the alliance than did the Returned Students. One ex-Communist maintains that at the time of the October negotiations, the Returned Students and Chou En-lai wanted to send two regiments to Fukien immediately, in order to strengthen the will of the Nineteenth Route Army and help weed out wavering elements. According to this version, Mao argued successfully for the cautious, wait-and-see approach reflected by the Preliminary Agreement.[23] If this is true, Mao may have been concerned about dispersing Red Army units just at the time of the KMT's fifth extermination campaign, already in its preliminary stages.

Orthodox Maoist history, of course, lays the failure to form a sincere alliance with the Fukien group at the door of the Returned Students, claiming that this was an outstanding example of their leftist sectarianism. Yet the real attitude of Mao and his faction toward the Fukien uprising is far from clear. Statements coming from Juichin were less condescending and scornful than those of the Central Committee, but they expressed the same criticisms. Furthermore, at the Second National Soviet Congress (January

1934), Mao charged that the Fukien regime was simply a new trick to deceive the people into thinking that a middle course was possible. It had, he said, no revolutionary significance at all.[l]

Few other non-Communist military units were approached on the basis of the January 1933 appeal, and those that were seem to have received about the same treatment as the Fukien group. Even in Manchuria, where the Japanese were the only enemy, the CCP seems to have proposed a united front on these terms.[24] The quasi-official Communist historian Hu Chiao-mu maintains that it was in cooperation with the CCP that Feng Yü-hsiang organized the People's Anti-Japanese Allied Army in May 1933.[25] Recent scholarship concedes the possibility of some participation by the CCP in this matter, but concludes that "it seems not to have been significant."[26]

Officially, the united front from below was still the policy of the Comintern and the CCP. In the speeches of Ch'en Shao-yü and K'ang Sheng to the Thirteenth ECCI Plenum (December 1933) there is no hint of a change.[27] Both Ch'en and K'ang described a rising tide of revolution against domestic fascism and Japanese imperialism. But K'ang admitted: "The work of winning the workers of the yellow and Kuomintang trade unions and the work of organizing the unemployed has only been started. . . . The tactic of the united front from below is not yet employed to a sufficient extent. The CC of our Party . . . has pointed out these weak spots and shortcomings and has taken decisive measures to overcome them."[28]

These speeches were decidedly visionary. In reality, workers, students, and others were simply not willing to respond to the policy that underlay the united front from below. The fact was that the CCP had virtually nothing to offer its potential allies—except an opportunity to be persecuted by the authorities and criticized by the Party. Nationalistic sentiments were present in the united front

[l] *Hung-se Chung-hua* (January 31, 1934), p. 1. John Rue interprets Mao's attitude as quite sympathetic toward a real alliance; these remarks, he believes, were simply a pro forma agreement with the Returned Student line, after the collapse of the Fukien regime had made continued disagreement futile. Rue, p. 261.

from below, but they were badly obscured by other elements of the policy. Thus, although resistance to Japanese imperialism took first place in Comintern-CCP statements after the Twelfth ECCI Plenum, this resistance was predicated on the prior overthrow of the KMT and the Nanking Government.

Nevertheless, it appears that the small influence the Party retained among students, the intelligentsia, and some small sections of the workers was the result of the CCP's openly announced anti-imperialist position, flawed though it was.[29] It was also much safer to speak in anti-Japanese terms, for only the most pro-Japanese elements could claim that *all* such sentiments were Communist-inspired; thus front organizations frequently spoke in nationalistic terms, as in the "Six-Point Program for Resisting Japan and Saving the Nation," published in May 1934 over the signature of Mme. Sun Yat-sen and others. The effectiveness of anti-Japanese boycotts during this period (as in Shanghai in late 1931) showed how widespread anti-Japanese feelings were.

Meanwhile, in Kiangsi during the spring and summer of 1934, the KMT's fifth extermination campaign was slowly strangling the Soviet regime with a military and economic blockade. In the face of threatened annihilation, the issues involved in any united front must have seemed remote indeed. Once the Long March began in October (on the pretext of marching north to fight the Japanese), hardships and perils made any reconsideration of united-front policy impossible. We do not yet know the full story of the Tsun-yi Conference, at which Mao Tse-tung took the reins of the Party; but even if united-front issues were involved, no action could have been taken at that time. This was still the situation in the summer of 1935, when the Comintern began assembling for its Seventh World Congress.

Chapter 4

Toward the United Front

THE EVOLUTION of the anti-Japanese united front began in August 1935, with almost simultaneous declarations by the CCP and by the famous Seventh World Congress of the Comintern. Two years later, between July and September 1937, the united front was a reality in China, but a reality fundamentally unlike the earlier alliance between the CCP and the KMT, for now the Communists had power—an army, territory, and party organization—fully independent of Kuomintang control. Now, too, China was faced with Japanese invasion, which, if successful, threatened to cancel all meaning the domestic power struggle might have for both contenders. This new united front, far broader from the CCP's standpoint than simple two-party collaboration, was both a goal achieved and a new beginning. It marked an early stage in the development of a set of policies and techniques for enlisting allies and isolating opponents, for expressing the Communist program in nationalistic terms, and for deferring (but not forsaking) revolutionary objectives. The united front merged at the lowest level with the CCP's mass program and the mobilization of the countryside; it operated at middle levels with students and intellectuals, non-Communist armed forces, and regional power structures; and it expressed itself at the top in the CCP's relation to the KMT and the Central Government.

Developments between 1935 and 1937 are extremely complex: crucial evidence is often missing; existing evidence is frequently contradictory, distorted, or ambiguous. We can only attempt here to fit a reconstruction to as many points of certain or probable evidence as possible. The principal problems of interpretation involve how and why the Chinese Communist Party eventually made such extensive changes in its policies and offered such apparently extensive concessions to get a united front. There are two main views. The first is that major policy decisions were made in Moscow and were carried out by a reluctantly obedient CCP. The second, argued here, is that the CCP (not without misgivings and internal disputes) adopted these policies independently, for reasons that had more to do with Chinese realities than with Russian desires. In this view, Comintern directives were an important, but not decisive, consideration.[a]

The Comintern and the United Front

When the Communist International convened its Seventh (and last) World Congress on July 25, 1935, it gave general expression to a popular front policy that had, in fact, been in piecemeal existence for more than a year. For the Comintern itself, and for most of the Communist parties of the West, the Seventh Congress was less the start of a wholly new policy than the complete official adoption of an existing one.

Since the Sixth Congress in 1928 the Comintern had taken a strongly leftist line. During this period, fascism was viewed as simply the most oppressive form of bourgeois dictatorship; as such, it would so sharpen class antagonisms that the masses would be driven to the left, would repudiate their perfidious Socialist leaders, and would bring about the revolution under Communist direction. This was the Comintern view of Hitler, whom the Communists—and many others—considered a flash in the pan. *Rundschau,* the German voice of the Comintern, had this to say on April 1, 1933, following the Reichstag fire and the outlawing of the German Communist Party: "The momentary calm after the victory of fascism is only a passing phenomenon. The rise of the revolutionary tide in

[a] The first interpretation is argued by Thomson in "Communist Policy." The second interpretation is essentially that of McLane's *Soviet Policy and the Chinese Communists.* These are the two best and most nearly complete accounts of the events of these years.

Germany will inevitably continue. The resistance of the masses against fascism will inevitably increase. The open dictatorship of fascism destroys all democratic illusions, frees the masses from the influence of the Social-Democratic Party and thus accelerates the speed of Germany's march towards the proletarian revolution."[1] A full account of the change in this sectarian view cannot be given here, but its elements were approximately these: a shift from "united front from below" to alliance with existing Socialist organizations, including their leaders; increasing Russian, as distinct from Comintern, overtures to bourgeois-democratic governments, especially those of the former Allied Powers; and finally, the merging of these two into a general united-front policy. The first two trends, already under way, were brought together at the Seventh Congress.[b]

Even during the period of the "united front from below," overtures had sometimes been exchanged between Socialist and Communist groups. These usually came to nothing because the Communists wanted to destroy Socialist leadership of the labor movement, while the Socialists wanted the Communists to merge with their own much larger organizations and hence give up their separate identity. Each blamed the other for the triumph of fascism.

The change came, hesitantly and full of the most contradictory argument, during the first half of 1934. It began in France, in February, when a financial and political scandal produced joint action by the Communists and the Socialists—a few days after a combination of Communists and extreme right-wing groups had forced the government to resign.[2] Jacques Doriot, the French Communist leader who had engineered this brief ad hoc united front from above, was rebuked and finally expelled from the French party for his collaboration with "social-fascists." But desire for some sort of

[b] The difficulties involved in this development will not be treated here. Suffice it to say that success in the united front of the labor movement often led workers to make demands that conflicted with the Russian desire to appear no longer as exporters of radicalism and revolution. This problem was very acute in Spain, where the Communists actually suppressed the left wing in order not to frighten off the Republicans, but it also existed in France and elsewhere.

meaningful unity in the labor movement was growing among both Communists and Socialists.

In late June and early July 1934, the French Communist Party, with Moscow's approval, concluded a kind of nonaggression pact with the Socialists and agreed to carry on a joint struggle against fascism and imperialist war. Similar proposals were made by the Communists of Spain, Czechoslovakia, Austria, and Switzerland. Furthermore, manifestos issued in early July by the central committees of the French, British, German, and Polish parties dropped all reference to "social-fascism" and appealed for unity in the workers' movement, "whatever party or trade union you belong to."[3]

Perhaps even more significant was a speech drafted by Georgi Dimitrov in June, a few days before these manifestos were issued. Dimitrov, who was to become the Secretary General of the Comintern at the Seventh Congress, was a Bulgarian Communist who was catapulted to prominence as a result of his impassioned defense at the Reichstag Trial, where he and others were charged with complicity in setting the fire. Dimitrov had impaled Goering with his barbs during the trial, and thus projected a strong anti-fascist image. His June draft had added significance because it was the speech he intended to make at the Seventh Congress, then scheduled for the fall of 1934 but later postponed. Dimitrov asked that the terms "social-fascist" and "social-democratic treachery" be dropped; he further suggested that an exclusively united-front-from-below policy be abandoned.[4]

This somewhat tentative shift in policy was given considerable impetus in October by a joint Socialist-Communist uprising in Asturias, Spain. Though put down within a fortnight, the insurrection developed real mass support and won back some of the Communists' previously lost prestige.[5]

Meanwhile, it had become the policy of the Russian Government to seek international recognition and support. Although Stalin continued to feel that an accommodation with Hitler's Germany might be possible, the situation was sufficiently unclear to persuade him to hedge his bets. Recognition by the United States came in November 1933, in return for a Soviet promise to abstain from revolutionary propaganda in that country. During 1934, existing nonaggression pacts with Poland and the Baltic States were extended, and agreements were signed with Czechoslovakia and Rumania. In September 1934, in the largest international shift to date, Russia joined the League of Nations. And in May 1935, Russia signed treaties with France and Czechoslovakia that were widely interpreted as being directed against Hitler.

Thus, on the eve of the Seventh Congress, the Comintern united front with the reformist labor movement was quite extensive. The Comintern had not yet announced a policy of defending bourgeois democracy, but this was implicit in what had already occurred. The Socialist movement was parliamentary in nature, and despite its frequent lack of militancy it was committed to a defense of democracy. Moreover, Stalin's attempt to create a system of defensive alliances required that Russia be acceptable to the democracies; this in turn implied an ostensible disavowal of Russia's subversive and revolutionary strategy ("a tragicomic misunderstanding," Stalin called it in April 1936).

The Seventh Congress (July 25–August 20, 1935) was probably the calmest ever held, reflecting the Comintern's role as an instrument of Russian foreign policy and Stalin's absolute control of the organization. No Zinoviev or Bukharin was to be purged, nor were there any fundamental disagreements among the 371 voting delegates. All decisions, resolutions, and elections were unanimous.[6] A great deal of verbiage was produced to prove that past Comintern policy had been correct, despite present changes in that policy. Some of the terminology of the past inevitably intruded into the speeches of the Congress, though shorn of its extreme epithets. But the governing mood and the dominant phrases were those of the united front—a united front based on the labor movement as a whole, but also, where appropriate, based on cooperation with existing governments, when these were opposed to "fascism and reaction."

Dimitrov declared, near the end of the Congress, "Our attitude to bourgeois democracies is not the same under all conditions. . . . Now the fascist counterrevolution is attacking bourgeois democracy in an effort to establish the most barbaric regime of exploitation and suppression of the toiling masses. Now the toiling masses in a number of capitalist countries are faced with the necessity of making a *definite* choice, and of making it today, not between proletarian dictatorship and bourgeois democracy, but between bourgeois democracy and fascism."[7] Although Communist parties were called upon to maintain "complete independence from the bourgeoisie and the complete severance of the bloc between Social Democracy and the bourgeoisie,"[8] the Congress urged parliamentary action in country after country, for "defense of the republic and constitution."[9] If a united front government could be formed, even a non-Communist one, and if it would be anti-fascist and not anti-Communist, Communists should join and support it.[10] Sectarianism was condemned, not simply as an "infantile disorder" but as an "ingrained vice."[11]

During the course of the Congress, considerable attention was given to the Far East, and in particular to China. Dimitrov left most of this to Ch'en Shao-yü, who, as a member of the ECCI, was the principal spokesman for the colonial areas (other Chinese present were for the most part nonentities who had little of significance to say). But before turning the floor over to Ch'en, Dimitrov praised "the initiative taken by our courageous brother Party of China in the creation of a most extensive anti-imperialist united front against Japanese imperialism and its Chinese agents, jointly with all those organized forces existing on the territory of China which are ready to wage a real struggle for the salvation of their country and their people."[12]

Ch'en, always both glib and verbose, was at his best in his speech of August 7. Where other Chinese delegates had described organizational problems, the difficulties of the labor movement, and the KMT's reign of terror, Ch'en spoke at length of the significance of the struggle against imperialism. He asserted that only "the tactics of the anti-imperialist united people's front" could mobilize the populace against Japanese aggression and its Chinese lackeys. Ch'en placed responsibility for the current absence of such a front in China equally on the traitorous activities of the KMT and the mistakes of the CCP—though he spent much more time detailing the latter than condemning the former.[13]

Some scholars have seen in these statements the start of a Comintern policy (to which, perhaps, only a few were privy) in which "the path was left open for the Kuomintang if Chiang Kai-shek were to call off his anti-Communist campaigns and join in the fight against Japan."[14] According to this view, the decision to include Chiang Kai-shek was made in Moscow, with little regard for the opinions of the CCP leaders in China. One piece of negative evidence supporting this view is a Comintern resolution entitled "The Anti-Imperialist People's Front in Colonial and Semi-Colonial Countries," which does not list Chiang or the KMT as named enemies but refers simply to "Japanese imperialism and its Chinese servitors."[15] It is true that the Comintern, reflecting Stalin's desires, could take a position regarding its national sections without having to ponder all the problems this position might raise for the local leaders. It was for the Comintern to lay out the correct line in general terms, and for the national sections to apply the line concretely in their own countries. More important, Stalin did not see the united front in terms of the domestic needs of the national Communist parties, but as a defense against fascism and hence as part of the foreign-policy needs of the Soviet Union. This meant that as soon as Chiang Kai-shek could be seen as meeting some of these needs, he would become a candidate for inclusion in the united front.

But if the KMT as a whole was considered a possible ally at the time of the Seventh Congress, the written record is far from making this plain. The omission of the KMT as a named enemy is balanced by explicit condemnations. In his formal report, on August 2, Dimitrov had said: "The predatory attack of Japanese imperialism and the treason of the Nanking Government have brought into jeopardy the national existence of the great Chinese people. Only the Chinese soviets can act as a unifying center in the struggle against enslavement and partition."[16] The united front was of "decisive significance" to Ch'en Shao-yü, but he condemned the "unexampled, infamous national treachery of the Kuomintang."[17] Dimitrii Manuilsky pronounced the Chinese Communists willing, on certain conditions, to "enter into an agreement with any and every political or military group with a view to joint action against the imperialist invaders." But in the same breath he observed, "The successes of the Red Army are also evidence of the *inseparable ties* it has with the broad masses of the toilers in China, who render every possible assistance to the Red forces in their struggle against Chiang Kai-shek."[18] Finally, in a separate resolution, Communists everywhere were called upon to support "the Red Army of the Chinese Soviets in its struggle against the Japanese and other imperialists and the Kuomintang."[19]

Thus, the position of the Seventh Congress was that Japanese imperialism—the main threat to Russia in the Far East—now constituted the principal enemy of the Chinese people. The relative lack of attention to Chiang Kai-shek and the KMT was the result of this change in the primary enemy; it also reflected the generally low level of abuse emanating from the Congress. Anxiety over the fascist threat to Russia, however, made a rapid advance to a position that included Chiang far easier for the Comintern than for the CCP.

In one of its last pieces of business, the Congress elected a new slate of officers. Mao Tse-tung was elected to the ECCI, making him the ranking member of the Comintern actually present in China, though he was still below Ch'en Shao-yü, who was a member of the ECCI's Presidium.

The Chinese Communist Party and the United Front

The August First declaration was issued at Maoerhkai, Szechwan, during the Long March, shortly after Chang Kuo-t'ao's Fourth Front Army joined the Kiangsi group under Mao. Whatever may be new in this statement, there is no change in the CCP's attitude toward Chiang Kai-shek and the leaders of the KMT, men with "human faces but the hearts of beasts." "All arise," urged the authors, "smash through the thousandfold oppressions of the Japanese imperialists and Chiang Kai-shek, and valiantly fight together with the Chinese Soviet Government and anti-Japanese governments in various places in the northeast for the formation of a united national defense government."[20]

But there are some tentative new beginnings in the August First declaration. The first is the broad scope of the appeal, addressed to "men and women in all walks of life—labor, industry, agriculture, military affairs, politics, commerce and education."[21] No statement since 1927 had been so sweeping in scope or so neutral in class terminology. Second is the call to form a "united national defense government." This is the first suggestion that the CCP might even consider entering a political structure in which it was not the sole organized political participant.[22] Third and most significant was the absence of any conditions for alliance between the Red Army and Kuomintang or regional armies save the cessation of attack on soviet districts and willingness to fight Japan. No longer were the conditions of January 1933 a part of the united-front program of the CCP.

Yet the August First declaration might have attracted scant attention had it not coincided with the appeals of the Seventh Comintern Congress for the formation of united fronts against fascism. Was it to the August First declaration that Dimitrov was referring on August 2 when he praised the initiative taken by the CCP? We cannot be sure, but if he was, the almost simultaneous publication of the two statements suggests conscious collaboration. Or possibly Dimitrov was simply distorting earlier CCP statements on the united front from below to make them conform with the new content of the anti-imperialist, anti-fascist united front. This was commonly done at a later stage by the CCP itself, when it was anxious to pose as having supported an all-inclusive anti-Japanese policy as early as the Mukden Incident.

It seems possible that some sections of the CCP knew in at least a general way about the Seventh Congress and its agenda. Since the Congress had been scheduled for the previous autumn, instantaneous communications were probably not necessary. Chang Kuo-t'ao, who clashed with Mao Tse-tung at the Maoerhkai meeting, maintains that contact with Moscow was established at this time, but that so far as he knows, the CCP had no information concerning Comintern united-front policy until after the Seventh Congress.[23] At present, it seems impossible to resolve this difficulty in chronology.[c]

In August 1935, therefore, the positions taken by the Comintern and by the CCP were similar. Both called for greater attention to the problem of a united front against Japan. In Moscow, as in Maoerhkai, the leadership of the Nanking Government was looked upon as an enemy, not a potential ally. Both called for the formation of a popular front government under the leadership of the Chinese soviets; neither specified the form that this government—or indeed the united front—was to take. Later the Comintern advanced somewhat more rapidly, and certainly more easily, to a position including Chiang, but the differences that this change produced between the Comintern and the CCP had seemingly been adjusted when the Sian Incident revived all the old issues once more in a new and intense form. The resolution of the Sian Incident formed the prelude to the ultimate KMT-CCP rapprochement, which took place prior to the outbreak of war with Japan seven months later.

The earliest explicit indication that Chiang and the Kuomintang might under certain circumstances be included in the united front appears in an unofficial article by Ch'en Shao-yü published in November 1935.[24] Ch'en characterized as "crazy talk" the assertion that the Communists were willing to establish a united front with any general and any army, but not with the KMT itself. Of Chiang Kai-shek, Ch'en said: "We will publicly declare that although he has committed numerous crimes in betraying his country and his people, if he truly stops fighting the Red Army and turns his guns against the Japanese imperialists, [the CCP] will not only

[c] Mao, however, might well have known some things that Chang did not; given the conflict between the two men, a withholding of confidence is quite conceivable. Furthermore, the most prominent of the Returned Students (with their Moscow connections) and the headquarters of the Central Committee were traveling with Mao and the First Front Army, not with Chang's Fourth Front Army, which had taken a different route from a different starting point.

give him a chance to redeem his past sins against the people and the country, but is even willing to cooperate with his Nanking army and establish a united front against Japanese imperialism."[25]

It is difficult to assess the significance of this article. It does not appear in official Comintern sources, but Ch'en's eminence in the Comintern lends a certain weight to all his statements. Yet Ch'en may have been doing no more than striking a posture, for he went on to urge KMT military officers to desert with their armies should Chiang persist in opposition to the united front.[26]

Whatever Ch'en meant, it is not completely clear that Moscow had made up its mind by the end of the year. Voitinsky, an old China hand, wrote in December: "If I have spoken of Chinese resistance to Japan, I was speaking—I repeat—of the Chinese masses, of the working class under the guidance of the Communist Party, of the soviets and the Red Army, of partisans and volunteers, of the revolutionary students. In no sense was I referring to Wang Ching-wei and Chiang Kai-shek, the leaders of the Chinese counterrevolution."[27] Ch'en himself referred to the August First declaration as a "serious beginning in the application of this new policy," i.e., the united front, but went on to say that "one must not therefore draw the conclusion that the Communist Party of China and the Chinese Soviet will insist upon commencing to set up the united front only in this form."[28] Ch'en suggested no alternatives, but left the issue open.

Meanwhile, in China, Mao Tse-tung and his weary veterans had finally reached northern Shensi, linking up in October with the small Communist forces already in the area. During the last days of December, the Party's current position on the united front was hammered out in what must have been a stormy and bitter meeting of "Party activists" held at Wayaopao, "one of the most important ever held by the Party center."[29] This session, coming after the great student demonstrations in Peking earlier in the month (see below, pp. 65–66), was the CCP's equivalent to the Seventh Comintern Congress; like the Seventh Congress, it summed up earlier scattered trends and set forth a new strategic line. The August First declaration had been hortatory, public, and vague. The documents of the December Conference were orders to the Party, secret and explicit.[d] In this sense it can be said that the united front as a definite Party policy began in December, not in August.

The "broadest national united front," the resolution stated, "is the general tactical line."[30] This meant, among other things, the subordination of the class struggle to the fight against Japan; the determination to ally with the bourgeoisie, provided it opposed Japan and did not attack the CCP; the affirmation of the CCP's hegemony and ultimate goals, coupled with a candid recognition of its present weakness; insistence upon maintaining the Red Army and the territorial base as guarantees of independence; and tactical flexibility, with the strategic goal of enlisting maximum forces against an isolated enemy.

Many of the "activists" present were opposed to an about-face that might require them to collaborate with the very kinds of people they had for years been trying to destroy: factory owners, yellow trade-union leaders, merchants, local militarists, bourgeois intellectuals, KMT members, liberal reformers, and the rest. In a passage remarkable for its crushing force, Mao served notice that "closed-door sectarianism" would not be tolerated. It was, he said, dogmatic, infantile, inconsistent with Marxism-Leninism, and of direct, deliberate service to Japanese imperialism.[31] Opposition was not overcome once and for all, but there can be no question of the orientation Mao here gave to the CCP. Furthermore, the whole tone of this document, and the analysis it contains (to say nothing of the consistency with which it was later held), argue that Mao's position was genuinely his own, taken in response to the situation in China, and not adopted simply in obedience to Stalin's orders.

Yet although the scope of the united front was widened, and al-

[d] The standard statement on the Wayaopao meeting is Mao's "On Tactics Against Japanese Imperialism" (Dec. 27, 1935), *SW*, I, 153–78. I have been unable to find an original text of this inner-party document, and it is possible that the *SW* text has been altered. Therefore, I have used the original of another long resolution from this meeting, "Mu-ch'ien cheng-chih hsing-shih yü tang ti jen-wu chüeh-i" (Dec. 25, 1935). The text may be found in *Chih-nan* [CCP 4], Vol. I, and in Yü Ch'i, pp. 211–30. It is only briefly extracted in *SW*, I, 277–78. I have quoted from "On Tactics" only where it is consistent with the latter document.

though the determination of the Party's top leaders to pursue this policy was unequivocally stated, Chiang Kai-shek and the Japanese remained the joint enemies of the Chinese people. Chiang was described as the willing tool of the Japanese and excoriated in language of the greatest hatred and contempt. At year's end, therefore, Moscow and Pao-an agreed on the importance of the united front, but the Comintern appeared to view Nanking with flexibility, while the CCP remained unbending in its enmity.

The first indications of a possible shift in the CCP's position came in the spring of 1936. Statements issued in February and March simply omitted mention of Chiang and the KMT, but in an interview on March 14th, Mao told a correspondent (in language remarkably similar to that used by Ch'en Shao-yü the preceding November): "On behalf of the Chinese government, I hereby announce that if Chiang Kai-shek ceases his attack on the Red Army, the Chinese Red Army will also suspend all military action and start a war with Japan in order to meet the needs of the people."[32] This tentative step was followed on April 25, 1936, by the first proclamation that even nominally included the KMT as a whole.[33]

The CCP itself dates the shift in policy toward Nanking from May 5, 1936, when it issued a "Telegram from the Military Revolutionary Committee of the Red Army to the Nanking Government," a direct appeal for the termination of civil war and for the formation of a united front of all groups in China against the Japanese.[34] A recent Chinese commentator has said, "This telegram marked another momentous change in the tactics of the Chinese Communist Party—from 'resisting Japanese aggression and opposing Chiang Kai-shek' to 'forcing Chiang Kai-shek to fight the Japanese.' "[e]

It is possible that direct contacts were made between the CCP and the KMT sometime between December 1935 and the autumn of 1936. Later, after the KMT-CCP alliance was established, the Party recalled that it had "sent representatives to hold discussions with people from the Kuomintang side on many occasions, but

[e] Liu Ching-yu, Part 2, p. 28. The next stage, after the Sian Incident, was "to ally with Chiang to oppose Japan."

with as yet no results."[f] Furthermore, Mao told Edgar Snow during the summer of 1936: "At present negotiations are being conducted. While the Communist Party has no great positive hopes of persuading Nanking to resist Japan, it is nevertheless possible. As long as it is, the Communist Party will be ready to cooperate in all necessary measures. If Chiang Kai-shek prefers to continue the civil war, the Red Army will also receive him."[35]

Chiang himself presents a fairly detailed, but unconfirmed, account of these contacts.[36] In the "autumn and winter of 1935," according to this version, Chou En-lai approached Tseng Yang-fu, a government representative in Hong Kong. Chou wanted to negotiate with Nanking for cessation of the civil war and joint resistance to Japan; he reaffirmed this position in a letter dated September 1 (1935?). Chiang continues that following the May 5th telegram, Chou and P'an Han-nien—the latter allegedly a Comintern representative—met with Chang Ch'ün. P'an later went to Nanking to confer with Ch'en Li-fu. The government put forth four conditions (essentially the same four accepted by the CCP in February 1937). "After protracted discussions they finally accepted these four points. Understanding had then been reached on practically all the issues. I was then in Sian. All that remained to be done was to get my final approval as soon as I was to return to Nanking." This last statement makes the entire Sian Incident incomprehensible, particularly since Chiang asserts that Chang Hsüeh-liang was acting "under the influence of the Chinese Communists,"[37] unless Chiang means that it was after his detention that such "understanding" was reached and is confusing the sequence of events.

The timing of this tentative shift in policy toward Chiang may have also been influenced by the failure of the CCP's campaign in southern Shansi. Toward the end of February 1936, sizable ele-

[f] "Urgent Tasks Following the Establishment of Kuomintang-Communist Cooperation," *SW*, II, 36. The original, which carries the title "Urgent Tasks Following the Establishment of the KMT-CCP United Front," is found in *Chih-nan* [CCP 4], II, 68–79. The *SW* version has been considerably altered, but is generally accurate here (my translation, used here, differs slightly from that of *SW*). The original states that the KMT had been "requested" (*ch'ing-ch'iu*) to form a united front; *SW* has "demanded" (*yao-ch'iu*).

ments of the Red Army crossed the Yellow River into Shansi. The campaign was ostensibly an attempt to fight through to the Japanese-controlled areas, but its real purposes were probably to gain badly needed food, to test Yen Hsi-shan's strength in the province, and perhaps to enlarge the soviet areas. At first successful, the Red Army soon faced a coalition between Yen and Ch'en Ch'eng (representing Nanking) and was unable to hold the territory it had taken. At the same time, Yang Hu-ch'eng and Chang Hsüeh-liang were threatening the soviets from the west and southwest. By late March, the Communists were in retreat, bearing the body of their dead commander, Liu Chih-tan, back to his homeland in northern Shensi.[38]

The speculation that the disastrous results of this foray were related to the Party's united-front policy (perhaps that such militant action was driving the opposition together) is given some added force by emendations in Mao's *Selected Works*: "In May 1936, the Red Army *recalled its forces from Shansi, and the Soviet Central Government and the Revolutionary Military Committee of the Red Army* published a statement [*SW*: circular telegram] requesting [*SW*: demanding] the National Government [*SW*: Nanking Government] to stop the civil war and make common cause against Japan."[g] It may therefore be significant that the May 5th telegram refers at some length to the Shansi operation: "But after much deliberation, the Revolutionary Military Council and the Red Army decided that a battle to the finish between the two sides would only damage China's strength for national defense and delight the Japanese imperialists, whichever side emerged victorious. . . . Therefore [the Red Army] has withdrawn."[39]

Whatever the precise combination of factors—negotiations, the failure of the Shansi raid, direct Comintern pressure (if any), the realization that it was blatantly unreasonable to indict the KMT's civil-war policy while calling for the overthrow of Chiang and Nanking—the CCP had finally abandoned its principle of a dual enemy and ended the exclusion of Chiang Kai-shek. Indeed, it was only

[g] The italicized passage is omitted in *SW*, II, 35. See Note *f*, p. 61, for sources.

from this time on that the CCP gave itself any real chance to join in a united front against Japan. The Comintern had left the door open some months earlier.

During the summer of 1936, and particularly in August, the CCP showed that its attitude toward Chiang had changed still further. On August 25, in the least inflammatory statement so far, Chiang was even accorded qualified praise for his refusal to recognize the Japanese puppet government set up in North China.[40] The leader of the KMT was now addressed respectfully by his full title, not by the pejoratives that had regularly preceded his name in the past. As a sign of the new spirit, the CCP asked its erstwhile enemies to recall the glories of 1924–27, and to apply the same successful formula again, this time against the Japanese. The letter was not without criticism—the KMT was rebuked for its past policies, and some of the resolutions of the Second KMT Plenum, just concluded, were also taken under fire—but the general tone was quite conciliatory. After attacking the KMT concept of "centralization and opposition" and the draft constitution, the CCP offered to make the soviet government and the Red Army "integral parts" of a national defense government, provided that this government opposed Japan, was thoroughly democratized, and stressed improvement of the people's life.[41] It may be doubted that Chiang was greatly moved, but this open letter increased public pressure, already at a high pitch, for an end to civil war, and helped to develop this feeling within the KMT itself. The change in the CCP slogan from a "people's republic" to a "democratic republic" was the start of the process that finally resulted in CCP recognition of the Nanking regime, in return for de facto regional autonomy.[h]

[h] The policy of Communist participation in popular-front governments was a part of the Comintern program for Europe, where there were multi-party or coalition governments. It made little sense in a China ruled by the KMT during the Period of Tutelage. Hence the term "people's government" sounded very similar to the united front from below and attracted little new support for the CCP. The editors of *SW* claim that the shift to a call for a "democratic republic" meant "essentially the same thing despite the difference in wording" (*SW*, I, 331). But this is not true, for the new term recognized the important position of the KMT, relinquished the demand that the government be convened on soviet territory, and sought a much broader participation than the earlier proposal. It was

Mao Tse-tung reiterated his views in an interview with Edgar Snow just before Snow left Shensi in October 1936: "The seriousness of Japanese aggression . . . is so formidable a menace that before it all the forces of China must unite. Besides the Communist Party there are other parties and forces in China, and the strongest of these is the Kuomintang. Without its cooperation our strength at present is insufficient to resist Japan in war. Nanking must participate."[42] Because of these circumstances, Mao said, "We are obliged to reconsider in detail the concrete formula under which such cooperation can become possible."[43]

During these same months, from the spring of 1936 onward, the Comintern's policy also clearly crystallized in favor of Chiang Kai-shek and the Nanking Government.[44] Having decided that the most effective opposition to Japan would have to center around Chiang, the Comintern took a much more unconditional position of support for Nanking than did the CCP. One example is provided by the Comintern's criticism of the Kwangtung-Kwangsi military leaders of the Southwest Political Council (Li Tsung-jen, Pai Ch'ung-hsi, Ch'en Chi-t'ang) when they challenged Chiang's leadership during the summer of 1936. Despite the claims of these leaders that they were motivated by a desire to oppose Japan, *Izvestia* attributed the disturbance to Japanese machinations to divert attention from new encroachments in the north.[45] The militarists were accused of actually damaging the anti-Japanese movement by trying to split the KMT. Here Mao Tse-tung's stated response differed from Moscow's press reaction. Mao viewed the action of Li, Pai, and Ch'en with approval, and indicated his desire "to join them in action."[46] A very similar divergence of opinion was to take place at the time of the Sian Incident, six months later.

But apart from this rather minor difference in views, the Comintern and CCP lines remained very close together. Sometimes even

---

out of evolving policy concerning the "democratic republic" that the CCP gradually fashioned its domestic platform of political reform, and ultimately the New Democracy. The points in this platform (civil rights, multi-party and multi-class orientation, moderate social reform) were very persuasive, particularly in view of the KMT's inability or unwillingness to recognize their full force.

the language was the same. These close parallels suggest a conscious coordination of policy, but this may be true without assuming that the CCP was simply taking orders from Moscow. What is more likely is that Mao was taking a position for reasons of his own, but generally agreed with what Moscow wanted the CCP to do. Moscow, however, had definitely decided that resistance to Japan must center around Chiang Kai-shek, the strongest force in China, while the CCP envisioned a united front, led by itself, in which Chiang might or might not participate, depending on specific circumstances. The extent to which the Soviet Union was committing itself to Chiang is indicated by the secret negotiations carried on between Nanking and Moscow in the fall of 1936. The object of these negotiations was a nonaggression pact, which included clauses dealing with "Soviet military supplies to China, establishment of airlines, opening of new consulates, and 'no assistance' to the Chinese Communists."[47] Agreement was apparently near by the eve of the Sian Incident.[48]

The United Front and the Patriotic Movement

The CCP's call for a nationwide united front against Japan was not simply the result of policy decisions made in Moscow and Pao-an. It was strongly influenced by the powerful surge of nationalism that swept through China after the student uprisings of December 1935.[i] In November 1935, observing Japan's efforts to create an "autonomous" North China, Peiping's college and middle-school students could no longer restrain their resentment. Led in

[i] The most complete account available of the student movement in these years is to be found in Israel's *Student Nationalism in China, 1927–1937*. Mr. Israel has also prepared a bibliography on this subject: *The Chinese Student Movement, 1927–1937*. Edgar Snow and his wife, Helen F. Snow (Nym Wales), were intimately acquainted with the leaders of the December Ninth demonstration, and collected voluminous materials on the student movement as a whole. Miss Wales has deposited these materials in the library of the Hoover Institution, together with a lengthy essay entitled *Notes on the Chinese Student Movement, 1935–1936*. During the period that Mr. Israel was completing his work in Taiwan, I was preparing the present work. I am indebted to Mr. Israel for his valuable comments and suggestions on much of the material in this section.

part by young natives of Manchuria, whose hatred of Japan was the most intense, the students exploded in violent demonstrations on December 9 and 16. Carried on in bitter weather and countered by club-swinging police, fire hoses, and widespread arrests, these outbursts protested Japanese aggression, criticized Nanking's dilatory tactics, and demanded immediate resistance.

The disturbance, like the May Fourth and May Thirtieth movements, soon spread to other cities and regions. Shanghai in particular was swept along, partly because the foreign concessions provided a convenient haven for critics of Nanking's policy. Canton, Nanking, the Wuhan cities, and Sian were also affected. Demonstrations, parades, and speeches took place despite attempts to suppress them. Propaganda teams were organized and sent to the countryside to stir up anti-Japanese sentiment among the peasantry. Before long, student federations, patriotic groups, and other associations dedicated to resistance to Japan were organized in schools and colleges throughout China. In many places, the criticism of Chiang Kai-shek and his policies was nearly as bitter as the condemnation of Japan. Not only was China's youth finding its political voice after nearly four years of silence, but it was on the verge of repudiating the Nanking Government.

In its early stages, the December Ninth movement was neither initiated nor led by the CCP, but was instead a spontaneous response to Japanese aggression and to the frustrations of apparent Chinese helplessness. Given the extreme weakness of the CCP in Kuomintang-controlled regions, it is impossible to imagine a movement of such scope being under Communist control. Liu Shao-ch'i is given official credit for directing the student movement during this period, but very few details are available; the nature of his role, if any, in the December demonstrations remains unknown.

Once the movement had begun, however, the CCP had much to do with its later development, and this experience helped to set a pattern that was frequently followed in later years: "Through the December Ninth movement, the Communists learned how to work with, maneuver, and use China's talented, dedicated left-wing patriots, and the latter became accustomed to lean on the CCP's leadership."[49] For example, the strongest influence on the student union in Peiping ultimately came from the "Chinese National Liberation Vanguard, which was, in effect, an extension of the Communist Youth Corps."[50] The Vanguards were formed during the January 1936 propaganda campaign in the countryside.

Until the spring of 1936, the student movement remained more or less fragmented and uncoordinated; but on March 30, representatives from 16 cities assembled in Shanghai to found the first national student union since the days of the Northern Expedition. Peiping and Shanghai clearly emerged as the guiding centers of the movement. It was from this time, in Snow's words, that "the professionals took over."[51] This produced greatly superior coordination and direction, with increasing sophistication in matters of organization, agitation, etc. Among the "professionals" was the young Communist Yü Ch'i-wei. Yü had been active in Peiping and Tientsin, but had apparently been a bystander during the December demonstrations.

Perhaps the most important change that took place at about this time was a shift away from overt criticism of Nanking and Chiang Kai-shek. Instead, attention was focused on the need to oppose Japan, terminate civil war, and act with solidarity. On April 25, the newly reorganized Peiping Students National Salvation Union issued a manifesto that "heralded the beginning of a new policy, and pledged to seek guidance and cooperation from the public.... There was no further talk of strikes or demonstrations against the 'murderous' authorities; the union's strongest criticism was directed not against Chiang Kai-shek or Sung Che-yüan, but against the imperialistic 'dwarf slaves.' "[52] The call "to broaden the salvation front" was further implemented during the summer months, when the students were on vacation and able to devote full time to patriotic activities. In July, the same Peiping Union petitioned the Second Plenum of the Fifth KMT Central Executive Committee, exhorting the Kuomintang to prepare for war against Japan, terminate civil war, unshackle the patriotic movement, release political prisoners, and institute constitutional rule.[53] With occasional exceptions, this continued to be the program of the movement.

This line closely paralleled the development of the CCP's own policy. If, as is almost certainly the case, this was more than coincidental, two inferences may be drawn. The first is that the Party was, by the spring and summer of 1936, already exercising a considerable degree of leadership in the student movement. The second inference is to confirm that the CCP began to include Chiang Kaishek in its conception of the united front, in principle if not in practice, in the spring of 1936.

Very closely linked with the student movement, but broader in scope, was the National Salvation movement. It endorsed the students' platform—national solidarity, resistance to Japan, and criticism (explicit or implicit) of Nanking—but reached many other segments of the population. The Shanghai Cultural Circles National Salvation Association was formed on December 27, 1935, in direct response to the demonstrations of the 9th and 16th. Lawyers and journalists formed similar organizations, and a number of women's salvation groups were organized. A Workers' Anti-Japanese National Salvation Association was set up in Shanghai, and was promptly declared illegal.[54] Student propaganda teams in the countryside tried, with varying degrees of success, to organize the agricultural villages. Students themselves joined National Salvation groups, and some student federations changed their names to include the words "salvation" (*chiu-wang,* or *chiu-kuo*) or "resistance" (*k'ang-ti*).

At the beginning, National Salvation was more nearly an inflamed state of mind than a coordinated movement, and its organizational development was always fluid, in spite of unanimous agreement on basic issues. But on May 31, 1936, representatives from all over China met in Shanghai, the center of the movement, to form the All-China Federation of National Salvation Unions. In its initial statement, the Federation announced:

> We declare wholeheartedly to the nation: with the exception of traitors, we do not wish to see the slightest loss of influence of any group; we want to foster them, unite them, and strengthen them, and to turn them into a mighty force to fight against Japa-

> nese imperialism. . . . Hereafter in its speeches, the National Salvation Front will never make malicious attacks against any authorities, except that it will oppose their compromise with the enemy, their suppression of the people, of freedom of speech.[55]

The appeal further called for all parties and groups to terminate civil war, to release all political prisoners, and to form a united anti-Japanese political power.

The National Salvation Federation did not attempt to create a political party structure, or to exercise close control over the sprawling National Salvation movement. Instead, it acted as a kind of propaganda and ideological center for the many organizations that considered themselves part of the movement. The National Student Union in Shanghai was affiliated with the National Salvation Federation, thus giving the Union a natural avenue to an even wider audience.

The CCP's attitude toward both the student and National Salvation movements was strongly favorable from the start. Mao's instinct for mass enthusiasm could hardly fail to be aroused by the explosions of anti-Japanese feeling throughout the country. The fundamental position—opposition to Japan and termination of civil war—was completely consistent with CCP policy; and the new Party line on the united front made it imperative that the CCP seize the chance provided by the students and salvationists. Not since 1925–26 had the Party had such an opportunity to spread its influence in KMT-controlled areas.

On March 29, 1936, the day before the founding of the national student federation, Mao told an interviewer, "The Chinese Soviet Government has decided to render all possible assistance to the student movement in Shanghai and in other parts of China. . . . We have encouraged the students in the Chinese Soviet to take concerted action with the students in Shanghai. . . . The student movement at present is obviously a reaction to the unanimous will for national salvation. It is true that the students' slogan urging an immediate cessation of internal conflicts is the demand of the entire nation."[56] A few months later, on August 10, Mao directed a long and persuasive letter to the leaders of the National Salvation movement, praising their activities and inviting them to send delegates to participate in the soviet government. It was here that Mao also indicated his support for the action of the leaders of the Southwest Political Council.

The extent of Communist influence upon these movements is impossible to determine. There is no doubt that it was considerable, but it was probably indirect and suggestive, rather than a matter of direct control from Shensi. First of all, the Party was still outlawed, and was forced to work in complete secrecy. This limited the number and effectiveness of Party members who could be sent to penetrate and direct the mass movement. If firm control is to be exercised over a mass movement, the opportunity for at least semi-overt operation must exist. Moreover, evidence of Communist direction would compromise the movement. The anti-Communist press was constantly charging such direction in order to discredit the students and salvationists; but a classified KMT source, which contained detailed information on many popular organizations, stated that it was only after the Japanese invasion of Suiyuan in November 1936, when national feeling was running very high, that the CCP sent agents to organize National Salvation groups.[57]

Publication and propaganda, however, provided a way for the CCP to intrude its message into the writings of prominent National Salvation leaders. This was particularly effective, since many of the most enthusiastic salvationists were noted writers, journalists, or public figures—and some of them had long been critical of the KMT and of Chiang Kai-shek. The left-wing journalist Tsou T'ao-fen devoted much space in his *Ta-chung sheng-huo* ("Life of the Masses") to articles supporting the united front and the National Salvation movement. Ai Ssu-ch'i, a Communist theorist, was himself the editor of the Shanghai periodical *Tu-shu sheng-huo* ("Student Life"), and was active in National Salvation propaganda circles.[58] Chang Nai-ch'i, an important spokesman for National Salvation and a respected businessman, argued that "anyone who says the National Salvation movement has some 'background' [i.e., is manipulated by the CCP] has as his own background selling out the country."[59] P'ing Hsin called in strident tones for all-out war against Japan, confiscation of the property of Japanese sympathizers, encouragement of the patriotic movement, and so on.[60] Shao Han-ch'i discussed techniques to be used in creating mass National Salvation organizations.[61] By the summer of 1936, a busy time for both the student movement and the salvationists, the country was exposed to widespread and continuous agitation for opposition to Japan and a cessation of civil war.

During these months, Sian, the capital of Shensi and the site of the Bandit Suppression Headquarters charged with the anti-CCP campaign, was swept by National Salvation and united-front activity.[j] The man charged with suppression of the Communists was the patriotic but emotional Chang Hsüeh-liang; his Northeast Army was made up of violently anti-Japanese Manchurians. Nominally under Chang's command but at least equally powerful in Sian was Yang Hu-ch'eng, with his Northwest Army. The Northeast Army troops, particularly the younger officers, were very receptive to the sentiments of the student patriots, especially since most of them were also natives of Manchuria. Chang had clearly indicated that patriotic students could find a haven in Sian, and a branch of Northeastern University was set up in the city. In October, a Sian branch of the Vanguards was organized by cadres from Peiping; almost simultaneously the Northeastern Peoples National Salvation Association was established. Two hundred Manchurian students formed a special unit, and were enlisted in a training school under Col. Sun Ming-chiu, one of Chang's most ardently anti-Japanese officers (and the man who would later carry the injured Chiang Kai-shek down the slopes of Li-shan to his two weeks' captivity). Between mid-September and December 9, the anniversary of the Peiping outbursts, six large patriotic demonstrations were held in Sian.[62]

Sian was also subjected to united-front efforts from quite an-

[j] A detailed inside account of National Salvation work in Sian was published in that city during the course of the Incident. See *Chieh-fang jih pao* (Sian), Dec. 21, 1936. This extensive newspaper account was in the form of a press conference with Hsü Pin-ju of the Propaganda Section of the Northwest Federated All-Circles National Salvation Association.

other direction—from the CCP to the North. Well aware that neither Chang nor Yang had much stomach for civil war, the Communists pressed for a reduction or cessation of hostilities. The CCP put forward the simple and persuasive message that Chinese should not kill Chinese, but should conserve their strength for opposition to Japan. Negotiations were held between the CCP and Chang, or his representatives. Communist liaison officers were present at the headquarters of both Chang and Yang.[k] By June, or a little later, a virtual truce had been arranged between the Commander of the Bandit Suppression Headquarters and those he was supposed to suppress.[63]

Chiang Kai-shek was kept informed of these events by his appointee as governor of Shensi, Shao Li-tzu. To counteract their influence, Chiang flew into Sian in late October. He harangued Chang Hsüeh-liang and his officers on the need to eliminate the nearby enemy before thinking of the more distant Japanese, and ordered a continuation of the campaign against the Communists. Chang's requests that at least a part of his forces be sent to counter the Japanese in the threatened province of Suiyuan were adamantly refused. Even these direct orders, however, failed to put Chang and Yang in the field against the CCP during November; and on December 4, Chiang returned to Sian, to replace Chang if he could not command him to act.

But by this time, several events had further inflamed national sentiment for resistance to Japan and condemnation of Chiang's policies. First, the crisis in Suiyuan had broken into open combat, and a mood of frustrated anger was rising in the country. Associa-

[k] At this time, the CCP liaison officer with Chang's army was Liu Ting (a pseudonym?); at Yang's headquarters was Wang Ping-nan, more recently the Communist official in Warsaw delegated to carry on discussion with the United States. Wang was the son of an intimate friend of Yang. Edgar Snow, *Random Notes*, p. 4. Teng Fa, then or a little later the chief of the Red Army's internal security forces, was reported living in Chang's house. Edgar Snow, *The Other Side of the River*, p. 264. Miao Chien-ch'iu, a Manchurian close to Chang Hsüeh-liang, claims that on August 10, 1936, Chang flew secretly into the Communist areas and conferred with Chou En-lai, P'eng Te-huai, and Ho Lung on the need for a program of unified resistance to Japan. Miao believes that this visit helped persuade the Communists to give up their rebellion against Nanking. McLane, p. 80.

tions to aid or support the defenders of Suiyuan were formed everywhere, alongside the National Salvation and student groups. Some Peiping students even formed a special column and marched westward. Numerous appeals to fight the Japanese were sent to Chiang. Second, the anti-Communist campaign was going badly. When the Sian generals refused to move, Chiang had ordered General Hu Tsung-nan to attack the Reds from the west, through Kansu. On November 18, after a deceptively easy advance, elements of Hu's best division were ambushed and cut to pieces. In the Communist counterattack that followed, Hu was driven back, and the Communists expanded the territory under their control. It seemed to many that Nanking could not eliminate the Communists, despite Chiang's assertions that their destruction could be quickly and easily accomplished. Third, in an act that outraged the entire country, seven of the most prominent National Salvation leaders were arrested in Shanghai on November 22. The seven, one of whom (Shih Liang) was a woman, were immediately called the "Seven Gentlemen" (*ch'i chün-tzu*), suggesting their selfless conduct even in the face of great personal risk. These were not young students, but adults of substance and national reputation. Now it seemed to many that these men, like the radical Vanguards of Peiping, were being imprisoned for their patriotism.[l] Their criticism of Nanking's policy had been highly effective; now it was even more potent, for its authors became symbols as well as spokesmen for immediate resistance to Japan.

Thus, when Chiang Kai-shek arrived back in Sian on December 4, he entered a much more explosive situation than during his October visit. Chiang nevertheless continued his earlier policy. In a con-

[l] The Seven were Shen Chün-ju, a prominent lawyer and educator; Chang Nai-ch'i, a banker and financier; Tsou T'ao-fen, a well-known journalist and publisher; Li Kung-p'u, writer, publisher, and educator; Wang Tsao-shih, a publisher and a professor in various Shanghai universities, with a Ph.D. from Wisconsin; Shih Liang, one of China's first and most famous woman lawyers; and Sha Ch'ien-li, a journalist. These people were tried in Soochow in April 1937 on a charge of "endangering the Republic." They were released in July, after the start of the war. The most complete account of the arrests and legal proceedings, together with biographical information, is found in Shih-tai wen-hsien-she, *Chiu-kuo wu-tsui.*

ference with Chang and Yang on the 7th, he dismissed their pleas for a more aggressive anti-Japanese policy, and ordered them to increase their efforts to extirpate the Communists.[64]

Two days later, on the anniversary of the great demonstration in Peiping, students from Northeastern University and many middle schools staged a large parade. After presenting their views to the authorities in Sian, the demonstrators turned toward suburban Lin-t'ung, where Chiang was billeted. Their attempt to petition the Generalissimo in person was blocked by Sian's Police Commissioner, who ordered his men to fire on the students. Chang Hsüeh-liang hurried to address the now thoroughly aroused demonstrators, imploring them in an impassioned speech to return home but promising satisfaction within a week.[65]

Chiang Kai-shek met the next day in joint conference with the Sian leaders. At this meeting, Chiang relieved Chang Hsüeh-liang as commander of the Bandit Suppression Headquarters, replacing him with General Chiang Ting-wen. Issuance of a new order for resumption of the anti-Communist campaign was scheduled for December 12.[66] This was nearly the last possible moment for Chang to act. He risked losing the loyalty of his officers and men if he continued to follow Chiang Kai-shek's orders. Yang Hu-ch'eng, too, was being pressed by his own followers, and he had never felt the loyalty to Chiang that Chang had previously exhibited. Chang had now lost his command, and it was only a matter of time before he would lose the power to influence events.

Chapter 5

The Sian Incident, and After

The Sian Incident

Before dawn on December 12, 1936, picked men from General Chang Hsüeh-liang's bodyguard surrounded a compound at Huach'ing-ch'ih, where the T'ang emperor Ming Huang had once enjoyed the favors of Yang Kuei-fei. They had come to make a prisoner of their commander-in-chief. After a brief but sharp skirmish, Chang's men broke into the compound; but Chiang Kai-shek, awakened by the gunfire, had had time to slip out of his window, climb over the compound wall, and scramble up the slopes of Li-shan, clad only in his nightshirt. He was found a couple of hours later, bruised and shivering, and was carried down the hillside into captivity. By 9:00 A.M. it was all over. Two weeks later, in the gathering dusk of Christmas Day, Chiang Kai-shek and Chang Hsüeh-liang boarded Chang's private Boeing airplane at the Sian airfield and flew to Loyang. The next day the two men, their roles now reversed, flew on to Nanking. Chiang's safe return was celebrated throughout China.

Few events in modern Chinese history are more dramatic in their impact—or more obscure as to crucial details—than the Sian Incident. It seems clear that Chiang Kai-shek's two-week detention somehow resulted in eventual collaboration between the CCP and the KMT. But the role played by the CCP and by Moscow has been subject to different interpretations. The CCP itself has maintained that its ultimate position was its initial position: to work for peace and unity as the only way of achieving a nationwide united front. The Party has, in fact, claimed credit for Chiang's safe return to Nanking and for the peaceful resolution of the affair.

With the publication of new evidence on the Sian affair by Edgar Snow,[1] a radically different version has been suggested. In Snow's words: "The Politburo [of the CCP] at first meant to exploit it [the Sian Incident] as a means of setting up a national anti-Japanese government in Sian, isolating if not totally discrediting Chiang Kai-shek . . . Moscow's sudden intervention [ordering Chiang's release] undercut previous plans and left Mao momentarily without a clear line."[2] The view that the CCP meant to eliminate Chiang but was overruled by Moscow is also argued by Thomson.[3] While the evidence presented by Snow is certainly the most important recent contribution to our understanding of these events, we need not accept the interpretation that he draws from it. There is another interpretation of the Sian Incident that seems more in accord with both the available evidence and the logic of the situation. I will first present a skeletal reconstruction, and then proceed to indicate the evidence and reasoning upon which it is based.

Chiang's kidnapping took place in so finely balanced a situation that its results might have led in any one of several directions, depending upon the decisions and actions of the parties involved—of which the CCP was only one. Therefore, the Communists could not at once apply any specific policy without careful consideration of its feasibility and possible consequences. After a period of indecision, during which the Party observed the movement of events, Mao Tse-tung and other top CCP leaders decided to work for Chiang's release, while still preserving as much flexibility as possible. This decision was made essentially on its own merits, and not because of orders from Moscow. Such orders were probably issued and transmitted to Mao, but they only reinforced a decision that would have been made even without such a command.[a] The decision was strong-

[a] Aside from the evidence in *Random Notes,* the only Communist reference to an order from Moscow that I have been able to find is in Chang Hao, p. 1. After reviewing, rather inaccurately, the reasons why the CCP needed a peaceful resolution of the Sian Incident, Chang says: "Because the Communist Party is an international party, we had received a directive from the Third [International?] which also insisted upon a peaceful settlement as correct and beneficial." The authenticity of this text, however, is open to some question; it is discussed in more detail on pp. 157–59.

ly opposed by certain elements in the CCP; this opposition was overcome, but not entirely eradicated.

The news of Chiang's capture—or garbled versions of it—fell like a thunderbolt, both in China and abroad. No one had anticipated such an incredible event. Mao later recalled: "When we received the first telegraphic report, we were very suspicious that the telegrapher had made a mistake . . . but after receiving three or four similar telegrams on the same day, we had to believe it."[4]

The instinctive reaction of the CCP to the news of Chiang Kai-shek's kidnapping was one of jubilation, even among highly placed leaders. There was by no means universal understanding or approval of united-front policy in general.[5] And now, with the leader of the counterrevolution suddenly under arrest, there seemed a dramatic way to settle at one stroke the accounts of a decade of bloody suppression. Edgar Snow has told of receiving a postcard from Yenan that described a "huge meeting addressed by Mao Tse-tung and others [at which] a resolution was passed to demand a 'mass trial' of Chiang Kai-shek as a traitor."[b] This is confirmed in general terms by a pro-KMT source, which says that news of the arrest was greeted with joy and excitement when it was thought that revenge might be taken, but that later more sober thinking took over.[6]

The Party quickly sent plenipotentiaries to Sian to represent its interests. Chief among them were Chou En-lai, Ch'in Pang-hsien (Po Ku), and Yeh Chien-ying; the chronology of their movements is still unclear. A recent work asserts that they arrived on the 13th;[7] but Chiang Kai-shek has said that Chang sent a plane to Yenan to pick up Communist representatives three days after the kidnapping (i.e., on the 15th).[8] It is probable that there were considerable comings and goings between Sian and the Communist areas.

[b] *Random Notes,* p. 1. The postcard was from Dr. George Hatem, also known by the Chinese name Ma Hai-te. Hatem, an American of Syrian Jewish extraction, entered the Communist region in the summer of 1936. Though a very popular figure in Yenan, and sometimes a semiofficial translator, he was doubtless ignorant of high-level policy considerations. Much additional information on Hatem is contained in Edgar Snow, *The Other Side of the River,* pp. 261–71.

The suggestion that the CCP was somehow involved in, or knew of, the actual planning of the Sian Incident is denied by most sources, including Chiang Kai-shek himself; and it is not supported by presently available evidence.[c] On the contrary, Miao Chien-ch'iu, one of Chang Hsüeh-liang's younger staff officers, asserted that the CCP had no knowledge of the plot until after the Incident.[d] But in a larger sense, the affair can be put in the context of the CCP's united-front effort. This effort undoubtedly had a great influence on Chang and his officers, which must have contributed significantly to the atmosphere in which the specific decision was made.

Until the situation clarified itself, however, nothing was settled or certain. The first consideration for the Communists was that Chiang Kai-shek was Chang Hsüeh-liang's prisoner, not theirs. Because of this, the CCP was by no means a free agent in dealing with Chiang. Furthermore, Chang insisted that Chiang's safety be protected. This was part of the initial planning, was publicly and privately reiterated, and was confirmed by W. H. Donald, the first representative of Nanking to reach Sian (on December 14).[9] The telegram issued by Chang and Yang Hu-ch'eng on the 12th stated, "Therefore we have tendered our last advice to Marshal Chiang, *while guaranteeing his safety,* in order to stimulate his awakening."[e] On the afternoon of December 13, Chang met with his staff

[c] Chiang, p. 80. Edgar Snow says that "the Communists had encouraged Chang Hsüeh-liang to detain the Generalissimo" (*Random Notes,* Preface, p. 4), but he presents no evidence to support this assertion.

[d] McLane, p. 88. Bertram, whose main source was Miao, believes that the decision was made by a small group of Tung-pei and Hsi-pei officers on the night of the 11th.

[e] My italics. The text of the telegram is available in many sources; e.g., Bertram, pp. 126–27: "The eight demands made by Chang, Yang, and the other signatories (many of whom were members of Chiang's staff; they had signed under obvious duress in what proved to be an unwise tactical move) were as follows: (1) Reorganize the Nanking Government and admit all parties to share the joint responsibility of saving the nation. (2) Stop all kinds of civil wars. (3) Immediately release the patriotic leaders arrested in Shanghai. (4) Release all political prisoners throughout the country. (5) Emancipate the patriotic movement of the people. (6) Safeguard the political freedom of the people to organize and call meetings. (7) Actually carry out the will of Dr. Sun Yat-sen. (8) Immediately call a National Salvation Conference." These demands parallel very closely two statements issued by the CCP on December 1st. The first called for total mobilization of the armed forces for resistance to Japan; an end to civil

to review the events of the day before. He concluded an emotional speech by saying,

> At present Chairman Chiang is entirely safe. We harbor absolutely no personal hatred toward Chairman Chiang. We certainly do not oppose Chairman Chiang himself. What we oppose are Chairman Chiang's policies and methods. . . . Our action will bring absolutely no harm to Chairman Chiang! If Chairman Chiang can abandon his past policies, and truly take charge of the resistance, then we will immediately and unconditionally support and obey him! At such time, if he deems our acts to have been in rebellion and punishes us, we shall accept this with complete equanimity. What we are struggling for is a policy; if that policy can be put into operation, then our objective will have been achieved and nothing else will matter![f]

But Chang Hsüeh-liang's position in his own camp was delicate in the extreme. Within the walls of Sian, Yang Hu-ch'eng had more men and more power than Chang, and Yang's motives were widely suspected to be far less disinterested than Chang's. Yang's men had been responsible for seizing power inside the city, and for the arrest of Chiang's staff, which was housed there. The arrests were made, though one aide was shot and killed. The police and Blueshirts were disarmed and rounded up. But Yang's soldiers

---

war and offensive military operations against the Red Army; an end to repression of the popular movement and of democratic freedoms; and a National Defense Conference, made up of representatives from all classes and groups, "to discuss overall plans for national salvation." The second CCP statement was a letter to Chiang Kai-shek from Mao, Chu Teh, and other Communist leaders. Though critical of Chiang's past policies, it again proposed unified military action in Suiyuan: "We want those in ages to come to see in you the hero who rectified his mistakes and brought salvation to the nation and to the people. . . . 'The butcher becomes a Buddha once he lays down his cleaver.' " The letter ended, "We await your instructions." (Both CCP statements are in *I-nien-lai* [CCP 6].)

[f] [Sian] *Chieh-fang jih-pao,* Dec. 16, 1936, p. 2. This paper has no connection with the famous Communist paper of the same name, which had not yet begun publication. Previously the *Hsi-ching jih-pao,* the paper changed its name beginning with the issue for December 13, 1936. Chang made the same offer in a confidential telegram to the China correspondent of the London *Times* on December 19: "When he [Chiang] does return to Nanking, I am prepared, if a dispassionate and fair trial is possible, to go with him to stand before the nation." Bertram, *Sian Mutiny,* p. 136.

rampaged virtually out of control for several hours; there was much looting and much unnecessary shooting.[g] Ominously, Chiang Kai-shek was first taken to Yang's headquarters; Chang was very worried about Chiang's safety there, but it was not until two days later, after Donald interceded, that the obdurate Generalissimo agreed to move to a compound controlled by Chang's men. Furthermore, some of Chang's senior commanders (especially Wang I-che and Hu Chu-kuo) were highly critical of cooperation with the Communists, while many of the younger officers—who apparently had the support of the very radical Sian National Salvation student leaders—were so bitterly opposed to Chiang that they would have killed him happily. It was by no means certain that Chang Hsüeh-liang could protect his prisoner.

Therefore, even assuming that the CCP had sufficient influence in Sian to engineer Chiang's assassination or otherwise try to take over, its action would almost certainly have been opposed by Chang. The Party had no choice but to recognize that its freedom of action was definitely limited. Moreover, the CCP had recently been calling for a united front that would include Chiang Kai-shek and all anti-Japanese elements in the Nanking Government. To be implicated now in the elimination of the defenseless Generalissimo would expose the CCP as the worst kind of hypocrite, and would invalidate all the propaganda the Party had issued concerning the need for national solidarity and cessation of civil war.

Events in Nanking during the first few days following Chiang's detention must have convinced CCP leaders that any hopes of "setting up a national anti-Japanese government in Sian, isolating if not totally discrediting Chiang Kai-shek," were quite impossible.[10] As soon as Chiang was taken captive, a factional struggle began in Nanking. Two main groups emerged almost immediately, with most of the real military power in the hands of those eager to launch a punitive expedition against the kidnappers and press vig-

[g] I have not yet been able to determine the precise balance of forces in Sian. Bertram (*Sian Mutiny*, p. 108) claims that Yang had about 40,000 men in the local area. Most of Chang's command was dispersed in Kansu; one unit was even in southern Hopei. Agnes Smedley, perhaps the only westerner in Sian at the time, had her possessions taken from her by one of Yang's soldiers. See Smedley, pp. 141–45.

orously ahead with the anti-Communist extermination campaign.[11] This group, led by Ho Ying-ch'in and Tai Chi-t'ao, argued that Nanking could not deal with mutineers and Communists, and must take the strongest possible action. Meanwhile, Madame Chiang, T. V. Soong, and H. H. Kung were trying to hold them back and work for moderation.[12] With Chiang dead (which the extremists insisted must already be the case, even though no news had come from Sian), this disorder could be expected to become more pronounced. Even after Donald confirmed on December 15 that Chiang was alive and safe, the extremists continued to insist on "punitive action," which clearly endangered his life. Although the moderates were able to prevent direct attack on Sian, the nearby city of Weinan was heavily bombed, and Central Army troops began pushing westward along the Lunghai rail line toward Sian.

From a military standpoint, this was of the utmost importance. Sian and the Northwest (Shensi, Kansu) were safe from invasion only if the defenders held T'ung-kuan. There, where the Yellow River makes its great turn from south to east, the only avenue to Sian and the province of Shensi can be blocked. The Lunghai rail line runs through this corridor. But by December 16, Central troops had already reached Hua-hsien, about 40 miles west of T'ung-kuan, where they clashed briefly with Yang's men and then halted. On December 18, Chiang Ting-wen arrived in Nanking from Sian with Chiang Kai-shek's order to cease bombing operations and halt the Punitive Expedition. But it was clear by the 16th that any reasonable hope of detaching the Northwest from Central control was gone.

Even in the absence of explicit orders from Moscow, there could be no doubt how Stalin felt about the affair. The Russian press began reacting as early as December 14. Opinions varied spectacularly, but all favored the unconditional release of Chiang Kai-shek. Chang Hsüeh-liang and Yang Hu-ch'eng were denounced as "rascals" or "traitors."[h] Most Russian papers attributed the kidnap-

[h] A summary of Russian press reaction will be found in McLane, pp. 82–86. Edgar Snow has shown that Moscow's line could not have been the result of simple misinformation, since the Russian correspondent in Peiping knew Chang Hsüeh-liang's true feelings. See *Random Notes*, p. 3.

ping to the machinations of the Japanese, or to the work of pro-Japanese elements, notably Wang Ching-wei. *Inprecor* praised the punitive campaign against Sian, and criticized Madame Chiang and T. V. Soong for holding it back. Moscow's press reaction, in Snow's words, "enormously weakened the Chinese Communists in their relations with [Chang] . . . in a quarter where Chang had expected help and understanding."[13]

The CCP made its first public statement on the Sian Incident in a circular telegram dated December 19.[14] The fact that no public statement was made by the CCP until a full week after Chiang's kidnapping indicates the difficulties inherent in the situation. But the CCP had to take action before too long. Everyone believed that the CCP was involved in one way or another, and expected the Party to clarify its position. To remain silent was to risk losing all initiative. Furthermore, the coverage of the Incident in the Russian press made it imperative that the CCP prevent the impression that these were also its views. The telegram expressed the conviction that "the Sian leaders acted from patriotic sincerity and zeal, wishing quickly to formulate a national policy of immediate resistance to Japan." An immediate truce between Nanking and Sian was proposed, pending the convocation of an all-party peace conference in Nanking; prior to this certain things would be settled, among them the disposition of Chiang Kai-shek.[i] The telegram was unequivocal in its support for Chang and Yang, and was therefore directly opposed to Moscow's position.

[i] The telegram reads at this point: "Tsai ho-p'ing hui-i ch'ien, yü ko tang ko p'ai ko chieh ko chün hsien t'i k'ang-Jih chiu-wang ts'ao-an, ping t'ao-lun Chiang Chieh-shih hsien-sheng ch'u-chih wen-t'i, tan chi-pen kang-ling ying shih t'uan-chieh ch'üan-kuo, fan-tui i-ch'ieh nei-chan, i-chih k'ang-Jih." ("Prior to the peace conference, all parties, groups, circles, and armed forces will bring forward their draft proposals concerning resistance to Japan and national salvation, and will discuss the question of the disposition of Mr. Chiang Kai-shek; but the fundamental program should be unification of the entire nation, opposition to all civil war, and unanimous resistance to Japan.") The crucial term here is "ch'u-chih." It implies the investigation of a situation and the taking of appropriate action; sometimes it suggests legal action, as in the prosecution of a case. But it seems to me that it is being used here with deliberate ambiguity, and that the whole tone of the telegram is to stress national unity without making the removal of Chiang a condition. Note also that the CCP suggests the conference be held in Nanking.

This brings us to the crucial question of CCP policy and Moscow's influence upon it. The statement concerning Chiang's "disposition" has been interpreted to mean that the CCP sought to eliminate him. The implication found in Edgar Snow's *Random Notes on Red China* is that Stalin's order to release Chiang reached Mao *after* the release of the December 19th telegram and in effect countermanded a plan to discredit or eliminate Chiang. But no concrete evidence supports this hypothesis. Moscow's public reaction had come with extreme speed. News of the Sian Incident could hardly have reached the Russian capital much before noon on Saturday, December 12. In order for *Pravda* to denounce the coup in its Monday issue, decisions of editorial policy had to be made quickly. If Stalin was as strongly committed to Chiang as his reaction suggests (and as is claimed by Snow, Thomson, Dallin, and others), it hardly seems possible that he would have waited a full week to communicate his will to the CCP—a week in which events might render the order meaningless.

If we make the contrary—more likely—assumption that Stalin's order reached Mao *before* December 19, then the telegram appears in a very different light, as evidence of Mao's determination to make his own decision independently of Moscow. It is my opinion that such was the case. In this light, the December 19th telegram was a temporizing document. The Party had first of all to consider the policies it would adopt if various possible situations arose. Conditions in Sian, and Sian's relations with Nanking, were highly fluid and largely beyond Communist control. What if Chang Hsüeh-liang were unable to control the situation in Sian, and Chiang were killed? What if Nanking should launch an all-out attack on Sian? Could any concessions be wrung from Chiang Kai-shek? If the CCP worked either for Chiang's elimination or for his release, could they succeed? These vital questions required very different answers, and the Party did not wish to make any statement until there was some clarification—much less commit themselves to a policy they might not be able to carry out.

The telegram can be read so as to be consistent with several possible alternatives. Peace and unity seem to be the keynotes, but this "unity" might or might not include Nanking, and might or might not include Chiang Kai-shek. The call for a termination of civil war ("peace") was one that could be maintained even in the face of stepped-up military campaigns against the CCP. Mao is reported to have flown into a rage upon receipt of Stalin's order.[15] But one need not assume that his temper resulted from a forced change of policy. Moscow's denunciation and brusque intervention provided grounds for anger, regardless of what Mao intended to do.

The question of concessions and counter-concessions was clearly of cardinal importance. The evidence indicates that Chang, Yang, and the CCP were substantially in agreement as to what these should be. Publicly, Chiang Kai-shek could only refuse to consider any demands made upon him under duress. And if the Sian authorities and the CCP were seriously trying to conclude some agreement with Chiang, they had to be careful not to compromise him by extracting public concessions. No source has ever suggested that there were any signed documents, or any written record of the discussions. This leaves the question of verbal agreements. Chiang has always maintained that he never reached any understanding, express or implied, with his captors; he denies having spoken to Chou En-lai or any other member of the CCP.[16] The CCP, on the other hand, has claimed that Chiang "accepted the demand of Generals Chang Hsüeh-liang and Yang Hu-ch'eng and the people of the Northwest for resistance to Japan, and as an initial step ordered the troops engaged in the civil war to withdraw from the provinces of Shensi and Kansu."[17]

Despite this obdurate public posture, the less formal utterances of both Chiang and Mme. Chiang suggest a vaguely conciliatory position. Mme. Chiang told Chang on December 23: "As we are all Chinese, we should not fight each other. Internal problems should be solved by political means and not by military force. That had been the policy of the Generalissimo and was so even in the case of the Communists."[18] Chiang later recalled that during his detention, "The problem which merited careful study was how to make the Communists really resist Japan with the rest of the nation."[19] The Communist leader Ch'in Pang-hsien (Po Ku), who was in Sian during the kidnapping, told Edgar Snow that Chiang's first words to Chou En-lai were "We must not have any more civil war."[20] From the standpoint of the Chinese Communists, this was, perhaps, the crucial step, from which all others might be taken.

It is possible that Chiang went not much further than this. Ch'in Pang-hsien claims that he had been directed to get further assurances from Chiang, but was prevented from doing so by Chang's "premature" release of the Generalissimo.[j] According to one source, Chou En-lai sought to convince Yang Hu-ch'eng that more explicit concessions were not necessary, and that Yang should not oppose Chiang's release.[21]

There are, therefore, excellent reasons why the Communists should have decided to work for Chiang's release and a peaceful settlement of the Sian Incident: the possibility that they could not prevent his release; the risk that an attempt to eliminate Chiang would cause a split in Sian without producing a favorable result in Nanking; the apparent increase in the power of pro-Japanese, anti-Communist elements in Nanking who could be controlled only by Chiang; and Chiang's probable willingness to consider a rapprochement with the CCP if it recognized his leadership. Lastly, of course, there was the command from Stalin. (A few weeks after Chiang's release, Hu Shih charged that the Generalissimo's arrest was a traitorous act, and had received no support in Moscow; Ho K'o-ch'uan (K'ai-feng) answered, with evident discomfort, that neither the USSR nor the CCP could make policy for the other, but that the Russian position was actually similar to that of the CCP, since both favored a peaceful settlement.)[22] All in all, it is hard to see how a rational process of decision could have come to any other conclusion than that the CCP should work for Chiang's release.

Several things, however, made the decision extremely difficult and risky. The first was opposition in the Party to letting the arch-enemy escape and stand recognized as the leader of the whole Chinese people. Next was the fact that right up until the last minute,

[j] Edgar Snow, *Random Notes,* pp. 12–13. Ch'in (Po Ku) maintained that Chang released Chiang completely on his own initiative—another indication that CCP power was limited in Sian.

the action of any one of several participants could radically change the situation and require a different course on the part of the CCP. Finally, the CCP's decision could be justified only as a bet on the future. If Chiang had resumed the anti-Communist campaign, repudiating in action the indefinite and uncertifiable "understanding" reached in Sian, Mao's action would have appeared a tremendous error. Except for the pressure of public opinion and the continuing threat of the Japanese, the CCP had no way of forcing Chiang to come through after his release. It is no wonder that Chou En-lai told Wang Ping-nan that "We didn't sleep for a week, trying to decide. . . . It was the most difficult decision of our whole lives."[23]

The CCP has made no secret of the fact that there was opposition within the Party to the peaceful resolution of the Sian Incident and the release of Chiang Kai-shek. Unfortunately, we know very little of the range of attitudes within the Politburo. After his defection, Chang Kuo-t'ao was charged with such recklessness: "Certain reputedly 'Left' people in the Party, like Chang Kuo-t'ao, then urged that the Red Army should 'fight its way out through T'ung-kuan,' which meant that the Red Army should mount an offensive against the Kuomintang troops. This proposal ran counter to the Central Committee's policy for a peaceful settlement of the Sian Incident."[24] Liu Shao-ch'i, too, has noted that "some comrades" opposed a peaceful solution: "They simply thought that if some other way of resolving the Sian Incident were adopted, or if it were not resolved, then the KMT and CCP could still cooperate or could cooperate even better. But they were only guilty of certain specific errors, which were easily corrected later on."[25]

It is possible, also, to get some glimpse of the disagreement and confusion that the Sian Incident produced among the rank and file. In a manifesto dated December 28, 1936 (three days after Chiang's release), the Northern Bureau of the Party deplored the Sian Incident, and went on to say that the Party

> from the start of the Sian Incident, had already stated that it did not approve of the measures adopted by Chang and Yang to detain Chiang Kai-shek by force in Sian. . . . This was because we felt that the impetuous measures taken by Chang and Yang at Sian

> would lead to civil war and disintegration in China, and would make it even more difficult to unify all sides in opposition to Japan; meanwhile Nanking's armed punitive action would directly touch off civil war. This would run the unparalleled danger of giving Japanese imperialism an opening it could exploit in order to destroy China. . . . From the start we did not approve of the measures adopted by Chang and Yang in the Sian Incident, and we believe that this was a most unfortunate affair for China.[26]

Although the statement does not call Chang and Yang "rascals," the tone of the document is much closer to that of Moscow than that of Yenan.

Following the release of Chiang Kai-shek, the Party center found it necessary to explain its policy during the Sian Incident in secret dispatches to local Party organs. One such, reprinted by local authorities, stated that during the Incident two erroneous opinions were widespread.[27] The first held that "if Chiang were dead, or were detained for a few days, Nanking would collapse, and the nationwide coalition would naturally emerge victorious." The second believed that "the 'Punitive Campaign' under the orders of Ho Ying-ch'in would collaborate with Japanese and puppet forces, and would be sufficient to wipe out the Northwest anti-Japanese power; the united front would suffer complete defeat."[28] The document explained that the former underestimated the continuing strength of Nanking, and the latter underestimated the strength of the anti-Japanese masses. Furthermore, "After Chiang's arrest, we observed, along with the insane suicidal struggle touched off by the 'Punitive Campaign Group' under Ho Ying-ch'in, that the Japanese imperialists were calling with unparalleled strength for 'opposition to peaceful settlement by the Nanking Government' . . ."[29] The main reasons why the CCP worked for Chiang's release were to frustrate those who hoped for civil war in China and to prevent the possibility of a Nanking-Japanese coalition against the CCP. Finally, it was explained that Chiang could not openly accept the demands of Chang and Yang and still regain his position: he would first have to repair his damaged prestige by acting in a manner apparently contrary to these demands. Later, however, Chiang would tacitly and indirectly move toward domestic peace and joint resistance.

Aftermath

Chiang Kai-shek's statement, upon his release, was worded with suitable lofty independence: "Since today you have shown due regard for the welfare of the nation and have decided to send me back to Nanking and no longer try to make any special demands or force me to make any promise or give any orders, it marks a turning point in the life of the nation and is also an indication of the high moral and cultural standards of the Chinese people."[k] He tried repeatedly to resign from all his offices. The Government would not permit him to do so; but it finally granted him leave to recuperate. Chang Hsüeh-liang was stripped of his offices and tried by the Military Affairs Commission, headed by Ho Ying-ch'in. He was sentenced to ten years' imprisonment and five years' loss of civil rights. Chiang requested that a special pardon be issued, and Chang was in effect turned over to the custody of his former prisoner.[l]

Chiang Kai-shek's semi-official biographer summed up the attitude of his chief:

> President Chiang's attitude toward the "Communist Party" remained unchanged after the Sian Incident. But in view of the unstable situation in the northwest, he felt that the gain would not justify the cost, if the Government was to spend all the resources at its disposal on another military operation against the so-called Communist Party. Being versatile in expedients, President

---

[k] Chiang and Soong, p. 177. This is supposedly Chiang's admonition to Chang and Yang prior to leaving Sian. It is doubtful that he made such a speech at the airfield, as claimed, but the sentiments are surely his.

[l] One can only speculate on why Chang Hsüeh-liang returned to Nanking with Chiang Kai-shek. Some possibilities: (a) Chang may have thought that he would be hailed as a hero and given an important command; (b) Chang wanted to prove the purity of his motives, a point he had stressed from the beginning; (c) Chang wanted to use himself as hostage to ensure that Chiang would not revert to his earlier policies of unification before resistance; (d) Chang wanted to help Chiang repair his damaged prestige, so that he could more effectively regain control in Nanking and lead the nation in resistance to Japan.

> Chiang began to consider whether it would be of national interest to come to an agreement with Mao Tse-tung and his followers in order to obtain their cooperation in case of a war with Japan.[30]

On January 6, the Bandit Suppression Headquarters in Sian was quietly abolished.[31] But Central forces under Ku Chu-t'ung moved into the area, and anti-Communist sentiments continued to be expressed by the KMT and the Government.

A mood of anticlimax and letdown was dominant in Sian. Prior to his departure, Chang Hsüeh-liang had appointed Yü Hsüeh-chung, one of his most trusted commanders and concurrently the Governor of Kansu, to take command of the Tung-pei forces. But Yü was unable to maintain the precarious unity that had existed in the Manchurian Army. It soon became clear that while the campaign against the Red Army would not be resumed, neither would Chang be returning to Sian. Meanwhile, Central armies were moving in, and the Tung-pei and Hsi-pei forces were about to be transferred and dispersed. The young radical officers became convinced that some of the senior unit commanders were negotiating privately with the Nanking men; on February 2, they took action into their own hands. General Wang I-che was assassinated, as were several lesser commanders. But the principal target, General Ho Chu-kuo, narrowly escaped, reportedly with the aid of Yang Hu-ch'eng.[m]

There was also the feeling in Sian that the CCP, having put its stakes on KMT-CCP unity, could no longer afford to concern itself with the fate of the Manchurian forces, or of Chang Hsüehliang himself. Those who had made the Sian Incident possible were the chief losers. The CCP was going for two birds in the bush; in doing so, it had to give up one in the hand. But it was not themselves they were sacrificing.

[m] Bertram, *Sian Mutiny,* pp. 257–59. If it was Yang's intention to curry favor with Nanking, the plan did not work. He soon left Sian for T'ung-kuan, and subsequently for the Japanese-held city of Dairen in Manchuria. He returned to China after the start of the war and was held under confinement. He was still in Chungking in 1949, where he died under mysterious circumstances. The CCP claims that he was murdered by KMT special agents before the fall of the city to the Communists.

In Yenan, 150 miles to the north, Mao Tse-tung was mixing exhortation with criticism. On December 28, he criticized Chiang's first post-Sian statement, but pledged CCP support if Chiang and the KMT ceased collaboration with the Japanese, terminated the civil war, and immediately entered an all-party anti-Japanese united front.[32] On January 6, the Central Committee and the soviet government wired the Nanking authorities that the CCP was dissatisfied with the trend of events: Chiang in temporary retirement at Fenghua, Chang under arrest, and forces commanded by pro-Japanese elements advancing on Sian. The authors of the telegram called upon Chiang to come forward and control the situation—and expressed confidence that he could do so. But they pointed out that this would be a "serious test of Mr. Chiang's political integrity and of his own dictum that 'words require fidelity; acts require results.' "[33]

Meanwhile, direct negotiations were under way, looking toward the convocation of the KMT CEC's Third Plenum in early February.[34] On February 10, the CCP dispatched a telegram to the Plenum in which four concessions were offered, in return for which the KMT was to terminate civil war, oppose Japan, grant civil liberties, release political prisoners, call an all-party conference to determine measures for resistance, etc. The four CCP concessions were: (1) to cease all efforts to overthrow the National Government; (2) to rename the soviet government as the government of the "special region" of the Republic of China; and to designate the Red Army as a unit of the National Revolutionary Army, which would accept "guidance" directly from the Central Government; (3) to put into effect in the special region a democratic system based on universal suffrage; and (4) to abolish confiscation of landlords' land.[35]

The Plenum took no formal notice of the telegram, but countered with its own demands, also four in number, which closely paralleled the concessions offered by the CCP. These provided the basis for the eventual achievement of KMT-CCP collaboration after the Marco Polo Bridge affair. Negotiations and interchanges between the two erstwhile adversaries increased during this period of tacit truce; CCP representatives were frequently sent to Nanking, and KMT groups visited Yenan. However, the reunion of the old enemies was not yet complete. The CCP betrayed concern that Chiang might cancel the progress that had been made, and resume his earlier policies. Even very slightly conciliatory actions by Japan were hotly denounced, not only as a smoke screen for aggression, but also as ammunition for those in the KMT who opposed the policy to which Mao was now definitely committed—and where he might be proved extremely vulnerable. On April 15, the CCP Central Committee issued a statement to all Party members that laid out the current line and explained its significance. The conflict between China and Japan was now of primary importance, overshadowing domestic feuds; the consolidation of domestic peace and unity and the achievement of democracy were the present tasks of the Party. In order to achieve these objectives, the CCP had offered four concessions to the KMT. These concessions were not a CCP surrender, as some had charged, because they did not surrender military and political independence, or freedom of action. The concessions would enable the CCP to achieve legality and nationwide operation, and would thus enhance the influence of the Party. It was essential that a genuine alliance be achieved with the KMT, for only in this way could civil war be avoided.[36]

But Mao's concern also showed through, during the spring of 1937: "They [the opponents of Mao's policy] say, 'Japan is retreating and Nanking is wavering more than ever; the contradiction between the two countries is becoming weaker and the contradiction within the country is growing sharper.' . . . I think this view incorrect. In saying that peace has been attained, we do not mean that it is consolidated; on the contrary we have said that it is not consolidated. . . . We say that the Kuomintang has begun to change and we also say that it has not changed completely."[37]

Chapter 6

The Wartime Development of the United Front

In this chapter, I shall attempt to trace the development of the united-front approach in general terms, up to about 1940. By this time, the main lines of the policy were clearly worked out, and the Party understood its principal applications. I shall also describe the United Front Work Department, the specific Party organization created to give overall direction to this work (it will become clear, however, that the uses of the united front were so broad that it could not be confined within any one department). The following three chapters will offer selected examples of the range and variety of problems to which the united front was applied. These will be hardly more than sketches; each of the topics is worthy of full-scale treatment, and the united front was only one facet of a many-sided approach. Nevertheless, even such cursory treatment may suggest the remarkable success of the CCP in combining pragmatic flexibility with general consistency of policy.

The Marco Polo Bridge episode of July 7, 1937, did not signal the immediate outbreak of large-scale hostilities or the final conclusion of two-party collaboration. There ensued a month of sparring, with rumors of a negotiated settlement between Nanking and Tokyo, before the Japanese attack on Shanghai irrevocably set off the war. The final touches were put to the KMT-CCP agreement during August and September. On August 25, the Red Army became the Eighth Route Army (later also called the Eighteenth Group Army), under the nominal command of the National Government. On September 22, the National Government released the CCP's "Manifesto on KMT-CCP Cooperation," which reiterated the CCP's concessions: (a) to strive for the realization of Sun Yat-sen's Three People's Principles (*San-min chu-i*); (b) to abandon its policies of armed revolt, sovietization, and forcible confiscation of landlords' land; (c) to abolish the present soviet government; and (d) to abolish the term "Red Army" and place Communist troops under government command. Chiang Kai-shek responded the following day, praising the statement as a "triumph of national sentiment over every other consideration."[1]

Thus, at the beginning of the Sino-Japanese War, the united front was seen, above all, as an anti-Japanese policy. During the eight years that followed, the CCP increased its military strength from roughly 30,000 to nearly 1 million, and the people it governed from about 2 million to 96 million. Yet when the Japanese threat was gone, the united front, with a change in emphasis and target, was applied effectively to the struggle against the KMT. Whatever role the Comintern may have played in the formation of a united front up to 1937, there can be no question of outside pressure to continue its use a decade or so later. The CCP did so because it had found that policy to be valuable. During the years of war, the united front grew in strategic importance until it came to occupy a permanent place in Chinese Communist practice and ideology.

Summary of KMT-CCP Relations

The first 14 months of the war set the high-water marks of internal unity and of KMT-CCP cooperation. Much of this was the result of a public opinion full of patriotic fervor, which longed for genuine unity and made the most of all signs that it had been achieved. Under the pressures of nationalism and necessity, the two parties gave a number of such signs during these months.

In early 1938, the KMT authorized the publication of the *Hsin-hua jih-pao* by the Communists in Hankow, and, according to one source, gave it financial aid.[a] On January 30, 1938, Chiang Kai-

[a] Rosinger, *China's Wartime Politics,* p. 29. The paper was later moved to Chungking and continued, though heavily censored, to publish throughout the war years.

shek and the government (willingly or not) approved the formation of the Chin-Ch'a-Chi Border Region. For the first couple of years of the war, the government allocated a portion of its scanty war matériel to the Eighth Route Army, and also provided pay for three divisions. Meanwhile, reports of sincere Communist cooperation were frequent, and foreign observers were impressed with the CCP's "scrupulous adherence" to the new policy.[2] Though not without reservation and criticism, Communist propaganda organs praised Chiang, affirmed the San-min chu-i, and proclaimed their determination to resist to the end beside the Central Government.

On the political side, civil liberties were considerably extended by the National Government's Program of Armed Resistance and National Reconstruction, and large numbers of political prisoners were released. Participation in the government was somewhat widened by the formation (August 1937) of the Supreme National Defense Council, with a 25-member Advisory Council composed of representatives from a number of political groups, including the CCP. In the following spring, this body was expanded to include 200 members, and its name was changed to the People's Political Council (PPC). Chou En-lai was made one of the 17 members of the Presidium of the Extraordinary National Congress of the KMT in March 1938, and was also appointed Vice-Minister of the Political Training Board of the National Military Council, a position he held until 1940.[3]

But despite this apparently smooth beginning—and the volumes of propaganda issued by both parties to support it—there were early instances of friction. Bookstores and newspapers in Sian were harassed or shut down.[4] Non-KMT youth organizations were required to register with the government in May 1938.[5] Other mass organizations were disbanded in August, and the *Hsin-hua jih-pao* was shut down for three days as a result of its protests. There were occasional forays across the ill-defined perimeter of the Shen-Kan-Ning border region; and during the formation of the base and guerrilla areas, there were constant disagreements.

The era of relative good feeling gradually came to an end after the fall of Hankow and the withdrawal of the government to Szechwan. As it surveyed the course of the war, the KMT was painfully aware that it had borne the brunt of the Japanese offensive, and that the most advanced regions of China had been lost. Meanwhile, the Japanese had paid less attention to the CCP, which was still regaining its feet after the rigors of the years just past. The Japanese seized major cities and lines of communication, but the Communists barely felt the loss of things they had never possessed. They took advantage of the thinness of the Japanese occupation, depending on the support of an increasingly aroused populace, and areas under Communist control or influence expanded rapidly, particularly in North China. The KMT was too weak to undertake a counteroffensive against the Japanese, and unable or unwilling to compete effectively with the CCP behind Japanese lines. Left without a positive policy, the KMT adopted a negative one: to restrict as much as possible the areas of CCP control, and to suppress Communist activities in areas controlled by itself.

True unity, the KMT argued, required that the Central Government should exercise effective and complete authority over all areas and all military forces subject to Chinese control, that it should determine areas of legitimate political activity, and that it should command the unquestioning loyalty and obedience of all patriotic Chinese. The Central Government was necessarily an extension of the Kuomintang, and this circumstance was justified by Sun's theory of the Period of Tutelage. China had an established government, supposedly recognized by all parties and groups. For what reason, then, did these groups refuse to genuinely accept and carry out the will of the government, whose mandate they publicly acknowledged? How could the Central Government prosecute the war and coordinate its domestic policies when large and expanding areas were in fact ruled by a rival regime?

The first serious clashes between the two parties came in 1939. A collision between guerrilla forces in Shantung in April was followed by bloodletting in Hunan and Hopei during June. In November, several hundred civilians and New Fourth Army soldiers were killed in Honan. Matters came to a head between December 1939 and March 1940. The "First Anti-Communist Upsurge," as the CCP called it, began with KMT capture of exposed areas on the outskirts of the Shen-Kan-Ning region, and reached its height when Yen Hsi-shan split with the CCP (see below, pp. 130–42). According to the CCP, this anti-Communist upsurge was terminated when elements of the Eighth Route Army defeated the forces of Chu Huai-ping in the T'ai-hang Mountains.[6]

The CCP marks a "Second Anti-Communist Upsurge," during which the New Fourth Incident of January 1941 took place.[b] The government maintained that the New Fourth Army had consistently violated orders concerning its areas of operation, and that instead of fighting the Japanese it had been spending most of its time clearing regions south of the Yangtze for CCP political influence to enter. The CCP could hardly deny some of these allegations, but countered that the New Fourth Army was the only effective anti-Japanese force in the area, and that to order it out would simply mean surrendering large regions to the Japanese. The CCP also claimed, with ostensible justification, that it was obeying the Central Government directives at the time of the attack (in fact, it was responding to orders from its own upper echelons to move north). Neither side was really talking to the other; rather, both were trying to convince the Chinese public—and the CCP was somewhat more successful in its posture of the martyred patriot than was the Central Government in its role as a commander of mutinous subordinates. Each side recoiled somewhat from the impact of this event. But though there was no further internal strife on this scale, its causes remained the same.

These military actions were paralleled, in the areas subject to KMT control, by civil actions designed to still criticism and to compel acquiescence. There was, therefore, a growing retreat from the freedoms of the early days of the war. In 1939, the KMT passed a series of acts aimed mainly at the CCP that also hamstrung the ac-

[b] An excellent account of the "incident" (in which an estimated 10,000 were killed) is contained in Johnson, pp. 136–40.

tivities of other political groups.[c] A tight lid was placed on virtually all criticism, and any form of organizational activity was regarded with deep mistrust.[d] Pronouncements concerning the relations between the two parties became increasingly bitter and accusatory. In November 1942, for example, Chiang said—with scant hope, one imagines—that the CCP would be treated like everyone else, "as long as they would, from now on, obey all laws and orders, refrain from disturbing the social order, organize no army of their own, cease the occupation of places by force, keep from hindering the prosecution of the war or undermining national unity."[7] And his famous statement of the following summer, after a plenary session of the CEC (KMT), was scarcely more than a disclaimer of immediate armed conflict: "I am of the opinion that first of all we should clearly recognize that the Communist problem is a purely political problem and should be solved by political means." It is a measure of the nearness of civil war that this pronouncement occasioned considerable relief.[e]

Some loosening of the ban on political activity took place in 1944, a dark year for the KMT and a year of recovery for the CCP. The two parties began apparently serious negotiations, which were carried on more or less continuously until September, when they were reported stalemated in the PPC. Although no results had been achieved, the atmosphere was widely felt to be hopeful. The points under discussion were: (1) the disposition, size, command, and training of the CCP armies; (2) the relationship between the CCP

[c] These were: (a) Measures to Restrict the Activities of Alien Parties (Hsien-chih i-tang huo-tung pan-fa), January. (b) Measures to Deal with the Communist Problem (Kung-tang wen-t'i ch'u-chih pan-fa), February. (c) Measures for Guarding Against Communist Activities in the Japanese-Occupied Areas (Lun-hsien-ch'ü fang-fan kung-tang huo-tung pan-fa), February. The texts of these and other measures may be found in *Mo-ts'a ts'ung-ho erh lai?* [CCP 12].

[d] See below for a discussion of the difficulties of the group that later became the Democratic League.

[e] *White Paper,* p. 54. See also Rosinger, *China's Crisis,* p. 101. Chiang preceded this statement with the words, "If you share my opinion . . . ." Since this was an address to the CEC, it has been suggested that this conditional clause indicated a body of opinion in the CEC that favored a military solution of the Communist problem.

and KMT regions; and (3) political problems, involving civil rights, legalization of the CCP, and coalition government.[f]

Following the arrival of General Patrick Hurley, President Roosevelt's Special Representative (later Ambassador), negotiations between Chungking and Yenan were resumed, and continued intermittently from November 1944 until March of the following year. As before, no conclusions were reached, but the issues were considerably simplified and clarified. November and December brought forth the CCP's Five Point Draft Agreement, and the KMT's counterproposal, the Three Point Plan. The CCP position was that if *first* (a) the KMT surrendered control of the National Government; (b) the government, including the military administration, was reorganized as a coalition including the CCP and other groups; and (c) the CCP and other groups were fully legalized, and civil rights were guaranteed; *then* the CCP would recognize the authority of this government and turn its armed forces over to its command. The KMT position, on the other hand, was that if *first* the CCP and its military forces would submit themselves to the existing National Government, *then* the KMT and that government would take measures to institute constitutional government with multi-party representation, legalize the CCP, protect civil rights, etc. The CCP throughout conducted itself as an established and sovereign entity, while the KMT viewed it as an illegal political party with a dissident armed force.

During the last months of the war, the KMT's position recovered somewhat from the dark days of 1944. George Atcheson, American Chargé d'Affaires, listed the causes:

> rapid development of United States Army plans for rebuilding the armies of Chiang Kai-shek, the increase of additional aid . . .

---

[f] *White Paper,* p. 55, and cited annexes. The lengthy public reports given by Chang Ch'ün and Lin Tsu-han to the PPC were the first authoritative discussion of the negotiations, which up to this time had been carried on in secret. The reports were quite detailed, dispassionate, and lacking in the name-calling and tendentious argumentation which had been (and was to be) so common. Lin's opportunity to get his case heard was the most impressive forum the CCP had had in Chungking for years.

> the cessation of Japanese offensives, the opening of the road into China, the expectation that the Central Government will participate at San Francisco in making important decisions, the conviction that we are determined upon definite support and strengthening of the Central Government alone and as the sole possible channel for assistance to other groups . . . the hopes of an early settlement with the Soviet Union without settlement of the Communist problem.[8]

Both sides knew by now that Japan would be defeated, and both sides were preparing their positions for the postwar power struggle that was certain to take place.

The Development of United-Front Policy

The theory and practice of the wartime united front were worked out during the first three years of the conflict (until 1940, when *On the New Democracy* appeared). By the end of the war, the potentialities of the united-front approach were understood, and its application to the civil war was anticipated by the analysis contained in *On Coalition Government.*

One of the first problems that the CCP now solved once and for all was the relation of the class struggle in China to the national struggle against Japan. Mao wrote: "In a struggle that is national in character, the class struggle takes the form of national struggle, which demonstrates the identity between the two."[9] The invasion of China by Japan meant that the class struggle "must be subordinated to, and must not conflict with, the interests of the War of Resistance."[10] He went on to say, later, that "United front policy *is* class policy, and the two are inseparable; whoever is unclear on this will be unclear on many other problems."[11] It was doubtless with a great sense of emotional release and satisfaction that the Communists were able to conclude, "Patriotism is simply an application of internationalism in the war of national liberation."[12] This sounds very similar to Lenin's formulation at the Second Comintern Congress, but the emphasis is quite different. For Lenin, nationalism and patriotism had no ultimate value (they were part of the bourgeois ideology of the state), though he recognized their power and saw ways in which they could be employed. But for the CCP, nationalism was—and is—an ultimate value. Though the solution derived from Lenin, his name was never invoked. The CCP was beginning to view the problem of nationalism and revolution in specifically Chinese terms. Because of China's semi-feudal, semi-colonial nature, "(1) The proletariat either forms a united front with the bourgeoisie or is forced to break it up; and (2) armed struggle is the principal form of the revolution. These have become the two basic characteristics of the Chinese proletariat and the Chinese Communist Party during the bourgeois-democratic revolution."[13] These peculiarities were "not found in the history of the Communist parties in capitalistic countries."[14]

The CCP continued to affirm that this was to be a nationwide, mass united front:

> Should the Anti-Japanese National United Front be confined to the Kuomintang and the Communist Party? No, it should be a united front of the whole nation, with the two parties only a small part of this united front. The two parties are unquestionably the leading components in this great united front, but they will always be only a part of it. The Anti-Japanese National United Front is one of all parties and groups, of people in all walks of life and of all armed forces, a united front of all patriots—workers, peasants, businessmen, intellectuals, and soldiers.[15]

The Party's united-front analysis (November 1937) divided Chinese society into the customary three blocs. (1) The left wing was composed of the Communist-led masses: the proletariat, the peasantry, and the urban petty bourgeoisie. This bloc was to be expanded and consolidated as the basis for reform of the KMT, the government, and the army; for the creation of a democratic republic; and for the defeat of Japan. (2) The middle forces were the national bourgeoisie and the upper strata of the petty bourgeoisie. This group included such elements as the Shanghai commercial class, parts of the Fu-hsing She (popularly called the "Blueshirts"), and parts of the CC Clique. All were vacillating but moving toward the left, or toward reform; this tendency was to be accelerated. (3) The right wing was composed of the big landlords and the big bourgeoisie—potential collaborators and capitulators. Some had already gone over to the enemy; others would do so before long. This group was steadfastly anti-Communist, but might be used as long as it remained anti-Japanese.[16] In the countryside, the poor peasants and the middle peasants were usually placed on the left; rich peasants and cooperative landlords ("enlightened gentry") comprised the middle forces; hostile landlords and other collaborators or active anti-Communists were placed on the right.

It is clear that this characterization was based less on abstract class analysis than on the actual attitudes of various people toward the CCP. Those who were committed or friendly were members of the left wing. Those who were neutral or not overtly hostile were in the middle. Those who were actively opposed to the CCP were the right wing. This analysis had operational value because, as we shall see, the Party formed specific policies and directives precisely in terms of these categories. The key was to determine, at any point in time, who was in which category, and how to increase the left and middle at the expense of the right.

The analysis was applied again, two years later, when KMT-CCP relations were deteriorating badly and the split with Yen Hsi-shan was imminent.[17] It is significant that in this hostile environment Mao called for more, not less, attention to the united front. Here, the peasantry appeared as the sure and permanent ally of the proletariat (i.e., the Party). A slightly less firm place was given to the urban petty bourgeoisie. These three, especially the peasantry, were the hard core of mass support around the CCP center. Other elements of the united front were relegated to subordinate, conditional places. The bourgeoisie "will vacillate and defect under other historical circumstances because of its economic and political flabbiness. Therefore, the composition of China's revolutionary united front cannot remain constant at all times, but is liable to change. At one time the bourgeoisie may be included, at another it may not."[18] Opposition was seen not as breaking up the united front, but as deserting it: "We will never allow a section of people to disrupt or break up the Anti-Japanese National United Front, which has been forged through the common effort of the whole nation."[19]

Coupled with this analysis of the forces opposing Japan was the CCP's defense of its own independence and autonomy within the united front, and of its role as the leader of this front. In practice, these points were never really questioned. All CCP commentators and spokesmen affirmed the Party's right to exist, and to its freedom to criticize; privately they agreed that "The Party is to maintain its organizational and political independence . . . the Eighth Route Army and the New Fourth Army are to be under Party leadership in the fight against Japan."[20] These were two absolute conditions. Still there was a definite problem to be solved. If the CCP maintained that everything should be "subordinated to the interest of resistance to Japan," and if, furthermore, it recognized the position of the Kuomintang, San-min chu-i, and Chiang Kai-shek, then by what argument could the CCP justify the separate operation of what amounted to a rival regime? Why not, as Yeh Ch'ing tauntingly suggested, dissolve the CCP and *really* get behind the KMT?[g]

The Communists had several answers. First, they emphasized their commitment to the war, the sacrifices they were making, and the exemplary and heroic performance of their armed forces. It would obviously be of great detriment to the war effort, they said, if such a dedicated and effective organization were broken up. In any case, as Mao pointed out in early 1938, the KMT had been unable to get rid of the CCP in ten years of civil war; it could hardly hope to accomplish this now. Any attempt to do so would surely lead to a renewal of internal strife, which no patriot (least of all Chiang) could want.[21] A second, more significant justification for the independence of the CCP lay in its domestic political program.

[g] Yeh Ch'ing, "Kuan-yü cheng-chih tang-p'ai," in Mao, et al., pp. 66ff. Yeh Ch'ing is the pseudonym of Jen Cho-hsüan, a former Communist who at one point barely escaped execution by the Nanking authorities. He later left the Party and was branded a renegade and Trotskyite; then he moved toward the KMT and became one of its pamphleteers and theoreticians. He is presently editor of *Chung-yang jih-pao,* the KMT organ in Taiwan.

In order to be effective, this program had to have several characteristics: it could not resemble too closely the radical approaches that the CCP had suspended or abolished; it had to be distinct from, but not in open conflict with, the KMT program; it had to be believable and to command respect (if not with dedicated anti-Communists, then with the general population); and it had to be worded in such a way that should the KMT accept all or part of it, the CCP could use these concessions as a basis for further growth and further demands.

Therefore the domestic platform was a serious, integral part of the united front. From the start there was no clear demarcation between internal reform and external resistance. The Ten Great Policies of August 15, 1937, for example, have usually been seen, not incorrectly but incompletely, as an anti-Japanese program. But only two of the ten policies (overthrow of Japanese imperialism; anti-Japanese foreign policy), together with their supporting clauses, were directed wholly at the national enemy. All the others called, in varying degrees, for domestic changes. Many of these were sweeping in their implications. Consider the following:

> *Total Mobilization of the Entire Nation:*
>
> Everyone, except traitors, should have freedom of speech, publication, assembly, association, and of armed resistance in the anti-Japanese fight for national salvation.
>
> Abolish all old laws and regulations prohibiting patriotic popular movements and promulgate new, revolutionary laws and regulations.
>
> Release from prison all patriotic and revolutionary political prisoners and permit political parties to function.
>
> All the people of China should be mobilized and armed to participate in the war of resistance. Those who have strength should contribute their strength; those who have money, money; those who have weapons, weapons; and those who have knowledge, knowledge.
>
> Mobilize Mongolians, Moslems, and other minority groups for a common struggle against Japan on the basis of the principles of self-determination and self-government.

Reform of Political Mechanism:

Convene a National Assembly truly representative of the people; enact a truly democratic constitution; draft a program for fighting against Japan and saving the nation; and elect a national defence government.

The national defence government should contain the revolutionary elements of all parties, groups, and popular organizations, and should exclude pro-Japanese factions. . . .

Ensure local autonomy; oust corrupt officials and set up governments of integrity.[22]

Whatever the enactment of these proposals might have done to increase Chinese resistance to Japan, they would have vastly improved the position of the CCP. Their purpose was to establish a Communist claim to domestic leadership and independence:

> Will the proletariat lead the bourgeoisie in the united front, or the bourgeoisie the proletariat? Will the Kuomintang draw over the Communist Party, or the Communist Party the Kuomintang? In relation to the current specific political task this question means: Is the Kuomintang to be raised to the level of the Ten-Point Program for Resisting Japan and Saving the Nation, to the level of the total resistance advocated by the Communist Party? Or is the Communist Party to sink to the level of the Kuomintang dictatorship of the landlords and bourgeoisie, to the level of partial resistance?[23]

The issue of independence was not simply a matter of public propaganda. There were differences in the Party concerning the extent of cooperation with the KMT, and the way in which specific decisions should be implemented. As early as November 1937, Mao wrote:

> 17. With regard to the Party's line of an Anti-Japanese National United Front, the main danger inside the Party before the Lukouchiao Incident was "Left" opportunism, that is, closed-doorism, the reason being chiefly that the Kuomintang had not yet begun to resist Japan.
>
> 18. Since the Lukouchiao Incident the main danger inside the

> Party is no longer "Left" closed-doorism but Right opportunism, that is, capitulationism, the reason being chiefly that the Kuomintang has begun to resist Japan.[24]

It was held that the "key to leading the anti-Japanese national revolutionary war to victory is to explain, apply, and uphold the principle of 'independence and initiative within the united front.' "[25] This was designed to "hold the ground we have already won," but "Our chief purpose is to extend the ground already won and to realize the positive aim of 'winning the masses in their millions for the Anti-Japanese National United Front and the overthrow of Japanese imperialism.' "[26] Obviously this referred in part to the Communist-led regimes then being set up behind Japanese lines, even where this was unauthorized or opposed by the Central Government. Other examples of recent expansion were cited: "In the last few months, many more left-wing members of the petty bourgeoisie have become united under our influence, the new forces in the Kuomintang camp have grown, the mass struggle in Shansi has developed, and our Party organizations have expanded in many places."[27] Despite these successes, no split with the KMT was to be considered. KMT-CCP cooperation, nominal though it might become, was the capstone of the Communist appeal to the nation. Were the Party, then or later, to initiate an irrevocable split with the KMT, it would itself bear the onus for the ensuing civil strife. If the CCP denied solidarity under nominal KMT leadership, it could not claim solidarity under its own actual leadership. Dialectically, it was only by admitting the KMT that the KMT might be isolated.

These issues were thrashed out again at the Sixth Plenum of the Sixth Central Committee, held in November 1938 (shortly after the fall of Hankow and Canton and the transfer of the capital to Chungking). Put coldly, the CCP policy was to act independently and in self-interest up to a point just short of the line at which the other side would initiate a break. Liu Shao-ch'i is quoted as saying that if "everything through the united front" meant through Chiang Kai-shek and Yen Hsi-shan, then this was submission rather than unity.[28] To illustrate the proper approach, Mao suggested that if an action were one the KMT would approve, prior approval should be requested. More questionable measures should be carried out before approval was asked. Finally, some steps should be taken without ever asking for approval. Moreover, "There are still other things which, for the time being, we shall neither do nor report, for they are likely to jeopardize the whole situation. In short, we must not split the united front, but neither should we allow ourselves to be bound hand and foot."[h]

[h] Mao, *SW,* II, 216. Chang Kuo-t'ao and Ch'en Shao-yü are said to have advocated closer cooperation with the KMT than Mao desired. Although the evidence is far from conclusive (and it is impossible to present the evidence here), it is my belief that in neither case was disagreement over the united front the main cause of contention.

Chang, who defected to the KMT in the spring of 1938, had not seriously rivaled Mao's authority since the end of the Long March. After his arrival in Nanking, Chang claimed that he stood for a truly sincere acceptance of KMT leadership—"victory for all" (CCP and KMT over Japan), instead of Mao's cynical "defeat for all" (of Japan and the KMT by the CCP). This is not confirmed by other sources, and was, I believe, an explanation presented to the KMT to cover the real reason for his flight—his loss of power in the Party to a coalition of Mao, the military, and the Returned Students.

Significantly, Chang was listed in December 1937 as seventh in a 25-member preparatory committee for the Seventh CCP Congress. The Congress was scheduled to meet sometime in 1938, but was later postponed until 1945. The first task set by the Politburo for the Congress was "how to achieve ultimate victory over Japan on the basis of the united front and KMT-CCP cooperation." It is unlikely that Mao would have permitted Chang such a position if there had been a severe clash on united-front policy at the Lochwan conference (August 1937), as Chang claims. See *Kuan-yü chun-pei chao-chi tang ti-ch'i-tz'u ch'üan-kuo tai-piao ta-hui ti chüeh-i* [CCP 7].

Ch'en Shao-yü, on the other hand, was charged with rightist capitulationism during his ten months in Hankow, from January to November 1938. He was said to have issued unauthorized statements, made concessions to the KMT's antipopular policies, shirked from launching mass struggles, etc. Orthodox Party history dates the correction of this tendency to the Sixth Plenum. It is true that Ch'en's decline began at about this time, but a close examination of the available evidence provides no clear support for the official position. (Most of the criticism of Ch'en during the 1940's was related to his earlier leftist line.) On the contrary, Ch'en's Wuhan Defense Committee and the mass organizations related to it were so effective that the Government broke them up in August 1938. His statements supported the KMT and the united front; but so did those from Yenan, and Ch'en seems no slower than other comrades to affirm that the CCP "frankly announces that it does not reject its unique struggle for Communism."

After Ch'en's return to China from Moscow in December 1937 (he may have been a representative of the Comintern) the Returned Students were quite strongly placed: Ch'en had high international status, Chang Wen-t'ien was Secretary-General of the Party, Ch'in Pang-hsien was a CC member. In Moscow, Ch'en had criticized Mao's leadership (without mentioning Mao by name) and may have strongly influenced the formation of the united front in China. In Hankow, Ch'en was still somewhat beyond Mao's direct control, and gave the impression of

Sometimes, under exceptional circumstances, instructions to carry out independent action could be very urgent, as in the directive sent to Hsiang Ying shortly before he was killed in the New Fourth Army Incident:

> To expand means to reach out into all enemy-occupied areas and not be bound by the Kuomintang's restrictions but to go beyond the limits allowed by the Kuomintang, not to expect official appointments from them or depend on the higher-ups for financial support but instead to expand the armed forces freely and independently, set up base areas unhesitatingly, independently arouse the masses in those areas to action and build up united front organs of political power under the leadership of the Communist Party.[i]

So far as the record shows, this was the last time the Party center had to push the united front to the left. By early 1940, in the wake of the "first anti-Communist onslaught," party members at the lower levels seem to have been too leftist in their view of the KMT. Therefore, the Central Committee cautioned:

> The Kuomintang is a heterogeneous party which includes diehards, middle elements, and progressives; *taken as a whole, it must not be equated with the diehards.* Some people regard the Kuomintang as consisting entirely of diehards because its Central Executive Committee has . . . mobilized every ounce of its strength for counterrevolutionary friction-mongering in the ideological, political, and military spheres throughout the country. But this is a mistaken view. The diehards in the Kuomintang are still in a position to dictate its policies, but numerically they are in a minority. . . . This point must be clearly recognized if

---

taking the major credit for the united front. It is my tentative conclusion that Mao's move against Ch'en was more a matter of factionalism than of doctrinal disagreement. No purge was carried out, but the Returned Students, the last group standing in the way of Mao's complete control of the Party, were probably reduced in importance and forced to recognize Mao's supremacy.

[i] "Freely Expand the Anti-Japanese Forces and Resist the Onslaughts of the Anti-Communist Die-Hards," *SW,* II, 431. This was an isolated exception, stemming from the New Fourth Army's anomalous geographical position. After 1938, the problem was to slow cadres down, not stir them up.

> we are to take advantage of the contradictions within the Kuomintang, follow a policy of differentiating between its different sections, and do our utmost to unite with its middle and progressive sections.[29]

The Central Committee repeated incessantly that the Party had to avoid Ch'en Tu-hsiu's right opportunism and capitulationism, and the Returned Students' left closed-door sectarianism. The former was criticized as being all unity and no struggle; the latter as all struggle and no unity. What was needed for the united front was a revolutionary dual policy that involved *both* unity and struggle (possibly, but not necessarily, armed struggle): "Best a hit and a tug, to hit again and tug again. When hard, do not be so hard as to split the united front; when soft, do not be so soft as to lose our own standpoint."[30] The feasibility of this course depended on the existence of the territorial base and Communist-controlled armed forces.

The years 1939 and 1940 saw the mature development of the wartime united front. The excitement and fluidity of the first years of the war were now past. The Party was finding the policy as useful in times of stalemate and difficulty as in moments of enthusiasm and expansion. Party united-front organizations and tasks were expanded and systematized; tactical refinements were added; the permanence of the policy was affirmed; and the policy as a whole was closely meshed with other major elements of strategy. Furthermore, this period was the beginning of several years of acute hardship for the CCP and for those living in the areas it had penetrated —a time when the CCP could ill afford to alienate any possible ally or neutral.

Two major statements, which reflect and summarize this concern with the united front, were issued in 1940. The first was *Current Problems of Tactics in the Anti-Japanese United Front,* the text of a report made at a Yenan meeting of high-level cadres in March 1940.[31] This is a systematic and businesslike review of the current situation, together with a functional analysis of Chinese society and a program for continued united-front work.

The two most important characteristics of the current situation were the onset of strategic stalemate and the fact of enormous CCP political, military, and territorial expansion. The CCP believed that the Japanese were now unable to launch large-scale military offensives designed to force China to surrender.[32] Instead, they would aim at a political solution, i.e., to induce as many Chinese as possible to follow the example of Wang Ching-wei, Chou Fu-hai, and others. Japan had indicated that she would once again be willing to deal with Chiang. (There is no indication that he ever wavered, but there was plenty of suspicion that Wang Ching-wei had kept in close contact with some influential KMT elements.) One of the principal inducements to Sino-Japanese collaboration was a Japanese program for vigorous anti-Communist action. Meanwhile, the CCP now had much more to protect, much more to lose. And the relative stabilization of the war certainly meant that some of the pressure that the KMT had been taking would now be shifted against the Communists. (This document is perhaps unintentionally revealing when it states that in recent months, "Communist armed forces are fighting against *almost as many troops as the Kuomintang armed forces are doing*."[33]) Therefore, the CCP wanted to maximize the opposition to Japan in order to minimize the opposition to itself. It was by no means out of selfless love of its allies that the CCP was willing—even determined—to work with middle elements and diehards. But it is a mistake to think, as many have done, that because the CCP did not sincerely like its allies its united-front policy was therefore insincere.

The approach to all sections of the middle group was to win them over, but only "as allies against imperialism."[34] The national bourgeoisie and the "enlightened gentry" could help establish an anti-Japanese democratic political power, but they were afraid of the agrarian revolution. Temporary neutrality was the most that could be expected from powerful provincial leaders. Winning all these elements over required "(1) that we have ample strength; (2) that we respect their interests; and (3) that we are resolute in our struggle against the diehards and steadily win victories."[35] This policy was of great importance, because the middle forces "may often be the decisive factor in our struggle against the diehards; we must therefore be prudent in dealing with them."[36]

The right wing in the united-front classification was, as before, composed of those whose antipathy for the CCP was nearly as great as for the Japanese. Still willing to oppose Japan, they were prepared to do so only while simultaneously working against the Communists. These were the diehards. Class labels (big bourgeoisie, big landlords) were naturally applied to them, but the significant factor was their attitude toward the CCP. Their inclusion could only be temporary, but they should be induced to "prolong their participation" in the united front, thus averting "a large-scale civil war of the kind that broke out before."[37] So long as they opposed Japan, they tied up forces that might otherwise be sent against the CCP. Refusing to initiate a split reduced the possibility of a KMT-Japanese rapprochement directed at the Communists. In the event of a clash, this approach would maintain the image of the CCP as a martyr to patriotism, stabbed in the back by traitors.

Yet conflict with the diehards was necessary to discourage their anti-Communist operations and to present them in an unfavorable light to the nation as a whole. The principles of this struggle were now set forth. First, self-defense: never attack unless deliberately provoked, but *always* counter when provoked. Second, victory: never strike until success is assured; do not take on too many diehard elements at once, but attack the most reactionary and unpopular first. Third, truce: after the successful counterpunch and before the diehards can regroup, "take the initiative in seeking unity with the diehards, and if they concur, we should make a peace agreement with them."[38] This was called the policy of "justifiability, expediency, and restraint." By the use of this approach, "We can develop the progressive forces, win over the middle forces, and isolate the diehard forces, and we can also make the diehards think twice before attacking us, compromising with the enemy, or starting large-scale civil war."[j]

[j] *SW*, II, 427. "Justifiability, expediency, and restraint" is the language of the International Publishers edition. The Foreign Language Press edition has "on just grounds, to our advantage, and with restraint."

The second important statement issued in 1940 was the Central Committee's *On Policy* (*Lun cheng-ts'e*), dated December 25. Together with *Current Problems of Tactics in the Anti-Japanese United Front,* this essay indicates the full and mature integration of united-front policy with other elements of CCP operation. *On Policy* is such a concise statement that it would be impossible to paraphrase it without virtual reproduction of the text. It adds little that is new, but rather suggests the extent to which the united front had by this time become a part of nearly every CCP policy. For all these reasons, it is included as Appendix 3, despite the fact that it is readily available in the *Selected Works.*[39]

The same year, 1940, also saw the publication of *On the New Democracy*. The ancestor of the New Democracy was the democratic republic that the CCP had called for in 1936, and its lineage can be traced down through *On Coalition Government* and *On the People's Democratic Dictatorship*. It provided the theoretical framework that tied together the actual actions of the CCP in the areas under its control and the actions it was calling for in areas under KMT control. New Democracy was, therefore, an important part of the domestic political program that has already been discussed. A couple of months after the appearance of this treatise, the Party instructed: "On the question of political power in the anti-Japanese base areas, we must make sure that the political power established there is that of the Anti-Japanese National United Front. No such political power exists as yet in the Kuomintang areas. It is the political power of all who support both resistance and democracy, i.e., the joint democratic dictatorship of several revolutionary classes over the traitors and reactionaries."[40] Thus the united front was the explicit characteristic of CCP wartime political organization. On the one hand, this provided the base for Communist-led political institutions in the extensive areas coming under CCP control. On the other hand, in the KMT areas, it gave a more systematic underpinning to the demands for the extension of bourgeois democracy (i.e., constitutionalism, multi-party rule, civil rights, etc.).

It has been said of *On the New Democracy* that "the work appeared precisely at the time (in early 1940) when ominous cracks were beginning to appear in the structure of this precarious KMT-CCP alliance. . . . It is thus probable that *On the New Democracy* was written not simply in order to provide the united-front strategy with a theoretical framework, but also to prepare the Party for the possible disintegration of the alliance in the future."[41] A possible split with the KMT did worry the Party, but the significance of this treatise lay precisely in the idea that "disintegration of the alliance" with the KMT *did not* necessarily represent a breakdown of united-front strategy. If the KMT were properly isolated, then this would leave the CCP as the leading element in a coalition including or neutralizing almost everyone else. The CCP of course realized that this was for the present impossible—although it is just about what happened eight years later. The immediate goal was to prevent this split as dangerous to the CCP, or to minimize its effect by united-front activities aimed at those who might initiate it.

The timing of *On the New Democracy,* the substance of which was anticipated in earlier statements,[42] was influenced by the constitutional movement in KMT China. The September 1939 session of the PPC had passed a resolution (sponsored by the CCP and others) that requested constitutional rule. In November, the KMT announced plans to convene a National Constitutional Assembly in November 1940. *On the New Democracy* therefore appears as the CCP entry in this contest, one that it would certainly not wish to leave to the KMT alone. It was both a bid for support (away from the KMT) and a statement of the kind of multi-class coalition regime that the CCP desired to lead and to expand. The apparently rational and moderate tone of *On the New Democracy* persuaded many Chinese that the CCP either had forsaken its revolutionary objectives or had deferred them to such a distant future that they need not any longer be taken seriously. If *On Policy* and *Current Problems* exhibited the maturity of the united front in an operational sense, "Introducing *The Communist,*" *On the New Democracy,* and *The Chinese Revolution and the Chinese Communist Party* did the same in the historical and ideological realms.

Thus far, we have discussed the united front in terms of the Communists' relations with people outside the Party. This is undoubtedly its principal significance, but it also had an important function within the Party. Indeed, without some such device, how could a revolutionary party successfully rationalize, for itself and its cadres, a long period of essentially reformist policies? It was easy enough for a Party cadre to understand that Japan was the primary enemy, and that all patriotic Chinese must join hands. But when the same hard-bitten veteran of the Long March was directed to tell a landlord that he could keep his land, to compose pro-KMT propaganda, or to collaborate with an inexperienced young intellectual from a rich Shanghai family, problems arose. Perhaps this is one reason why the united front often worked more smoothly at upper levels than at lower levels. The united-front approach was often used to curb excessive leftism inside the Party. To the cadre, chafing under orders to persuade where he wanted to execute, the united front was invoked to explain how revolution and reform could be combined without ultimate compromise. One example, among many, is drawn from a simply written cadre training manual:

> Q: I feel that the united front and KMT-CCP collaboration are too great an about-face. It would be better to strike down the village bosses and divide the land. If we moved quickly, the revolution could easily be accomplished, isn't that so?
>
> A: This is incorrect, because to act in such a way today would certainly bring about the outbreak of civil war. If we fight each other, we won't be able to fight Japan. We would then be destroyed by Japan. Were the nation to perish and fall into Japanese hands, carrying out Communism would be very difficult. The realization of Communism requires national independence.[43]

This dual nature, this schizophrenia imposed by Japanese aggression and rendered whole by the united-front strategy, has been viewed differently by different observers. To the KMT, Bolshevik cynicism has always been foremost: the united front was simply a trick to deceive people. To many others, at that time, the Menshevism of agrarian reform, coalition government, and broad democracy were most obvious. Because both aspects were parts of a single policy, both analyses were wrong.

The success of any united front depended on a community of interest between the potential allies and the CCP. Nationalism, the patriotic struggle against Japan, clearly provided the broadest issue. But without concrete incentives, nationalism *by itself* could hardly have held such support through eight years of agony and weariness. For this the Party had to give sustained attention to the specific interests and needs of the particular groups from which allies were to be recruited. This undramatic, routine work (best done face-to-face) has frequently been underestimated, perhaps because of its prosaic and pervasive nature. Yet care for the "pressing needs" of potential friends probably won as much support for the CCP as any element of doctrine, including nationalism. Lack of attention to this point would certainly have killed the effect of the call to patriotic sacrifice (as it ultimately did in the case of the KMT). What made the difference, as the war dragged on into stalemate, was not that the KMT ceased to proclaim its patriotism, but that the CCP was far more effective in fleshing out its claims with the kind of action that made people believe that the Party cared about them, and hence made them willing to accept its leadership.

Countless articles and injunctions emphasized the patient cultivation of support. Sometimes cadres were criticized for failing to be sufficiently attentive: "In the past, the methods of winning over middle elements leaned heavily on political propaganda and our own requirements. Very rarely did we pay attention to the social position of the middle elements and to their immediate interests, even causing some people to get the idea that they were being used. From now on, we must seriously and attentively protect the social position and concerns of the middle elements, share their adversities with them, and win them over to prolonged cooperation with us."[44] Every time a Communist-led detachment observed strict discipline and concern for the needs of the villagers in whose midst they found themselves, all elements of CCP strategy were gaining in effectiveness. Every time a united-front cadre behaved with solicitude toward a university professor, the Party widened its influence. As Mao later said: "The leading class and the leading party must fulfill two conditions in order to exercise their leadership in the classes, strata, political parties, and people's organizations which are being led: (a) lead those who are led (allies) to wage resolute struggles against the common enemy and achieve victories; (b) bring material benefits to those who are led, or at least do not damage their interests, and at the same time give them political education."[45] All this was apart from propaganda and specific policies, but it gave meaning to both; for propaganda is effective only to the extent that it is believed. Doubtless the Party's ideal cadre was as rarely achieved as are other ideals; but the CCP made determined efforts, with quite impressive success, to move in the direction of the ideal.

Too often the united front has been dismissed as "just propaganda"; but if it had been no more than verbal assertion unsupported by concrete action, it would not have been effective. This was not a question of good faith so much as one of long-range self-interest. Although the CCP never denied its ultimate goals and the ideology that underlay them, many uncommitted people evaluated the Party instead in terms of its present behavior and performance.

Thus, by 1940, the united front was closely meshed to other elements of CCP strategy. In "Introducing *The Communist*," Mao wrote: "Therefore the united front, armed struggle, and Party building are the three fundamental questions for our Party in the Chinese revolution. Having a correct grasp of these three questions and their interrelations is tantamount to giving correct leadership to the whole Chinese revolution. We are now able to draw correct conclusions concerning these three questions by virtue of our abundant experience in the eighteen years of our Party's history."[46] The united front defined the enemy in terms as manageable as possible and sought to isolate him. It sought allies or neutrals. The armed struggle was then turned against the enemy, once the united front had done its work. Armed strength also induced waverers to either get in line or remain neutral. Party building ensured a stable and disciplined center, a hard core immune to the impurities of united-front allies, unable to be swayed from ultimate goals yet able to defer them for a prolonged period.

In this sense, the *cheng-feng* (Party reform) movement can be seen as the inverse of the united front—the organizational and doctrinal tightening of the Party necessary to mold the many new members and to offset the diversion of the Party from direct revolutionary activity. This was partly a matter of dedication and commitment. But it was also a separation of the leading element, somewhat like the Manchus' setting themselves apart from the Chinese even while carrying on a "united front" with them in the governance of the empire. But the CCP wanted to take no chances of ending like the Manchus, submerged in what they were supposed to lead. Therefore, the CCP tightened its organization, concentrated on improving its work style, and reaffirmed its revolutionary program.

There is an essential difference between the united front in the 1920's and early 1930's and the united front as it came to be developed by 1940. In the earlier period, the united front *itself* was seen as tactical and temporary because the alliances that composed it could not be permanent; in the later period, the united front came to transcend particular alliances. An alliance might still be temporary; but the concept of alliance, the united front, was permanent: "Our eighteen years of experience show that the united front and armed struggle are the two basic weapons for defeating the enemy. The united front is a united front for carrying on armed struggle. And the Party is the heroic warrior wielding the two weapons, the united front and the armed struggle, to storm and shatter the enemy's positions. That is how the three are related to each other."[47]

The Organization of United Front Work Departments

In CCP directives, one frequently encounters the assertion that the united front is everyone's business, that in the winning of friends no one is without responsibility. Each agency in each branch —Party, government, army—likewise had its united-front functions. But given the importance of united-front work, some systematization was necessary. This was provided by the creation of the United Front Department (sometimes United Front Work

Department: *t'ung-i chan-hsien* [*kung-tso*] *pu*), attached directly to the Party apparatus and found nowhere else. At the highest level, this department was directly controlled by the Politburo of the Central Committee. It was in existence by 1938, and was probably set up in that year.[48] Its director was Ch'en Shao-yü; his vice-directors were K'o Ch'ing-shih and Nan Han-chen.

Of the functions of this agency, the KMT's Bureau of Investigation and Statistics had this to say:

> Similar to a Ministry of Foreign Affairs. This Bureau is concerned solely with united-front work, and all relations with other parties, groups, and armies are attached to it. . . .
>
> Whenever Central Government personnel go to Yenan, they are entertained by the Reception Offices of the so-called Border Region Government and the Eighth Route Army Rear Area Garrison. But in fact, the Reception Offices are also under the direction of the United Front Department.
>
> At present in Yenan, those workers who are not Party members are called "non-Party cadres." None of them have any connections with the Organization Department; all are attached to the United Front Department.[49]

The last function, that of handling the non-Party cadres, is one of particular interest, although detailed information is lacking. Hsü I-hsin, head of the Non-Party Cadre Section, instructed his fellow Party members on working with such cadres: appreciate their abilities, employ them properly, trust them (but keep a "benevolent check" on them), and reeducate them in Marxism-Leninism. Nearly all non-Party cadres had come voluntarily, Hsü concluded, and were to be treasured as a real asset.[50]

This is an illustration of one of the functions of the united front, here seen in its organizational aspect: outsiders can be employed and controlled without the danger of excessive dilution of the Party, or of involving purely Party organizations with non-Party groups and functions (which might impair discipline, morale, etc., or create a security problem). Other sections in the UFWD at this time were the Secretary-General's Office, General Affairs Section,

Friendly Parties Section, Friendly Armies Section, and Research Materials Section. There is little additional information concerning this organization until the spring of 1940, when it appears that Ch'en Shao-yü was relieved of his position as its director. The reasons for his ouster are not entirely clear; it may have been connected with his loss of power in the Party, or it may have resulted from an illness, of which there were persistent rumors. His place was taken by K'o Ch'ing-shih.[51]

Because of the deterioration of the "united front from above" with the KMT, 1940 stands as an important year in the expansion of united-front organizations, and in the criticism of the work done by organizations already in existence: "Especially since the Kuomintang began carrying out its anti-Communist policy, many cadres —even including some leading cadres—have come to feel that the Kuomintang and the Central Armies are all diehards, and that our line is one of opposition, struggle, and preparation for a split. . . . Some people regard directives of the Central Committee that call for the strengthening of the united front as prattle, gobbledygook that makes little sense."[52] The Central Committee was "waiting for a report from you of a generalized nature on united-front work, especially emphasizing work with respect to friendly armies, to be issued via telegraph within a month of receiving this directive."[53]

At the same time, all provincial and regional Party committees received orders to establish United Front Departments where this had not already been done.[54] Division into sections was to be similar to that of the Central UFWD (Party/Group, Friendly Army, United Front Cadre). Hsien and municipal CCP committees were to set up UFWD if the local situation warranted. In addition, a United Front Problems Committee might be established. This group was called upon to investigate and discuss united-front problems, and was to include, apart from UFWD members, representatives from cultural, youth, and women's activities. In CCP-controlled regions, army and government authorities were also directed to participate.

This structure required relatively great freedom to work openly. Under conditions of secrecy, a streamlined and simplified organization was called for. No Problems Committee was to be set up under these circumstances. In the UFWD itself a system of functionally separate Operatives (*kung-tso kan-shih*) might replace the more formal and cumbersome sections. Greater security was also called for, and the following principles were to apply:

> 1. Separation of cadres engaged in overt work from those engaged in covert work.
> 2. Separation of Party from non-Party cadres.
> 3. Separation of upper levels from lower levels.
> 4. A control system of individual contacts; the identity of the Party contact man to be concealed.
> 5. To preserve secrecy, united-front cadres engaged solely in carrying on united-front work in general will not participate in ordinary cell life; their Party relations are controlled at higher levels.[55]

The Party maintained close touch with all united-front activities. The director of the UFWD was to confer regularly with the Secretary of the Party Committee and follow his directives. "Particularly important persons connected with the united front in friendly armies and friendly parties should revert directly to the control of the responsible person in the Central Committee United Front Department."[56]

The united-front cadre was sometimes told to take a cover occupation, and was given specific advice that had little to do with political ideology: "Use all possible social connections (relatives and family, fellow townsmen, classmates, colleagues, etc.) and customs (sending presents, celebrating festivals, sharing adversities, mutual aid, etc.), not only to form political friendships with the subjects, but also to become personal friends with them."[57] If captured, the cadre was to rely on this sort of connection, and not on his Party affiliation, to secure his release. Meanwhile, he should represent himself as a simple patriot.

The targets of this united-front work were many and varied: (a) parties and groups—KMT, Third Party, National-Socialist Party, National Salvation Association, Vocational Education Society, Livelihood Education Society, Rural Education Society; (b) all regional powers: (c) friendly armies; (d) all local circles, intellectual and otherwise; (e) gentry; (f) members of each government agency, including *pao-chia,* in each locality.[58] To provide the information necessary for united-front work, "a many-sided, deep, and detailed investigation" of important persons in each of these categories was to be made. A written record was to be compiled, to include name, age, native place, financial activities, history, changes in thought, political activities, habits, character, peculiarities, social relationships, etc.[59]

It is difficult to know how systematically these directives were carried out. United-front work was largely secret (this was sometimes true even in CCP-controlled areas), and therefore poorly documented.[k] Many of our materials come from a time of great peril (1940), when the CCP was almost desperately seeking as many friends as possible. Thus these documents may overstate the failures of the past and the expectations for the future.

Information concerning lower-level UFWD organization and operation in areas controlled by the CCP is particularly scarce. It may well be that they were less significant in these regions than in KMT or contested areas. Nevertheless, they undoubtedly existed. For example, a detailed KMT intelligence report concerning the Lung-tung (eastern Kansu) and Kuan-chung (central Shensi) regions shows the local UFWD as ranking with other sections of these special regional Party committees (organization, propaganda, youth, women, mass movement). In the Kuan-chung area, the same person was identified as heading both the UFWD and the propaganda section.[60] Furthermore, none of the directives cited above distinguish between CCP and KMT areas. Clearly, some of the structures—e.g., the United Front Problems Committee—could hardly have been set up extensively outside the Communist regions.

What is most striking is the way the united-front approach was embedded in so many aspects of the Party's work in securely held areas. Analysis of classes and agrarian policy were frequently put in united-front terms.[61] The Communist governmental structure was conceived as a united-front organization. The question of mili-

[k] Periodic reports from regional and provincial UFWD to the CC were called for, but none are held by the KMT Bureau of Investigation. I suspect that at lower levels very few documents were prepared, as a security measure. Some reports may have been revised, declassified, and published. A possible example is Chang Chih-i, *K'ang-chan chung ti cheng-tang ho p'ai-pieh.*

tary-civilian relations was expressed in this way. P'eng Chen even discussed the elimination of traitors in Chin-Ch'a-Chi as the work of relying upon and expanding the united front.[62] The impression is one of general pervasiveness, of an attitude, a work style, a policy that informed and shaped many organizations and actions.

We can summarize by observing that the united front had become a genuine element of long-range strategy, with the following characteristics:

1. It was under CCP leadership and was based on independent CCP power, neither of which could be compromised. Its content was to be determined by the Party alone; when the Party acted as its allies desired, it did so for its own reasons.

2. It did not represent an abandonment of the Party's ultimate goals, but was rather a way of seeking a position from which they could be achieved.

3. It reflected the Party's awareness of its own weakness, and hence its need for active, sustained, and genuine non-Party support, and its need to keep the enemies of the Party as limited in number and as fragmented as possible.

4. It was based on the twin appeals of resistance to Japan (nationalism) and domestic reform—the latter operating both nationally and locally, both politically and economically.

5. It operated through, and under, qualified cooperation with the Kuomintang, but this cooperation was a means to greater CCP power, not an end in itself.

6. In order to gain the support, neutrality, or suspended hostility of the maximum number of people, the Party was ready to make and conscientiously carry out extensive changes in policy, *provided* these did not involve real concessions in the areas of 1 and 2; in fact, the integrity of 1 and 2 made it feasible to undertake policies that superficially looked like very great concessions.

7. It was prepared to use the negative inducement of force as well as the positive inducements of nationalism and reform.

8. It had taken organizational form through the UFWD, but was no more limited to one department than were the other two elements of strategy with which the united front was linked, armed struggle and Party building.

Chapter 7

Examples of Unity and Struggle

IN THIS CHAPTER, I shall describe the CCP's general approach to so-called "friendly armies," and then consider the application of this and other united-front techniques to the relations with Yen Hsi-shan in Shansi—a united front that split at the end of 1939. Finally, I shall examine the operation of the "three-thirds" system as an aspect of the united front in areas controlled by the CCP. These sections are meant to suggest some of the ways in which the policy was used in and near the Communist-led bases.

FRIENDLY ARMY WORK

During the Sino-Japanese War, relations between Communist-led military units and non-Communist forces were a matter of cardinal importance. Needless to say, these relations ran the gamut from professed cordiality to open hostility. Probably there was a greater tendency toward the latter than the former. Expansion of Communist armies, and of the territory under their control, brought the Party into conflict not only with Japanese and puppet (or quasi-puppet) forces, but often with Central Government forces as well. In their efforts to reverse this expansion, the government forces just as often initiated attacks on the Communists.[1]

Nevertheless, below the level of armed conflict, the CCP made persistent efforts to influence, persuade, or win over "friendly armies" (*yu-chün*)—the Communist term designating military forces not subject to Japanese or puppet command, regardless of the degree of their actual friendship with the CCP. The Party defined these efforts as one aspect of united-front work: "Hence friendly army work is a historical category that follows along with the birth and development of the united front, and with the relations of the KMT and CCP in general."[a] The CCP had been strikingly successful in this work before the war, when it had worked out a truce with Chang Hsüeh-liang and Yang Hu-ch'eng. Even greater successes were to be won in the postwar struggle for supremacy. Friendly army work during the war linked these two periods.

Such work was carried on by several Party agencies. As a part of overall military policy, it was under the ultimate supervision of the Politburo's Military Affairs Committee. As we have seen, UFWD set up Friendly Army sections at all levels. In addition, regional and local Party committees established Departments of Armed Struggle.[b] There were a number of CCP military liaison offices, in Wuhan, Chungking, Sian, and Kweilin; the last of these was shut down shortly before the New Fourth Army Incident.[2] Finally, many friendly army activities were undoubtedly handled on an ad hoc and pragmatic basis by the military themselves, and therefore fell outside any formal organizational structure.

There were three main sources of cadres for this work. First were experienced Red Army cadres who because of age or disability were no longer able to undergo the rigors of regular army operations. Second, many of the graduates of K'ang-ta (Resistance University) were assigned to this work. Third, some retired soldiers were given on-the-spot training.[3] Cadres might be sent anywhere; frequently they were returned to their homes, where they were intimately acquainted with local conditions.

A CCP treatise on friendly army work is quoted as saying that

[a] "Chung-kung chün-yün kung-tso ti hsin ts'e-lüeh," appended to Kung-lun ch'u-pan-she, p. 13. Much material that bears on this subject is presented by Johnson in *Peasant Nationalism.* He is concerned mainly with the establishment and expansion of Communist-controlled areas, operations that frequently involved the incorporation of local non-Communist forces, as well as contacts—friendly or otherwise—with Central forces. This section stresses general principles of the policy, and is intended to demonstrate that the CCP placed much of the expansion and mobilization of which Johnson speaks in the context of the united front.

[b] Kung-lun ch'u-pan-she, p. 2. According to Chung-kuo kuo-fang-pu hsin-wen-chü, pp. 19a–21a, Mao and Chou En-lai were Chairman and Vice-Chairman, respectively, of the Military Affairs Committee in 1939.

friendly army operations were to be directed against the forces that during a given stage (even a very short stage) exercised important political and military functions; if work were successful here, it could produce great political and military changes, perhaps even decisive ones.[4] The work stated that

> The central purpose of friendly army work is the same as that of our work generally, an offensive against the weakest links under Kuomintang political leadership . . . those links that are dissatisfied with current conditions, with the government, and with the KMT, for these forces will most easily abandon the leadership of the government and the KMT. . . . Forces that have a local character, forces that are discriminated against by the Central Government, forces that are not trusted by the Central Government, forces that find themselves in the midst of great hardships—those who most have these characteristics provide opportunities for work.[5]

Friendly army work was carried on in the area that the KMT viewed as its very basis of power and was therefore most anxious to keep free of CCP influence. Hence the work had to be characterized by secrecy, flexibility, and persistence. Since it was also carried on in the midst of an "unceasing struggle against Japan," it should not be permitted to split the united front.[6]

Until 1939, relations between the CCP and many KMT forces were relatively friendly. When this was the case, the CCP sought contacts with commanders and other influential officers (especially those responsible for training, intelligence, and political affairs) as an avenue to the common soldier. This approach was coordinated with work at lower levels. As the environment became more hostile to the CCP, the balance gradually shifted toward secret work. From 1939 on, consolidation and protection of the slender CCP resources in KMT armies were called for. Therefore, instead of trying to widen the scope of action, Party members were instructed to seek promotion, more strategic placement, etc., without undertaking anything that would compromise their true affiliation.[7]

A consistent distinction in friendly army work, which can be seen throughout, was that between well-trained armies under tight Central control and those that were less disciplined and less firm in their allegiance to the Central Government, especially provincial and former warlord forces. In the former, there was not much chance for direct persuasion or influence; contact at the officer level was difficult, but could sometimes be established. Shen Chien (from 1960 to 1964 the Chinese ambassador to Cuba), for example, worked during the war in the research office of the Sian branch of the Central Military Academy. At the same time, he was assistant English-language secretary to General Hu Tsung-nan, who was in charge of the forces blockading Shen-Kan-Ning. He was in frequent contact with agents of the Eighth Route Army.[8]

Aside from cases like Shen Chien's, penetration of the KMT armies was carried on principally through new recruits. Special efforts were made to get them into military schools, propaganda units, and political departments. Most of these recruits had previously received some training, and most were more intelligent and better educated than the average conscript. As a result, the KMT itself acknowledged, they rapidly became noncommissioned officers, and often had considerable influence with the troops.[9]

It was otherwise in poorly trained armies, the "troops of miscellaneous brands." There, the CCP promoted work at all levels. In the case of officers, and higher-ranking officers in particular, social contacts were used. Higher cadres were sent to serve with them, become a part of their staff, and work conscientiously to gain their trust.[c] Once this had been done, influence was exerted to bring in CCP members at the middle and lower levels. When the lower levels had been suitably influenced, it was time to consider bringing the whole army over to the Communist side. At this point, the original officer corps had lost control, either submitting or being isolated.[10] The work of a Party member named Wan I provides an illustration of the technique. During the first two years of the war, Wan was a brigade commander in the Nationalist Army's 111th Division under Ch'ang En-to. Operating in the Shantung-Kiangsu region,

[c] The success of this initial contact was, of course, decisive; it was not a simple matter to establish the kind of relationship necessary to go on to later steps.

he used his following of over 1,500 men to force Ch'ang to turn himself over to the CCP in 1939. Wan was elected an alternate member of the CCP's Seventh Central Committee in 1945.[11]

An even better example is provided by the fate of General Wan Fu-lin, formerly one of Chang Hsüeh-liang's senior commanders in the Northeast (Manchurian) Army, and in 1938 the head of the Central Government's 53rd Army in central Hopei:

> He attended the Fu-p'ing Conference [at which the Chin-Ch'a-Chi Border Region was established] with the remnants of his troops in January 1938. . . . Returning to central Hopei from the Fu-p'ing Conference, he was accompanied by a "political director" from the Eighth Route Army. Together they organized the area and recruited a new army. The work was as much political as military. . . . Simultaneously with this military occupation of central Hopei by Wan Fu-lin's forces, political organizers were sent to each village, and they arranged for the election of Mobilization Committees, the formation of units of the People's Self-Defense Corps, and other mass organizations. These mass organizations gave such support to the Communist sponsored economic reforms that within about a year the Communists obtained the dominant position in central Hopei. And since the new 53rd Army was recruited from the local people and obtained its political indoctrination from the Communist political director, it became as loyal to the Communists as the people as a whole. Exactly what happened to General Wan in the course of 1938 is not known. In April 1939, however, he was reported to have been "relieved" from his command. By that time the Eighth Route Army was in full control of General Wan's former areas in central Hopei.[12]

Perhaps, this source suggested, such experiences "may in part explain why Kuomintang generals now fear to engage in united front action with the Communists."

Regardless of time or place, friendly army work had a number of consistent characteristics. Key Party members in non-Communist forces were always controlled directly by higher Party organs, and cells were rarely set up. Instead, there were separate vertical lines of control; horizontal contact was discouraged for reasons of security.[d] This practice, incidentally, throws an ironic sidelight on at least one of the CCP's wartime promises. In 1940, commemorating the third anniversary of the war, a CC declaration stated disingenuously: "We continue to uphold the decision of the Sixth Plenum of the Party held in November 1938 not to develop Party organizations in any friendly army. Certain local Party bureaus that have not strictly carried out this decision should immediately make corrections."[e]

Other tactics and principles of operation included the following: Party members working at upper levels were strictly separated from those at lower levels; cells or groups, if set up at all, were set up only at lower levels. Overt opportunities for work were sought, including public meetings, songfests, and theatrical performances. "Gray" status was maintained at all times; non-Party activists were often persuaded to carry out duties that might compromise a Party member. When possible, propaganda materials were to come from openly published sources, KMT political journals, etc., and were not to violate the principles of the united front. Consolation Corps (*wei-lao tui*) and Propaganda Corps established contact with the troops, and propaganda materials might be included in comfort items. Work was carried on among wounded soldiers; cadres were sent into hospitals as nurses, orderlies, etc. Party members and Vanguards made special efforts to get into Central training schools, particularly mechanized training units—both to augment the CCP's scanty knowledge of mechanized warfare and to carry on work among these units.[13]

It is perhaps not surprising that the CCP carried on friendly army operations. The point, however, is that the CCP saw such

[d] Kung-lun ch'u-pan-she, p. 16. Provision was made for properly covered relations with the provincial committee.

[e] "Chung-kuo kung-ch'an-tang chung-yang wei-yuan-hui wei k'ang-chan san-chou-nien chi-nien tui shih-chü hsüan-yen," in Chung-kuo kuo-fang-pu hsin-wen-chü, Vol. II. The document goes on to say, in a rather thinly veiled threat, that no organization having anything to do with a friendly army should attempt to infiltrate the CCP armies either. This last is omitted in the version that appears in *SW,* III, 213.

work as a specific part of its united-front operations—in conception, and frequently in organization and implementation as well. It is often easier to trace friendly army work in a general rather than in a specific way. Because of the secrecy that characterized this work, our documentation is frequently inadequate; but one example is presented in a document prepared by the Huai-pei Party Committee and dating from early 1944.[14] It is not concerned with secret penetration of friendly armies, but with somewhat more formal and open relations. The document was written during a period of relative calm in the contacts between the two parties. Noted here in particular was the effect of the KMT's Tenth Plenum, which had taken place the preceding November. At that time, Chiang Kai-shek had said that if the CCP observed certain principles, it would be treated like any other group. This highly conditional statement, the Huai-pei document said, had had little effect at top levels; but middle and lower strata in friendly armies had been favorably influenced, and relations had taken a distinct turn for the better in the Huai-pei region.[15] Representatives were dispatched from the New Fourth Army to discuss problems of collaboration and cooperation with several high Central Army leaders (including T'ang En-po, Li Hsien-chou, Ho Chu-kuo, and Wang Chung-hsü). Though there is no indication of what was said, these military leaders were thought to be much more sympathetic than previously.[16] Several examples are also given of recent attempts at making friends with the "friendly armies." They usually took the form of aiding these armies when they entered CCP areas because of Japanese pressure: presenting them with food, assigning rest areas, helping their dependents, etc.[17]

The view from the KMT side is given in a very frank report concerning the Hupei-Honan Border Region and dating from 1944. The CCP, the report states, worked very hard at the united front with the guerrilla forces of the Central Government. But if they could not be won over, then the CCP tried to destroy them. "The larger the guerrilla forces, the better the chance for the CCP to increase its armed strength and territory. The principal source of rifles in the border region was the guerrilla force led by Ch'eng Ju-huai in eastern Hupei, which they disarmed entirely."[18] There were several reasons why guerrilla forces were attacked, the report went on. Their fighting strength was low, and their military discipline was extremely bad. "They curse and abuse the populace, and even steal things, commit rape, etc."[19] In the Ta-wu-shan region (northeastern Hupei) there was a popular jingle, referring to the KMT guerrillas:

> When the Japanese come,
> There's a windy spell;
> But when the guerrillas come,
> Our homes are stripped as well.[f]

This gave the CCP a pretext for attacking Central Government guerrillas, and enabled the Communists to pose as the protectors of the common people.

It was somewhat otherwise with the regular armies, which were both stronger and better disciplined. The people disapproved of Communist attacks on a regular army, unless its discipline, too, had broken down: an example in which CCP elements under Li Hsien-nien did attack is cited.[20] But more generally, if a regular army entered an area under Communist control,

> The most important authorities do not show themselves, but stay to one side. They just send a few unimportant persons of lesser authority to make united-front contacts, or they send articles of consolation. They mobilize local gentry to come and talk things over. They are willing to cooperate and to supply such necessities as intelligence, laborers, guides, etc. But when a regular army arrives, whether or not it is within the united front, they will not open up their administrative areas, nor approve of [Communist] withdrawal.[21]

---

[f] *Yü-O pien-ch'ü hsien-wei tiao-ch'a tzu-liao,* Part 3, "Tui yu-chi-tui." The Chinese original for this bit of doggerel runs as follows:

日本人來了一陣風
游擊隊來了家家空

Thus the policy was one of selective conciliation and conflict, described above as one of "justifiability, expediency, and restraint." Its goals were to widen support for the CCP among the civilians in a given area and among other military units; to expand the areas under CCP control; and to reduce the number of those who might take overt anti-Communist action. Here, as elsewhere, it is clear that the formal relationships between the CCP and the KMT were only one phase of the united front as a whole; and the view that conflict between their military units indicated a rupture in the united front is an erroneous one, at least in the CCP's conception. The united front did not mean to the CCP that clashes could not occur; or that if they did occur, the united front was broken. On the contrary, the conflict itself became an integral part of the policy. In this sense, the New Fourth Army Incident did not signal the end of the united front; rather, this event forced the KMT to the reluctant conclusion that it could not simultaneously maintain a militantly anti-Japanese and a militantly anti-CCP posture. This was precisely what the united front was trying to achieve: isolation of opponents and creation of the most favorable conditions for expansion.

The Split with Yen Hsi-shan

As an example of wartime Chinese Communist policy in action, it would be hard to surpass the events in Shansi province. The combination of united front and armed struggle, directed by the Party, was used here with much success. Friendly army work was extensively employed. Economic, social, and political reforms were aimed at the poorer peasantry, and the appeals of nationalism were aimed at everyone. In essence, the CCP worked through the provincial authorities, holding them in place with a "united front from above." Meanwhile Communists were intruding their influence at lower levels, mobilizing and arming the populace in a "united front from below." Yen Hsi-shan, warlord, provincial governor, and commander of the Second War Zone, was very nearly isolated when he and his more conservative associates attempted to reassert control in 1939. This effort led in November and December to an open break and a considerable acquisition of strength for the Communists.[g]

Even before the CCP made its initially successful but ultimately ill-starred raid into Shansi in the spring of 1936, Yen Hsi-shan had created what he vainly hoped would be an effective anti-Communist mass organization. This was the "Force for the Promotion of Justice" (*Chu-chang kung-tao t'uan*). With Yen himself as chairman, and senior military and political officers as the principal cadres, the Justice Force established branches at all levels, county (*hsien*), sub-county (*hsiang*), and village (*ts'un*). In concept, it was a "mass anti-Communist organization, led by the provincial military and political authorities."[22] Gillin has shown how little success it had during the Communist invasion.[23] The organization of the Justice Force was quite loose; and even as early as this, it was infiltrated by younger and more liberal elements who would soon show how little they were in sympathy with its goals (prominent among them were Sung Shao-wen, Kuo T'ing-i, Chang Wen-ang, and Niu P'ei-tsung; it is possible that Chang was an underground Communist).[24]

By the autumn of 1936, Japanese pressure on Suiyuan was rapidly increasing, and the CCP's united-front proposals included not only men like Yen Hsi-shan, but even Chiang Kai-shek. In this atmosphere, the younger, liberal members of the Justice Force persuaded Yen to form a new organization, the "League for National Salvation through Sacrifice" (*Hsi-sheng chiu-kuo t'ung-meng-hui*). The Sacrifice League accordingly came into existence—on the anniversary of the Mukden Incident, September 18, 1936—and pledged itself

[g] A full account of these events has yet to be written. The two most useful studies in English are Johnson's (esp. pp. 92–109) and Gillin's "'Peasant Nationalism.'" Gillin disputes Johnson's analysis of the nature of the CCP appeal to the peasantry, but not the fact the Party won widespread support. Gillin also presents very extensive bibliographical material. In Chinese, an official and quite detailed history of all of the base areas is presented in *K'ang-Jih chan-cheng shih-ch'i chieh-fang-ch'ü kai-k'uang*. The most important new source used here is "Shan-hsi 'Hsin-chün' p'an-pien chen-hsiang." This long and detailed historical study, though written as an anti-Communist intelligence report, is impressively objective. It is consistent enough with known evidence to convince me that it is a highly reliable source for events that seem to be covered nowhere else. The report also has a certain literary merit. Hereafter cited as *Chen-hsiang*.

to support and carry out the anti-Japanese national united front. Though collaboration between Yen and the CCP does not seem to have been particularly close at this time, some sort of agreement may have been reached.[25] In any case, Yen accepted the propaganda and the principles of the united front. By the autumn of 1936, Shansi had become second only to the Sian area as a haven for those advocating opposition to Japan.[26] Thus, the united front came to Shansi earlier than it did to the nation as a whole.

Apparently Yen's motives in setting up the Sacrifice League were mixed. He wanted it to achieve what the Justice Force had failed to do: organize the masses under his own control.[27] But Yen was also concerned about Japanese pressure, and hoped to utilize anti-Japanese sentiment as a banner to attract men of ability who could help him control the people.[28] Gillin has shown that the poorer peasants in Shansi responded far more in social, economic, and personal terms than in terms of nationalism per se.[29] But Yen had little choice: he was unwilling or unable to undertake serious structural reforms; and moral-legal reform (enlisting "good men," exhortations to be honest, enforcing the laws against corruption and the drug traffic, etc.) had failed to make the masses unreceptive to the Communists. Nationalism, however, was an appeal he could try without undertaking institutional change. He perhaps did not realize the extent to which anti-Japanese nationalism was a two-edged sword, in that new forms of organization and new leaders could be justified on grounds chosen by Yen himself, thus making it difficult for him to oppose them.

The Sacrifice League was immediately successful in achieving one of its goals. It did attract a large number of able young men—simple patriots, liberals, leftists, and CCP members. One such group was led by Po I-po (who later had an important career in the CCP), Chang Wen-ang, and Han Chün.[h] These men, all from Shansi, had formed an association dating from their middle-school days in Taiyüan, the provincial capital. By the time of their graduation, about 1930, they may already have been CCP members. Po I-po joined the Party in 1927, then went to Peiping University; from 1932 to

[h] Also included were Jung Wu-sheng, Lei Jen-min, and Hou Chün-yen. See "Po I-po's 7-Man Group and His Dismissal," *RHKCP*, 184/53 (Oct. 6, 1953).

1935, he was imprisoned for "incitement to riot" in connection with anti-Japanese activities. It is reported that despite their background, Yen was impressed with them and induced them to renounce Communism.[30] They were in any case released, and soon became very active in the League. Other League leaders were Li Kung-p'u and Chou Hsin-min, both of whom were later prominent in the Democratic League (Li was assassinated in Kunming in 1946; see below, pp. 194–95). Many members of the Justice Force also joined the Sacrifice League, where the more conservative of them formed the "National Revolutionary Comrades Association" (*Kuo-min ko-ming t'ung-chih hui*). The Association did very little until early 1939, when it became the center of Yen Hsi-shan's efforts to reassert control of the mass movement. The Justice Force was not disbanded, but led an attenuated existence.

The League was, on paper, elaborately organized along hierarchical lines reaching down to the village level.[31] Probably the preexisting structure of the Justice Force was taken over to some extent. Village work was not handled by the League alone, but was also carried on by local bodies ("mobilization committees") or individuals ("village government assistance officials"). These were appointed by the provincial government and were for the most part League members.

Thus the Sacrifice League was halfway between a mass movement and a political party. Among its members were people of widely different political persuasions, including Communists. But there is no mistaking the virulent nationalistic temper of the organization as a whole, or the fact that young, left-wing activists were in substantial control. Some of these leaders were intimates of Yen Hsi-shan—his nephew and private secretary, Liang Hua-chih, was prominent—and the fact that they had his confidence undoubtedly did much to facilitate the work of the League.[i]

The statements and platforms issued by the League were very close in tone and content to the CCP and National Salvation united-

[i] *Chen-hsiang,* pp. 39a–39b, states that the following were very close to Yen: Liang Tun-hou (who remained loyal after the split), Chang Hsiao-liang, and Kuo T'ing-i. The last two were leftist in their sympathies. See also Gillin, *Warlord,* pp. 231–32.

front appeals. There was no hint of revolutionary ideology. Instead, they were typically patriotic and sweeping, with heavy stress on civil rights and an equitable sharing of burdens—the whole being justified by the need to mobilize the entire population for resistance. Nevertheless, an undertone of social and political change was there. As Jung Wu-sheng later put it, "In North China today the mass movement is growing and strong, but that does not mean that North China is Communist. The people are being mobilized for resistance *and reconstruction, and not strictly for political purposes.*"[32]

By early 1937, it was reported that there were 600,000 League members throughout the province, and about 450 cadres "who were able to operate independently." Furthermore, about 20,000 had been enrolled in some sort of military training by the 180 "village government assistance officials."[33] Thus when the war began in the fall of 1937, the League already had a considerable following. The CCP and the Eighth Route Army now returned to Shansi, under the united front, and gave both propaganda and military support to Yen Hsi-shan.[j]

It seems undeniable that Central and provincial forces took the brunt of the Japanese attack, though the record of the Shansi armies was spotty. Yen executed one of his generals for failing to make even a token defense of an important pass, and it was the collapse of provincial armies at Niangtzukuan that permitted the Japanese to outflank the stubborn provincial and Central defenders at Hsin-k'ou and thus take Taiyüan in early November 1937. During the battle of Hsin-k'ou, the Communists disrupted Japanese lines of communication, but were unable to break them entirely. After the fall of Taiyüan, the provincial forces virtually collapsed. In his account of the battle of P'inghsingkuan, where a joint Communist-provincial force had inflicted a heartening but not decisive defeat on the Japanese, Lin Piao was contemptuous of the fighting ability of provincial troops. With cold-blooded realism, he suggested that they be used to meet the enemy head on, while the Communists harried Japanese

[j] For an account of Communist military operations in Shansi, see Johnson, pp. 92ff. Gillin believes that Johnson slights the military contribution of the Shansi provincial forces and the Central Armies under General Wei Li-huang.

flanks and prepared for the counterattack.[34] James Bertram quotes a Communist officer as saying in 1938 that the Eighth Route Army had had little heavy fighting since the early engagements, and was conducting mobile or guerrilla warfare.[35]

With the fall of Taiyüan and the subsequent campaign against Yen's new headquarters at Lin-fen (southwest of Taiyüan), provincial administration crumbled. Yen was now more than willing to support and utilize whatever services, political or military, the Sacrifice League could offer in the combat zones or behind enemy lines. He was driven from Lin-fen in February 1938, and retired west of the Yellow River. But the Japanese did not remain in southwestern Shansi, and Yen was able to maintain a foothold there, subject to sporadic raids. Most of the northeastern quadrant of the province (north of the Shihchiachuang-Taiyüan rail line, and east of the Tatung-Taiyüan line) now fell behind Japanese lines and was completely lost to Yen. He did, however, retain some jurisdiction over the rest of Shansi.

It was in the Japanese-occupied northeastern area that the CCP's 115th Division, under Nieh Jung-chen, was operating. There were also a number of other anti-Japanese elements in the region, including Sung Shao-wen of the Sacrifice League.[k] It was here, and out of these varied groups, that the Chin-Ch'a-Chi Border Region was created in January 1938, with Sung as Chairman of the Administrative Committee. This base, one of the most important of all such regions, received formal (but unenthusiastic) approval from Yen Hsi-shan and Chiang Kai-shek.[36]

Prior to the fall of Taiyüan, as Japanese pressure mounted, Yen had allowed the Sacrifice League to step up the organization of military units, and had turned over to them a quantity of military equipment.[l] By the end of 1937, four "Dare-to-Die Columns" (*chüeh-ssu tsung-tui*) had been organized. They were commanded by Po I-po,

[k] Johnson, p. 100. Sung was not a Party member. A native of Shansi, he had graduated from Peiping University in 1935 and was imprisoned briefly in 1936 for his participation in anti-Japanese demonstrations in Taiyüan.

[l] But probably not as much as the 30,000 rifles that Johnson accepts (p. 100). *Chen-hsiang*'s data on the split indicate that the defectors were on the whole rather poorly armed.

Chang Wen-ang, Jung Wu-sheng, and Lei Jen-min; the commanders also served as political officers. The League also sought to organize local self-defense corps. One type, numbering 200–300 men per hsien, was to be composed of full-time militiamen. Along with its military expansion, the Sacrifice League increasingly assumed the local political functions that had been generally abandoned by the regular officials. Before long, 60 of Shansi's 105 hsien had magistrates who belonged to the League. The League also persuaded Yen to create Area Special Commissioners (*ch'ü chuan-yüan*), who had charge of several hsien. About half the territory still under Yen's jurisdiction thus came under the direct administrative control of Commissioners who were League members: Third Area (southeast), Po I-po; Fifth Area (south-southwest), Jung Wu-sheng; Sixth Area (west-northwest), Chang Wen-ang.[37]

The military forces were of average quality by Chinese standards. The American Marine officer Evans F. Carlson, apparently unaware that Po I-po was a Party member, got the impression in 1938 that "General Po's headquarters was friendly, but it lacked the democratic quality which was present in units of the Eighth Route Army. Officers held themselves aloof, and soldiers bore an attitude of subservience. All had the class-conscious bearing of old China." Carlson concluded, "I thought I saw the hand of the Eighth Route Army in a good deal of this. The form was much the same, but the leaders had not yet caught the spirit of self-sacrifice and devotion to the welfare of the people which made the Eighth Route Army system work."[38] Of this Army, Po I-po later recalled: "Its strong point was its close relations with the people; its weak point, its lack of unity, central leadership, and military experience. Such a force, composed of students who hardly knew how to fire rifles, professors who knew nothing of tactics, and farmers who knew neither tactics nor politics, was in danger of disintegrating for lack of a directing head and of being wiped out for the lack of technique."[39]

The League now suggested that a "united front" be created between the Sacrifice League and the Justice Force, and that the two organizations be merged at the top in a "Justice-Sacrifice General Committee." Yen Hsi-shan's nephew, Liang Hua-chih, of the

League, became Secretary-General of the Justice Force, and the leading organs of the joint committee were packed with League members.[m] Through the joint committee and the League itself, an effort was made to control the remaining provincial armed forces. It was about this time (mid-1938) that the expressions "New Army" (*hsin-chün,* led by the League) and "Old Army" (*chiu-chün*) became current. The "new" was praised and the "old" was criticized in Yen's own words: "The new can survive, the old must be eliminated."[40]

These various moves confirmed the suspicions and excited the hostility of the older and more conservative military-political leaders of Shansi, the most prominent of whom were Wang Ching-kuo (Yen's son-in-law), Sun Ch'u, and Chao Ch'eng-shou. Yen Hsi-shan, too, apparently began to feel that the growing power of the League should be curbed, for in October 1938 he called a meeting at which the New Army was strenuously attacked. Yen attempted to reorganize the Dare-to-Die Columns and the self-defense forces and to place them under his direct command, but was unsuccessful. The League criticized these efforts as unpatriotic; it charged that Wang, Sun, and Chao were potential collaborators, but there was no overt attack on Yen himself, whose leadership of the Shansi united front was supported. Otherwise, the League simply paid no attention and continued its work of organization and mobilization.

The following March, after a conference at Ch'iu-lin (across the provincial border in Shensi), a more vigorous effort was made to control the League. The National Revolutionary Comrades Association, composed of Old Army leaders in the League, was now revived as the means whereby the mass movement might be controlled from within. The League was to become " a front organization of the Comrades Association,"[41] which would control and direct all League activities. The Association planned to send its own representatives into the countryside, to restrict the authority of the

[m] *Chen-hsiang,* p. 14b. The author suggests that it was inexpedient to call for the dissolution of the Justice Force because it had been Yen's own invention. Liang Hua-chih had edited a series of essays on united-front work style, apparently to good purpose.

Area Special Commissioners, and to take charge of the local self-defense forces, enrolling them in Peace Preservation Corps or bringing them under provincial command. The Dare-to-Die Columns were broken up and reorganized into eight units commanded by Old Army men; other military units were similarly subdivided.[42] The solidarity of the Comrades Association later proved to be shaky. Hsü Fan-t'ing, perhaps the most prominent non-Party man in the later creation of the Shansi-Suiyuan Border Region, was one of the Directors of the Association, and Liang Hua-chih was also active. Furthermore, when the split came, a number of Association-appointed military commanders went over to the Communists.[n]

In a larger sense, this effort to bring the increasingly Communist-influenced mass movement under control reflected the stalemate into which the war had fallen. Hankow had by now been lost, and the government had moved to Chungking. The forward surge of the Japanese had ended. During that surge, the pressures of combat and the emotions generated by them had forced a kind of mutual dependence and trust that could not survive a long war of attrition and maneuver. This decompression into stalemate produced a kind of "bends," which now appeared in the political and military bloodstream of unoccupied Shansi.

Although the Old elements saw that it was necessary for them to regain firm control if they were not to lose control altogether, it was the New elements who were creating new forms of power in the ruins that the war had made of the traditional power structure. Thus it was one thing to call for the reassertion of control and quite another to carry it out. The ruins, of course, were not complete, and this determined effort had some success; but leaders who had failed to gain mass support in reasonably settled times could hardly hope to succeed now. As a contemporary Japanese source pointed out, "The intervention of Yen Hsi-shan was never really possible. The main instruments of mass mobilization in the surrendered areas

[n] Just how many did so is not clear from the tabular data in *Chen-hsiang,* pp. 17a, 30b–32b. Some Old Army commanders were killed, and in other cases it appears that units under these officers departed en masse. One or two may have been forced to go along, but this cannot be true of all nine men (out of a total of 13 Old Army commanders) listed by name.

were the Sacrifice League and the New Army. Therefore, control in the region evaded the grasp of the Shansi Army. The Old Army was isolated from the masses."[43]

Outside the Sacrifice League, the Eighth Route Army and Yenan kept up a stream of united-front propaganda support for Yen Hsi-shan, combined with criticism of his Old Army associates. For example, Kan Ssu-ch'i, a Russian-trained political officer in Ho Lung's 120th Division (operating in northwestern Shansi), praised Yen Hsi-shan and the success of the united front in the province. But he referred to a number of problems: the Japanese called for struggle against the Communists and the Central Armies, but not against Yen; they attacked areas controlled by the Sacrifice League, but not those controlled by the Justice Force; there were some corrupt and traitorous military and political officials who opposed the Communists; others were cooperative when an attack was impending but anti-Communist when the heat was off.[44]

As the tension grew during the summer of 1939, Old Army leaders were denounced as "legal traitors" and "diehards," both by the League and by the organs of CCP military forces in Shansi.[o] Things were clearly moving toward a climax. From the summer months on, there were armed clashes as the Old Army tried to take over the headquarters of the Dare-to-Die forces. One source reported that over 1,000 military and political officials of the League disappeared or were killed.[45] Whatever the accuracy of this figure, all sources report considerable bloodshed on both sides.

On October 10, the CCP Shansi Provincial Committee issued a statement on behalf of all patriotic elements in the province. While the statement affirmed the desire to continue the united front with Yen, it also made it clear that independent resistance would be carried on whatever the cost.[46] The following month, Chiang Kai-shek

[o] *Chan-hsiang,* pp. 36b–38a, lists and discusses eight periodicals published by the League, its military units, or the CCP (sometimes jointly). That the charges of collaboration were not without foundation is shown by Gillin, who illustrates how the Japanese succeeded in getting the support of many rich gentry. Quite a few Old Army leaders came from such a background, though their action was doubtless motivated in part by resentment at being bypassed and thrust aside.

assisted Yen by ordering Hu Tsung-nan to disarm the Dare-to-Die Columns. Efforts were now made to recall principal leaders to Yen's headquarters, where they could be suitably "retrained." To this, Chang Wen-ang and Han Chün replied in a telegram to Yen Hsi-shan dated November 28: "If you think we cannot be revolutionary, then we will not insist that you make the revolution with us. We will go wherever we please; if you are able to transfer any part of of the Second [Dare-to-Die] Column, then you may go ahead and do so."[p]

This was the signal for the revolt, which began that evening when elements of the Second Column broke through the units surrounding them.[q] One after another, Sacrifice League members and Dare-to-Die units broke entirely away from provincial control and completed their linkup with Communist forces (either Ho Lung's 120th Division in northwestern Shansi, or Liu Po-ch'eng's 129th Division in the southeast). Finally, on December 7, 1939, Han Chün, in the name of the students loyal to him, sent a telegram to Yen. The language was eminently correct, but the message was mutiny.

> The 61st Army has harassed us excessively, and is willing to turn traitor. The students swear that together with the more than 10,000 able-bodied youths of the Second Column, they will ever struggle for the great victory. December 12 is herewith set as the date on which the men will be instructed on their mission. For the next two weeks, we fear that there will be no time to report to your eminence, and there will also be orders that are not accepted. . . . One last word: the victorious outcome remains to be seen.[47]

---

[p] *Chen-hsiang,* p. 23a. The same source tells of a piece of clandestine work that is fantastic if true: Han and Chang dispatched two of their subordinate officers to Japanese headquarters at Lin-fen, posing as the representatives of the Old Army leader Ch'en Ch'ang-chieh. There they participated in a conference at which they indicated that Yen Hsi-shan was ready to compromise, and that Wang Ching-kuo and Ch'en would collaborate with the Japanese (p. 22b).

[q] In the resulting confusion, a provincial brigade commander was arrested by Central forces, and his brigade was disarmed. Eventually the matter was straightened out; but in the meantime, the League took advantage of this opportunity to create the impression that the Central Armies were trying to take over from all local forces, both Old and New. *Chen-hsiang,* pp. 23b–24a.

Most of the Dare-to-Die forces were either already in, or trying to make their way to, northwestern or southeastern Shansi. There they openly cooperated with the CCP forces with whom they had been quietly collaborating for nearly two years. How many men were involved? Surely far more than the 3,000 to which Chalmers Johnson refers.[48] The various units under Chang Wen-ang and Han Chün, which were the first to revolt, are reported as 11 regiments totaling about 15,000 men (with a fighting ability ranging from "weak" to "quite strong").[49] Apparently these units, which were located in southwestern Shansi near Yen's headquarters, suffered the greatest casualties. Apart from these forces, those that went over to the 120th Division in northwestern Shansi are listed as 14,000. Hsü Fan-t'ing was the principal League leader here. In the southeast, 21,000 are reported as defecting from provincial control. Po I-po was the most important member of the League in this area. Another 6,000 men in southwestern Shansi were also said to have responded.[r] These forces were reorganized and made a part of either Eighth Route Army units or local guerrilla forces. There is no indication that they objected to this reorganization, as they had to Yen Hsi-shan's.

It is quite possible that these figures were inflated for dramatic effect; but even if we impose a large correction, the Communist gain in Shansi was impressive. Within a fairly short time, border-region governments were in both corners of the province. The Shansi-Suiyuan Border Region (first created in early 1940, with Hsü Fan-t'ing as Administrative Chairman) was of considerable importance because it defended Shen-Kan-Ning and was the main corridor between Yenan and Chin-Ch'a-Chi. To the southeast, the Communists later established the Chin-Chi-Lu-Yü (Shansi-Hopei-Shantung-Honan) Border Region. Because this region guarded the routes from Shansi to the North China Plain, it was of great strategic significance. It also served as a link between Chin-Ch'a-Chi and the

[r] *Chen-hsiang,* pp. 32a–32b. One might speculate that the CCP's famous Hundred Regiments Offensive (August–November 1940), which involved the action of 115 regiments, mainly against Japanese communication lines, was facilitated by this accession of strength. The most important battles of this campaign were fought from southeastern Shansi.

Shantung base area. Meanwhile, Yen Hsi-shan was left with only the southwestern corner of Shansi and what remained of the united front from above. Hsü Fan-t'ing proclaimed the continued loyalty of the New Army to Yen in the newspaper of the CCP's 115th Division.[50] In February 1940, Mao Tse-tung communicated his hope that Yen would be magnanimous toward the New Army and would continue, as before, in command.[51]

It was the anonymous KMT author of *Chen-hsiang* who most aptly summed up the events in Shansi, in mingled terms of condemnation, grudging admiration, and helplessness:

> This is the way the Communists always work. At first they were full of sweet words, flattery, and obsequious distortions, in order to open things up and cover their actions. In this case, their "loyalty" and "hard work" far surpassed the ordinary. Furthermore, they often relinquished or would not assume positions of authority, but were quite willing to work without sparing themselves (seizing particularly on low-level work, for this is the heart of their policy). Their loyalty was like that of a dog; their docility like that of a sheep. Any lord who had such slaves would be delighted. But once they were fully fledged, and once the low-level base was really achieved, they turned at once and bit, acting with no hesitation. The more respectful and obedient they are in the beginning, the more terrible and ferocious they will be later on. . . . Two years ago, when we saw the many ways the Communist Party played up to Mr. Po-ch'uan [Yen Hsi-shan] and observed their extreme obedience, we already suspected the sky would fall around us. We guessed in our hearts that things would end like this. But we weren't aware of how fast events were moving . . . nor did we believe this could happen at the very moment when the CCP's calls for "united front" and "maintenance of unity for resistance" were filling the heavens.[52]

The Three-Thirds System

In areas controlled by the CCP, the united-front policy aimed at developing support for the Party and its measures, solidarity with the Communist-led armies, and active participation in the governments that the CCP was organizing behind enemy lines. Therefore, the united front was incorporated in a variety of specific movements and policies, most of which are outside the scope of this study. For example, the policy of rent and interest reduction combined with guaranteed payment was an important way of gaining the acquiescence, if not the active support, of the richer landowners. This was part of the treatment of the class struggle within the framework of the united front.

The political organization and mobilization of the villages required the close coordination and cooperation of Party and non-Party. We have already seen that the Party considered its program of political organization an express part of the united front. As one aspect of this political organization, the "three-thirds system" (*san-san-chih*) was put into effect in 1940. The system also had a social objective in mind—gaining the support of the middle and upper levels of rural society in CCP base areas.

If "three-thirds" had such an objective at the mass level, it almost certainly had other objectives as well. It was put forth after the split with Yen Hsi-shan, during the difficult winter of 1939–40, when it seemed possible that formal "united fronts from above" with Central and regional leaders might disintegrate. Instituted almost simultaneously with the publication of *On the New Democracy,* it was also a part of the CCP's political program: if the Kuomintang was preparing to institute constitutional rule, as it said it was, the CCP wanted an effective bargaining position. By seeming to make its own political structure more representative, the CCP could argue that the KMT ought to do likewise. If the KMT agreed, the CCP would benefit; if not, the KMT would compromise itself.

The first mention of the three-thirds system dates from March 6, 1940, when it was set forth in "On the Question of Political Power in the Anti-Japanese Base Areas." This directive, attributed to Mao, states:

> In accordance with the united-front principle concerning the organs of political power, the allocation of places should be one-third for Communists, one-third for non-Party left progressives,

> and one-third for the intermediate sections who are neither left nor right.
>
> We must make sure that the Communists play the leading role in the organs of political power, and therefore the Party members who occupy one-third of the places must be of high caliber. This will be enough to ensure the Party's leadership without a larger representation. Leadership is neither a slogan to be shouted from morning till night nor an arrogant demand for obedience; it consists rather in using the Party's correct policies and the example we set by our own work to convince and educate people outside the Party so that they willingly accept our proposals.[53]

This was, therefore, no relinquishment of Communist political leadership, but rather an attempt to make that leadership more acceptable. Like other united-front measures, it was designed to gain support and reduce the possible opponents the Party might face. In particular, this policy was aimed at the quite considerable rural population that might be opposed to or indifferent to the CCP.

Judging from documents from widely separated areas, it appears that the poorer peasantry had accepted the CCP with more or less enthusiasm from the very start.[54] But these same documents also make it clear that one did not have to rise very far above the lowest strata to encounter reactions ranging from hesitancy to hostility. Even assuming that the middle and upper levels were a minority of the population, they were extremely important because of their influence as traditional rural leaders, because they controlled much of the productive power and wealth of the countryside, and because their educational level was relatively high. Furthermore, under conditions of mobile and guerrilla war conducted against a superior enemy even a small hostile group can assume an importance out of all proportion to its numbers. Mao wrote:

> The non-Party progressives must be allocated one-third of the places because they are linked with the broad masses of the petty bourgeoisie. This will be of tremendous importance in winning the latter over.
>
> Our aim in allocating one-third of the places to the intermedi-

> ate sections is to win over the middle bourgeoisie and the enlightened gentry. Winning over these sections is an important step in isolating the diehards. At the present time, we must not fail to take the strength of these sections into account and must be circumspect in our relations with them.[55]

Chinese society, said one spokesman, was egg-shaped, large in the middle and small at the ends, and the three-thirds system was one way of dealing with this fact.[56]

The CCP insisted that the policy be carried out; and that it not be treated as a propaganda device, with non-Communists permitted only token representation. In Mao's words, "The allocation of places described above represents the genuine policy of the Party, and we must on no account be half-hearted about it."[57] Lower levels were not excepted. The idea that the three-thirds system need not be carried out at the village level was subjected to scathing criticism.[58] Similar statements were frequently combined with critical remarks concerning practical shortcomings, but nowhere was it suggested that the policy could be ignored.

Yet the three-thirds system was never elevated to the status of a legal requirement.[59] Nor was the composition of the non-CCP two-thirds described with either precision or consistency. Most frequently used, but not clearly defined, were the quasi-class terms employed by Mao above. But sometimes political party labels were employed (one-third CCP, one-third KMT, one-third non-party). Occasionally, even rightists or diehards were accorded a place, though never a full third.[60]

In practice, actual representation varied so widely that it is clear the policy was not enforced with dogmatic exactness. The directive itself had left the door ajar: "The above figures for the allocation of places are not rigid quotas to be filled mechanically; they are in the nature of a rough proportion, which each locality must apply according to its specific circumstances. At the lowest level, the ratio may be somewhat modified to prevent the landlords and evil gentry from sneaking into the organs of political power."[61] In both the organs of government and in the representative assemblies, composition was in fact "somewhat modified" within the general three-thirds guideline. Generally speaking, the assemblies came closer to achieving three-thirds proportions than the agencies of government.

For obvious reasons our data on the three-thirds system are fullest for the Shen-Kan-Ning Border Region. Yenan, the wartime capital of the CCP, was located there; and this base area lay to the west of the deepest Japanese penetration. Therefore, apart from KMT incursions around the periphery and the KMT blockade to the south and west, this region was not beset with the problems of politics under conditions of guerrilla warfare.

A comprehensive summary of the history and operation of the three-thirds system in the Shen-Kan-Ning area is presented in a 1944 report by Lin Po-ch'ü, Chairman of the Border Region government.[62] According to Lin, the system was first applied in the Lung-tung (eastern Kansu) and Sui-te (northeast Shensi) Special Regions in 1940, with reference to subregion provisional assemblies, hsien provisional assemblies, and government committees. In general, the method of invitation or co-option was used.[63] Both of these were "new" areas, on the outskirts of the Border Region, where land reform had not been carried out. In and after 1941, three-thirds was applied electorally at all levels throughout the Border Region, in accordance with a "directive from the Party center."[64]

Lin observed that the higher strata of rural society, especially the landlords and gentry, were very much in favor of three-thirds and felt that the Border Region government was now demonstrating its legitimacy. The peasants, on the other hand, especially the poor peasants and hired farm workers, had many misgivings about the system, stemming from the oppression they had suffered in the past. Even in areas where land had been distributed, Lin said, poor peasants lacked political experience and were afraid that the former landlords and gentry might regain control. This feeling was shared by middle-level and lower-level cadres—usually of worker or poor-peasant background—in those areas where the agrarian revolution had been carried out. They demanded that elections be carried out as in the past, and had no wish to relax control. They protested that bloody struggles had been waged to seize power from the landlords and local bullies, who were now being allowed to return to power.[65]

The report then went on to suggest how the benefits of three-thirds might be combined with continuing Party leadership to prevent the recrudescence of landlord-gentry control. A careful investigation of all non-Party nominees should be made, with unacceptable individuals barred from candidacy. The proper ratio, Lin said, was one-third CCP, one-third progressives, one-third middle elements. He deplored the common misconception that the ratio should be one-third CCP, one-third KMT, one-third non-party. He had even heard of one-third CCP, one-third KMT, one-third Ke-lao Hui (a secret society with many members among the peasantry in western and northwestern China).[66]

On the basis of the experience gained in the 1941 and 1942 elections, Lin recommended that CCP and progressive elements should make up more than a two-thirds majority in government councils at the hsiang and municipality levels, with "some places" left for moderate elements. Hsiang headmen (*hsiang-chang*) should be more than 50 per cent Party members, with non-Party progressives next, and finally "middle elements truly willing to follow the CCP."[67] He felt this was consistent with the spirit, if not the letter, of three-thirds, and with the class relations within the Border Region. In "old" areas where land reform had been carried out, this distribution of posts was appropriate because the number of moderate elements was small; the majority were supporting the Party, a minority were bitterly opposed to it, and middle elements were few. In "new" areas this distribution was also fair, since the landlords' social and economic position was still strong, and it was necessary to prevent them from gaining control of local government.[68]

All this was of pressing importance, for the report makes it clear that there were areas where CCP control was weak. In some places, coalitions of landlords, rich peasants, and KMT members were dominant. In many "new" areas, the Kuomintang continued to exist and to elect many representatives (though Lin acknowledged that there were both progressives and moderates among them). In one subregion of Lung-tung, for example, in the 1942 hsiang

Statistics for Assembly Representatives in Fourteen Hsien

Category	Ch'ing-chien	Sui-te	Mi-chih*	Ch'ing-yang	Ho-shui	Huan-hsien	Ch'ü-tzu	Ch'in-shui	Hsin-cheng	Hsin-ning	Ching-pien*	Chih-tan	Lu-hsien*	Yen-ch'ang*	Total
Landlord	10	23	8	12	7	8	47	...	...	14	...	2	...	3	134
Rich peasant	202	159	12	89	56	32	32	3	20	30	...	45	1	5	686
Middle peasant	502	578	33	325	166	137	181	65	185	115	5	101	14	30	2,437
Poor peasant	280	1,301	154	460	1,334	501	719	405	165	393	130	541	55	111	6,549
Tenant	...	...	7	...	...	...	...	5	13	19	...	...	...	...	44
Hired peasant	93	22	...	36	4	9	22	14	2	1	12	89	1	7	312
Worker	...	236	8	22	63	38	...	...	...	2	...	14	2	9	394
Merchant	...	127	3	27	6	6	...	2	1	...	...	3	...	2	177
Gentry	...	...	...	...	...	...	...	...	...	10	2	20	...	...	32
TOTAL	1,087	2,446	225	971	1,636	731	1,001	494	386	584	149	815	73	167	10,765
CCP	416	400	83	196	219	229	257	107	124	151	67	386	57	89	2,801
KMT	69	161	2	41	58	12	...	...	2	2	...	...	5	...	352
Non-party	1,402	2,075	140	732	361	516	744	387	188	487	165	439	64	73	7,773
TOTAL	1,887	2,636	225	969	638	757	1,001	...	314	640	252	825	126	162	10,926

In this table the same group of representatives is apparently enumerated in two ways, by class affiliation and by party membership. In a number of hsien, however, the two enumerations are inconsistent. The discrepancy could stem from a number of sources: simple errors in transcription (e.g., Ch'ing-chien and Ho-shui), errors in enumeration (several are very close), or the fact that some of the party-affiliated representatives were outsiders who were not assigned to a social class (military representatives, perhaps). The original table carried an "other" category but had no entries. Despite these discrepancies, the figures give an excellent picture of the social composition of the assemblies in these hsien. (An asterisk indicates that figures for a given hsien are limited to one or two districts.)

representative elections, there were 192 CCP, 41 KMT, 732 non-party; in 1943, the figures were 180 CCP, 101 KMT, 733 non-party.[69]

This wide variation from place to place is fully borne out by the quantitative data we have. Lin presents detailed information on 14 hsien in the Border Region (see the accompanying table). In eight of these, CCP representation was under one-third; in six it was over one-third. Lin gives simplified figures for another eight hsien in which Communist Party members comprised from 13.8 per cent (in Sui-te) to 29.1 per cent.[s] This variety of representation is confirmed in a general way by Hsieh Chüeh-tsai. In 1942, figures quoted for CCP hsiang representatives ranged from 20 per cent to 45 per cent. Hsiang government agencies, hsien, and municipalities were all consistently higher, sometimes ranging as high as 73 per cent.[70] These figures meant that

> Generally speaking, among representatives to hsien assemblies, the three-thirds system has not been completely carried out. With hsien government personnel, there is still a long way to go to reach the three-thirds system.
>
> In general, in new regions, the three-thirds system has been well done; even to the point that not merely do CCP members constitute only one-third, but sometimes KMT electees outnumber those of the CCP. . . . If people want to elect many Party members, there is nothing to be done. In older border regions, the number of Party members is high; in the past, those who worked in the government were mostly Party members.[71]

As one moves into higher-level assemblies, and later in time, the proportion of Party members, progressives, and moderates becomes consistently closer to the three-thirds guidelines, at least in Shen-Kan-Ning.[72] For example, when the foreign correspondents were allowed to visit Yenan for the first time in 1944, reporters found the Border Region Assembly a coalition body under CCP leadership.[73] But doubtless wide local variations continued to exist.

[s] Lin Po-ch'ü, p. 6. Is it possible that the CCP was using three-thirds to justify a *larger* Party representation in some areas?

In contested areas behind Japanese lines, three-thirds was apparently carried out much less thoroughly. In P'eng Chen's report concerning conditions in the Chin-Ch'a-Chi region up to the fall of 1941, statistics are given from typical hsien that illustrate the results of the system a year and a half after it was begun. Class representation in the assemblies of seven hsien was quite accurate: workers, poor peasants, and middle peasants constituted 92 per cent of the population and 81 per cent to 92 per cent of the representatives at village (*ts'un*), district (*hsiang*), and hsien levels. Rich peasants and landlords made up the remainder. But as for the three-thirds system, "It cannot be made a written regulation, because to fix the three-thirds system in legal terms would be in direct opposition to the principles of truly equal and universal suffrage."[74] Thirteen hsien in the Wu-t'ai region elected a minimum of 34 per cent CCP members and a high of 75 per cent.[75] Though CCP members were sometimes directed to withdraw in cases like these, P'eng does not say that this was done here.

An example drawn from central China illustrates a complete failure to implement the policy. A May 1944 report from T'ai-hsien (Kiangsu) makes no mention whatever of the policy, and presents the following figures.[t]

Members of hsiang government:	
Party members	86+ %
Middle elements	14−
Rightist elements	0
Chief hsiang representatives (i.e., village heads):	
Party members	60+ %
Progressive elements	24.5−
Middle elements	13−
Rightist elements	2.5
Class composition, hsiang governing authorities and above:	
Poor peasants	72− %
Middle peasants (including young intellectuals)	24−
Rich peasants	2+
Landlords	2

[t] T'ai-hsien hsien-wei-hui, p. 6. This region, a little north of the Yangtze and east of the Grand Canal, was located in one of the Japanese Model Peace Zones and was almost certainly a problem area for the CCP. A drive called the "Support

Are we therefore justified in thinking, with the Kuomintang, that three-thirds was a sham? It certainly was not universally or rigorously applied. The CCP consciously sought to use the policy in such a way that its leadership was strengthened, not diluted. It did not involve either the army or the Party itself, and thus did not admit outsiders to the inner circles of power. The government bodies and assemblies to which three-thirds applied were not policy-making bodies; rather, they were forums for discussing, transmitting, and implementing policy. The KMT might legitimately criticize the CCP for failure to live up to the letter of its own instructions; but these criticisms lose considerable force because the CCP, even so, probably had a better record of concessions in representation and participation than its critics. Furthermore, three-thirds helped strengthen the CCP's demand that the KMT carry out equally "democratic" reforms.

It is striking that the CCP instituted this policy at a time of great tension in the united front and insisted on its implementation even in the face of persistent opposition from precisely those elements of the peasantry on whom the Party depended most heavily. In this light, three-thirds demonstrates the extent to which the Party acted upon as well as proclaimed the united front. Like the united front as a whole, three-thirds was never intended to take such precedence that it would compromise Party control and leadership. Instead, it was designed to complement this leadership and make it more effective. Hsieh Chüeh-tsai stated that the main purpose of the policy was to avoid the alienation and passivity that usually resulted from the monopolization of government by one party.[76] He was not referring to the formulation of policy, but to its implementation. In any large, complex organization (especially one so physically dispersed as was the CCP during these years), the line be-

---

and Love Movement" (*yung-ai yün-tung*), which aimed at getting contributions of food, clothing, etc. for the army, "was not properly understood" (p. 2). The report was also critical of the scarcity of Party members and cadres volunteering for military service (only 42 out of 1,053 recruits were in these categories). Meanwhile, criminal cases numbered 1,404 for the spring season alone. The categories may be of interest: traitors, 170; KMT special agents, 41; collaborators, 228; narcotics offenders, 728; bandits and thieves, 237. Special movements aimed at the first two were then under way.

tween the two is indistinct. There was much work to be done that might be meaningful and important to both Party and non-Party.

Was three-thirds effective in widening the base of support and participation of the CCP? I think the answer is a qualified but definite yes. There were undoubtedly many people whose enmity or mistrust of the CCP was beyond the power of three-thirds to change. We have seen that there were many difficulties in carrying out the policy; but as an aspect of the approach to uncommitted, usually more affluent, rural elements in the areas controlled by the CCP three-thirds was one part of a fairly effective program, as Lin Po-ch'ü's testimony suggests. The principle of bringing large numbers of non-Party people into the active work of government was widely recognized and observed, and was very popular with these people. The most important element in this program was probably the agrarian policy, which put an end to confiscation of property and limited itself to rent and interest reduction. But even this relatively mild program was initially very unpopular with landlords and rich peasants. P'eng Chen observed that at the time the new democratic political power was being set up in Chin-Ch'a-Chi,

> The broad peasant masses, who had undergone thousands of years of oppression, suddenly attained liberty and could not avoid excessively leftist acts of vengeance. They went so far as to infringe the personal, political, property, and land rights of the landlord class; and this produced anger and fear on the part of the landlords. They weren't sure how we and the basic masses would treat them in the end. But when we brought up and implemented the "three-thirds" system of political power, and strictly guaranteed the political rights and property rights of all anti-Japanese people, the landlords finally felt like supporting the anti-Japanese democratic regime and participating in it.[77]

Besides, he noted with heavy irony, "The landlords' land is in the villages and can't be carried off to the cities."[78]

Finally, testimony from the CCP's adversaries is provided by a classified KMT report on the Hupei-Hunan Border Region. In connection with united-front work and the three-thirds system, a series of "Policy Correction Meetings" (*cheng-ts'e chiu-cheng hui*) were held during April 1944. The gentry and landlords were the principal guests. "These conferences," wrote the KMT operatives, "were very effective. Gentry who in the past had been dissatisfied, after participating in such conferences, filled the skies with praise, feeling that the [CCP] government wasn't so bad after all, that it could recognize its own mistakes and could ask for criticism. This was stranger than anything in all Chinese history. . . . The Central Government has been away from them too long."[79]

Chapter 8

The United Front in KMT Areas

White Area Operations

In regions controlled by the Kuomintang, the Party could not reinforce its extensive propaganda with a concrete program; this, however, left it free to make suggestions it did not have to carry out. During and after the war, the CCP operated on the assumption that it was entitled to full equality and independence with respect to the KMT. The Communists never admitted that the KMT had any moral superiority because of its relation to China's legally recognized government. In other words, the CCP viewed the KMT as a political party like itself, only not as worthy.

The themes of CCP propaganda were resistance to Japan, a program of democratic reform, and qualified recognition of Chiang Kai-shek and the Central Government.[a] The main CCP propaganda organs in the KMT-controlled regions were:

The New China Daily (*Hsin-hua jih-pao*), published in Hankow and Chungking throughout the war, under the editorship of P'an Tzu-nien. In 1940, it had a circulation of about 25,000.[1] The editorial offices of the paper also ran the New China News Service, which issued news releases, put out special pamphlets, etc. It was heavily censored during much of the time of its publication, but succeeded nevertheless in expressing the CCP point of view. There was also a Yenan branch edition.

The Masses (*Ch'un-chung*), also published in Hankow and

[a] A general survey of CCP propaganda in the KMT regions (from a source hostile to the CCP) up to the spring of 1941 may be found in Wang Ta-chung, *Chung-kuo kung-ch'an-tang hsüan-ch'uan kung-tso tsung chien-t'ao*. Also included is a list of CCP propaganda organs.

Chungking, at first as a weekly but later irregularly. Its contents included CCP policy and resolutions; writings by CCP leaders; analyses of current international and domestic affairs; war reports and descriptions of CCP action behind enemy lines; and scholarly articles on politics, philosophy, etc. Many of its articles were reprinted from *Liberation Daily*. It, too, was censored heavily.

Liberation Daily (*Chieh-fang jih-pao*), published in Yenan at approximately ten-day intervals until 1941, when it shifted to daily operation. This was by far the most important publication in the CCP areas. It had some circulation in KMT China, but was banned in 1939 and was thereafter distributed secretly, mainly to Party members.

In addition, there were a great many other less important newspapers and journals. One source, admittedly incomplete, listed 51, but most of these were confined to Communist-controlled localities.[2]

During the first two years or so of the conflict, CCP propaganda was positive and enthusiastic, in favor of the war and the alliance with the KMT. Occasional criticism was hortatory, and usually put the blame on local authorities. Chiang was accorded great respect. The CCP stressed the concessions it had made in the interests of unity.[b] In these early months, the KMT, whatever private misgivings it might have, could hardly disavow its confidence in CCP sincerity without compromising its own acceptance of the concessions.

As an appeal to the general public, the San-min chu-i came in for special consideration—and the procedure here shows how skillful the CCP was in introducing its own views. The Party agreed that "the San-min chu-i enunciated by Sun Yat-sen are the paramount need of China today. This Party is ready to strive for their thorough realization."[3] This invoked the sacrosanct name of Sun Yat-sen and seemed to suggest that the CCP was moving away from Marxism-Leninism. Public statements never explicitly said that the CCP's conception of Sun's legacy was not in substantial agreement with that of non-Communists.[4]

[b] These lines of propaganda can be traced very clearly in the ten-volume series entitled *K'ang-Jih min-tsu t'ung-i chan-hsien chih-nan* [CCP 4].

> (a) Carry out the Testament of Dr. Sun Yat-sen by arousing the masses for united resistance to Japan; (b) carry out the Principle of Nationalism by firmly resisting Japanese imperialism and striving for complete national liberation and the equality of all the nationalities within China; (c) carry out the Principle of Democracy by granting the people absolute freedom to resist Japan and save the nation, by enabling them to elect governments at all levels, and by establishing the revolutionary democratic political power of the Anti-Japanese National United Front; (d) carry out the Principle of the People's Livelihood by abolishing exorbitant taxes and miscellaneous levies, reducing land rent and interest, enforcing the eight-hour working day, developing agriculture, industry and commerce, and improving the livelihood of the people; and (e) carry out Chiang Kai-shek's declaration that "every person, young or old, in the north or in the south, must take up the responsibility of resisting Japan and defending our homeland."[5]

This, it was observed, "is a simple enough program and is widely known, yet many Communists fail to use it as a weapon for mobilizing the masses and isolating the diehards. . . . In acting according to this program we are within the law, and when the diehards oppose our carrying it out, it is they who are outside the law."[6] The CCP thus claimed the right to determine what Sun had meant, while allowing the general public to read into Party pronouncements whatever conceptions it might have. Many came to believe that CCP ideas were much closer to their own than was actually the case.

CCP propaganda also stressed that the united front was not a tactical measure, to be abandoned at any time. Instead, CCP wartime united-front policy was publicly viewed as a long-range (though not necessarily permanent) change in strategy. Ch'en Shao-yü wrote in March 1938, "The Chinese Communist Party, in the present revolutionary stage, has carried out a strategic change, a large and basic change in the plan for the disposition of revolutionary strength, not simply a single, partial change in the form of organization and struggle."[7] The public pronouncements of the Sixth Plenum, which, behind the scenes, was rebuking rightism in the united front, made the same point: "It is necessary to have permanent cooperation between the Kuomintang and the Communist Party as the foundation of the anti-Japanese national united front and the guarantee of the success of the big work of the war of resistance and national reconstruction. . . . Cooperation in the war of resistance serves as the foundation of cooperation after the war is won."[8]

There were plenty of accusations to the contrary, ranging from Chang Kuo-t'ao's tendentious exposé to the assertions of anti-Communist government spokesmen. Therefore, much CCP effort was devoted to countering the accusation that the war against Japan was simply a cynical cover for internal expansion and subversion. Also common was the assertion that it was the CCP's policy to devote 70 per cent of its efforts to expansion, 20 per cent to coping with the KMT, and 10 per cent to opposing Japan. These charges are still cited frequently by KMT spokesmen as evidence of CCP perfidy, but they have not been given serious attention by Western scholars.[9] A frequently cited piece of evidence in support of both charges is a pamphlet attributed to Chang Hao, entitled *The Tactical Line of the CCP* (*Chung-kung-tang ti ts'e-lüeh lu-hsien*).[c]

Chang Hao, whose real name was Lin Yü-ying, was a native of Hunan and an uncle of Lin Piao. His career lay not in the military, but in the labor movement. In Yenan, about 1940, he was principal of the Yenan Workers' School, a member of the Industrial Movement Committee, and the editor of the periodical *Chinese Worker*. (According to Chang Kuo-t'ao, someone named Lin Yü-ying came from the Comintern in 1936 with support for Chang in his clash with Mao;[d] but it is hard to see how this could be the same person.)

[c] The appendix to this volume, "Chung-kung tsai k'ang-chan ch'i-chien chih cheng-ko yin-mou," is the *locus classicus* for the 70-20-10 indictment. Other editions of Chang's book were published as early as April 1938, but these included no publication data whatever and did not carry the appendix.

[d] North, *Moscow and Chinese Communists,* p. 175. Chang Kuo-t'ao further claims that it was Lin Yü-ying who brought a copy of the Seventh Congress Resolution dealing with the united-front policy, which he says was previously unknown in China.

The book, which circulated in Hankow during the spring of 1938, purported to be the record of lectures delivered by Chang Hao at Resistance University in Yenan in February 1937. It took a view of the united front drastically different from that of publicly stated CCP policy. "Only with a true democratic republic," it said, "can we overthrow the one-party dictatorship of the Kuomintang. The realization of a true democratic republic will be the start of the dictatorship of the proletariat, the starting point from which socialism will be set up."[10] Internationalism was stressed above nationalism; CCP weakness and imminent defeat were motives for the united front; and the San-min chu-i were recommended as a smoke screen to cover continuation of the agrarian revolution. Japan was grudgingly given first place as an enemy, but the greatest hatred was reserved for the KMT.

The CCP could not allow this sort of publicity to pass unchallenged, particularly when it came so close to Chang Kuo-t'ao's defection and his similar charges of duplicity in the united front. Chou En-lai officially denounced the entire work as a forgery.[11] Chou admitted, however, that Chang had delivered a series of lectures that contained errors similar to those in the book: "Comrade Chang Hao's error at that time was to consider the national anti-Japanese front to be a temporary tactical change, whereas the CC of the Party definitely views it as a revolutionary strategic change during a certain historical stage."[12] Chou claims, and the book admits, that Ch'in Pang-hsien administered an official rebuke. Therefore we cannot, like Chou En-lai, consider Chang's book a forgery designed to slander the CCP and disrupt the united front. But Chou is undoubtedly telling the truth when he says that the CCP had nothing to do with the editing and distribution of the booklet; that in fact genuine CCP materials were being suppressed, while this pamphlet was being sold on every street corner. It was probably written up (and perhaps slanted) by a KMT party or military agency on the basis of some such source as agent reports or defectors' notes.

What Chou En-lai and the CCP could not say was that such opinions, while straying from the official line, were present in the Party, and had been even more prevalent in the spring of 1937 than they were a year later. Whatever the room for controversy over specific points, *The Tactical Line of the Chinese Communist Party* more or less accurately reflected a current of opinion in the CCP that accepted the necessity of the united front but tended to understand it as a short-term tactical device, whose *immediate* goal was still the goal of the old united front from below—the isolation and destruction of the KMT.

On the other hand, the charge of 70-20-10 allocation of CCP efforts appears to be a fabrication. So far as is known, the original source was identified only as "X X-x," secretary of a Party cell in the 18th Group Army, who had defected when he saw the evil nature of Communist schemes. He claimed that Mao and Chu Teh discussed the principle publicly in the fall of 1937, with units of the 18th Group Army who were about to go to the front. Furthermore, all comrades were to be informed, so as to know what to do in case contact was lost. Yet all this is top secret. In addition, this defector summarized the comments of Mao and Chu on their plans for the conduct of the war.[e] Nothing even vaguely resembling this incident shows up anywhere else. It is true that the CCP was determined to expand behind Japanese lines; but this expansion constituted its main opposition to Japan, and the two could hardly be disentangled. Furthermore, it is impossible to believe that an entire wartime strategy quite different from public policy would be discussed in detail in front of a large group of soldiers—or that these vague plans could form a guideline for troops somehow separated from contact with Yenan.

[e] The war would go through three stages. At first, the CCP was to appear very self-sacrificing; it should be very respectful to KMT old-timers, since they were in opposition to the two KMT cliques most feared by the CCP (the CC clique and the Blueshirts). The Party should set KMT factions against one another, and the rank and file against the leadership. It should expand militarily along a northeast-southwest axis, thus splitting the Central armies and preparing for later stages. There would then be a stalemate, lasting probably two or three years, during which the political and military power of the National Government was to be eliminated north of the Yellow River. If CCP-KMT conflict strengthened the Japanese unduly, the CCP should again adopt a conciliatory attitude toward the KMT. In the third stage (duration undefined), CCP power should be pushed into central China, and bases like those in the North should be set up there. Then the CCP would be ready to fight the KMT for overall leadership.

By 1939–40, as the picture of inter-party collaboration developed serious cracks, the propaganda campaign gradually began to change. Each side had always pointed out the shortcomings of the other, but now denunciation, charge, and countercharge dominated the public statements. These reached their height of bitterness at the time of the New Fourth Army Incident:

> Certain people at home are engineering a new anti-Communist onslaught in an attempt to clear the way for capitulation.... They want to put an end to the War of Resistance by what they call Sino-Japanese cooperation in "suppressing the Communists." They want to substitute civil war for the War of Resistance, capitulation for independence, a split for unity, and darkness for light. Their activities are sinister, and their designs pernicious. People are telling each other the news and are horrified. Indeed, the situation has never been so critical as it is today.[13]

Denunciation of those who opposed the CCP was a major propaganda theme right up to the end of the war, paralleling demands for internal reforms and descriptions of CCP action against the Japanese. As it became clear that Japan would be defeated, the propaganda line became more exclusively directed against the KMT as a whole, despite the continuing belief that certain elements in that party could be won over or neutralized.

The propaganda effort of the CCP in the White areas was only one part of a coordinated operation, which had the same general contour as other related aspects of wartime policy: expansion during the first couple of years of the war; defense and growing secrecy until late in the war; a partial revival of activity in 1944 and 1945.

The problems of White-area operations were given serious attention even before the KMT-CCP alliance was finally concluded. Chang Wen-t'ien (Lo Fu), then Party Secretary-General, wrote a tract on this subject for a conference of White-area Party Representatives held shortly before the Lukouchiao Incident.[14] Now that two-party agreement was in the offing, and the prospects for increased legal activities were growing, work on both the mass level and the leadership level was possible. This involved the expansion of overt operations, and it is clear from Chang's discussion that exposed work, coming after years of illegal struggle carried on with utmost secrecy, found many Party members ill at ease and uncertain how to proceed. Chang called this new approach "the proper coordination of the united front from above with the united front from below."[15] It involved working with non-Communist leaders in order to win them over and to gain influence with their followers. Success came only when leadership by Communist Party members or those under their control had been attained; at that point, the original leaders had to either move in the desired direction or find themselves isolated. This differed from earlier policy, when the higher-ups in almost all non-Communist organizations were considered part of the enemy to be destroyed.

Chang particularly stressed the avoidance of excessively leftist activity, which he said the Party would not tolerate. The KMT was no longer the principal target of struggle, and overt, legal activities were of primary importance. For example, the CCP should organize, or get non-Communist sympathizers to organize, groups like those voluntarily set up by the people (mutual-aid societies, cooperatives, national salvation groups, etc.). Non-political groups should continue their regular functions, and should not undertake secret or illegal activities. Instead, they should adopt a friendly neutrality toward the CCP and the illegal struggle. Legal-overt activities should be strictly separated from illegal-secret operations. No one taking part in one should have anything whatever to do with the other.[f]

Whatever the situation, however, the Party was to maintain its position of leadership. In organizations where the CCP had gained the support of the general membership, Party members might assume top positions. Otherwise, activists should be put in these positions. "In any legal or illegal mass revolutionary struggle," wrote Chang, "it is important that it always be led by the secret Party; but

[f] Lo Fu, p. 30. Despite the stress on overt operations, the Party was always to maintain its secret structure. As one cadre manual put it, "If our Party were to become public, it would be as though we were a soldier who handed his rifle to the enemy, making it easy for him to shoot us. This we cannot do. Party secrecy can preserve and enlarge the Party's strength and render it difficult for the enemy to destroy us. This is of benefit to resistance against Japan and to the revolution." From *T'ao-lun ta-kang* [CCP 3], Question 23.

Party comrades among the masses must, as always, appear as members of the masses. Responsible Party comrades, so far as possible, should not be placed among the masses or attract the attention of others. In the struggle, they should consistently push active elements among the masses into positions of leadership."[16]

These techniques were used in Wuhan with a high degree of initial success. In November 1937, a National Salvation Youth Corps was established there, and its influence spread to other areas, among them Honan (National Salvation Youth Association) and Anhwei (Fight-the-Enemy Youth Association). These groups set up special schools, training groups, and lecture meetings to educate activists and to persuade some of them to go to the Communist areas.[17]

Overt activities were given a further boost in April 1938, when the KMT issued its Program of Resistance and Reconstruction, which pledged freedom of speech and association. Organizations like the National Emancipation Vanguards and the Ant Society sprang up.[18] Ch'en Shao-yü and other members of the CCP Representative Group established the Wuhan Defense Committee, which acted as a kind of general directorate for some 16 mass organizations. Communist spokesmen compared the Wuhan cities with Madrid, which was then under siege by Franco's forces. The Communists, though shunning positional warfare for themselves, called for defense of Wuhan to the last man, and for the arming of the working classes through the Defense Committee.[g] Rivalry grew up almost at once between the groups associated with the Defense Committee on the one hand and the Blueshirts and San-min chu-i Youth Corps on the other. This burgeoning mass movement was cut off in August, however, when the Hankow-Wuchang Defense General Headquarters dissolved the National Emancipation Vanguards, the Young Salvation Association, and the Ant Society.

[g] Johnson, p. 37. Spain was rarely compared to China, since in Spain the united front was bound up with civil war. This was what the CCP was trying to avoid. Hostile critics sometimes made this very point: that the CCP's united front was, like the united front in Spain, a civil-war tactic. It was specifically for this reason that the term "popular front" (*jen-min chan-hsien*) was avoided. See Ch'en Shao-yü, "Wan-chiu shih-chü ti kuan-chien."

This action was justified by the authorities on the ground that the Young Salvation Association had not been granted formal permission to organize and was therefore illegal. The other two were dissolved for "action detrimental to public order."[19] In October, the same fate overtook the National Salvation Youth Corps. Thus, the very success of the procedures set forth by Chang resulted in the suppression of these organizations and a deterioration in the conditions for further work.

CCP action toward the KMT itself was characterized by public separation and secret penetration. One type of infiltration (which both parties carried on ceaselessly) was solely for intelligence purposes, not to influence the infiltrated party. The agent was passive and individual, and it was neither necessary nor desirable that cells or fractions be set up. Another tactic was to try to flood the KMT with a low-level membership amenable to CCP leadership. This required at least the opportunity for semi-overt work, since so large an operation would be impossible to hide completely.

Here the CCP wavered in its policies, finally concluding by the end of 1938 that extensive infiltration of the KMT was not feasible. In the summer of 1937, Chang Wen-t'ien had recommended a program that must have reminded older cadres of Canton in 1926:

> Our objective is to reorganize the KMT. This requires that leftist, revolutionary elements enter [the KMT] in large numbers, thus creating the left wing of the KMT. Our purpose within the KMT is to solidify the left wing, push and join with the center, and split the right wing. . . . At the same time, the revolutionary masses should voluntarily enter the KMT, creating and reestablishing a low-level base. Then the strength of this low-level base will press upper levels to carry out inner-Party democracy, and ultimately our objective of reorganization. The CCP should not refuse to join the KMT, but when the KMT is not willing to allow CCP members to join it, they may enter secretly and should appear with left-KMT characteristics.[20]

But a few months later, in September, the Central Committee sent out a resolution that ordered CCP members not to participate in any of the organs of the Central Government, or in local government agencies under direct Central control. "Such participation only blurs the features of Communists and prolongs the Kuomintang's dictatorship, and does harm rather than any good to the promotion of the establishment of a united democratic government."[21] Party members were permitted, however, to take part in representative bodies and to use them as forums for the CCP viewpoint.[22] The decision may have been motivated by the fear that a bold policy of infiltration in the face of KMT opposition and CCP pledges not to do so would have a bad effect on the public image of the CCP.

But the hope of being able to introduce large numbers of leftists into the KMT was not abandoned so early. At the Sixth CCP Central Committee Plenum (November 1938), the CC telegraphed Chiang Kai-shek that it formally resolved "not to build secret organizations of the Communist Party in the Kuomintang and the Kuomintang troops."[23] But it continued: "The Chinese Communist Party considers it the best form of cooperation to have members of the Communist Party join the Kuomintang and the San-min chu-i Youth Corps. And the Communist Party will hand over the names to the leading organs of the Kuomintang of their members who have joined the Kuomintang and the San-min chu-i Youth Corps."[24] It is scarcely surprising that Chiang Kai-shek rejected this proposal.[25] From the end of 1938, then, nothing more is heard of the idea of influencing the KMT from within by changing the composition of its rank-and-file membership.

The early months of 1939 marked the end of relatively free and open CCP operations in the White areas and the beginning of greater caution and conservatism, combined with increased secret operations. The principal architect of the CCP's White-area operations during these years appears to have been Liu Shao-ch'i. In the fall of 1939, he published an extensive treatise, "On Overt Work and Secret Work," which set forth the general principles for directing and coordinating this work.[26] Liu made it clear that secret-illegal work (he equates the two terms in general, but notes that there may be exceptions) is very confining; and that it is adopted not by preference but because opportunities for overt-legal operations are absent or insufficient.[27] Yet he observed that the necessity for secret work would continue as long as enemies existed: even in CCP-controlled areas secret work was necessary, although there it was completely legal.[h] He stressed throughout the need for proper organization, the ability to shift back and forth from overt to covert work as the situation demanded, and avoidance of both the leftist error of impetuosity and the rightist error of passivity. Above all, undue or unwise risks must not be taken. Necessary risks should be preceded by preparations designed to reduce losses. Liu also devoted considerable space to the specific techniques of work in a secret and illegal environment, some of which have already been covered in the section on friendly army work: use of cover, control and organization methods, etc. It is clear that he had the current situation in mind, though the essay only occasionally becomes specific. Liu characterized the KMT areas as "semi-overt, semi-covert."[28]

In March 1940, a directive from the Party Center set the general line for the rest of the war:

> The Anti-Japanese National United Front is our policy for the whole country in the War of Resistance. . . .
>
> Our policy in the Kuomintang areas is different from that in the war zones and the areas behind enemy lines. In the Kuomintang areas our policy is to have well-selected cadres working underground for a long period, to accumulate strength and bide our time, and to avoid rashness and exposure. . . . If a member of our Party is forced to join the Kuomintang, let him do so; our members should penetrate the *pao chia* and the educational, economic and military organizations everywhere; they should develop extensive united-front work, i.e., make friends in the Central Army and among the troops of miscellaneous brands. In all the Kuomintang areas the Party's basic policy is likewise to develop the progressive forces (the Party organizations and the mass movements), to win over the middle forces (seven cate-

[h] Liu Shao-ch'i, pp. 11a ff. In this article, Liu makes it clear why we have so little information on this subject. He discourages the use of written reports, and directs that when used, they carry no place names, personal names, or numerical data.

> gories in all, namely, the national bourgeoisie, the enlightened gentry, the troops of miscellaneous brands, the intermediate sections in the Kuomintang, the intermediate sections in the Central Army, the upper stratum of the petty bourgeoisie, and the small political parties and groups) and isolate the diehard forces, in order to avert the danger of capitulation and bring about a favorable turn in the situation. . . . Our Party organizations in the Kuomintang areas must be kept strictly secret.[29]

At this time, the Party directed that further efforts be made to penetrate the masses and to draw in large numbers of intellectuals. It also criticized the tendency to "stress united-front activities among the upper strata and to neglect activities among the lower strata of the masses."[30] The Party must pay attention to the masses' concrete interests: "We must utilize government laws and regulations already extant and methods permitted by local custom . . . and lead them in political, economic, and cultural reform movements which will prove beneficial to the masses themselves as well as to the war of resistance. We should be content even to begin with very minor reforms."[31]

As for the intellectuals, the directive noted their enormous leverage in a backward country like China. They were to be recruited in increasing numbers, and to be given work commensurate with their abilities and political trustworthiness.

> In the main the principles stated above are also applicable in the Kuomintang areas and in the Japanese-occupied areas, except that, on admitting intellectuals into the Party, more attention must be paid to their degree of loyalty, so as to ensure still tighter Party organization in those areas. We should maintain suitable contact with the huge numbers of non-Party intellectuals who sympathize with us and organize them in the great struggle for resistance to Japan and for democracy, and in the cultural movement and the work of the united front.[32]

It was, however, difficult to move in both directions at once—to stress concealment and caution and at the same time stress expansion and development. In fact, the movement toward secrecy predominated during the years immediately following. In May 1940, the Party ordered: "Great care must be taken to protect our cadres, and whoever is in danger of being arrested and killed by the Kuomintang while working in an open or semi-open capacity should either be sent to some other locality and go underground or be transferred to the army."[33] We get only occasional glimpses of covert White-area operations once these directives went into effect.

A document issued by the Southern Bureau of the Party at about the same time specified in detail the tactics appropriate to work in a secret environment—including the use of cover occupations, relations between comrades on a need-to-know basis, and what to do if arrested.

> Following apprehension, comrades must not lightly confess to being Party members, but should defend themselves as anti-Japanese elements and common citizens. Employ family and social connections to effect rescue. Do not expect the organization to secure your release. If by some chance Party membership is admitted, make the admission for yourself only. You must not expose any Party secrets, or offer the identity of other comrades. Such an occurrence will constitute conduct in betrayal of the Party and will result in severe punishment and expulsion from the Party.[34]

Another glimpse is provided by a Party directive quoted in a document we have already cited.[35] The local Party committee here pointed out that although it was permissible for CCP members to serve as low-level public servants in KMT regions, in the past they had not survived long in such posts. They tended to be too leftist, to behave too much as though they were in the Shen-Kan-Ning area, to criticize the Central Government too much, and to have difficulty getting along with their colleagues.[36] It was all right for Party members to join the KMT or the San-min chu-i Youth Corps. If they did, they should try to qualify for special training; this would lead to much greater acceptance and more opportunities for work. But at all times a Party member had better be prepared for a fast exit.[37] Cadres engaged in secret work should be controlled by the secret apparatus, and should not be involved in the work of ordinary Party cells in their areas. When it was impossible to place Party members, moderates and progressives should be induced to come forward.

As a result of highly restrictive KMT policies, it was not long before almost the only legal CCP members in the White areas were those in Chungking, who were attached to the permanent Representative Group or to the staffs of the *New China Daily* and *The Masses*. But as we shall see, even this closely watched group was able to carry on some united-front work.

The conservative line was followed throughout the rest of the war, but the years 1944 and 1945 saw some revival of more overt CCP activity as a result of the reluctant concessions made by the KMT in the area of civil rights and the constitutional movement. Accordingly, Mao noted:

> In the Kuomintang-controlled areas . . . a vigorous movement embracing various social strata and democratic parties and individuals is gaining ground. . . .
>
> The democratic movement of all the oppressed classes, parties and groups should develop extensively, mustering gradually the scattered forces. . . . The Chinese Communist Party and the people of the liberated areas should give them every possible help.
>
> In the Kuomintang-controlled areas the Communists should continue to pursue the policy of a broad Anti-Japanese National United Front. To fight for the common cause we should cooperate with anybody who is not opposing us today, even though he did so only yesterday.[38]

By the war's end, therefore, the CCP was beginning to move away from holding operations and toward a more aggressive line. After its cautious expansion of the years immediately preceding, the CCP was not strong, but it was in a good position to press forward.

The United Front and Minor Parties

One of the most important united-front targets of the CCP in the Central Government areas was the coalition of minor parties and groups that came to be known as the China Democratic League (DL). These minor parties never had a very large active membership, or much actual power. But in one way or another they represented, spoke for, or influenced nearly all educated Chinese who were not irrevocably committed to the KMT or CCP. The minor parties were also involved in clique politics, and hence exerted a pull on disaffected members of the Kuomintang. For all these reasons, the various minor parties had a collective importance far beyond their actual numbers.

A study of these groups and their relations with the two major contenders illustrates many of the themes that were so much a part of the history of the 1940's: the difficulties of a neutral position, the dilemmas of the Kuomintang, the CCP's effective use of very slender resources. It seems likely that if the Kuomintang had undertaken more enlightened policies on its own initiative, the bulk of the DL would have remained with it instead of eventually going over to the CCP. But the combination of KMT errors and CCP effectiveness in dealing with the minor parties provides an almost classic example of successful united-front work.

From about the mid-1940's on, both during the civil war and after the establishment of the People's Republic, the minor parties were a prominent part of the Party's united front. For these reasons, we shall examine in some detail the minor-party coalitions that preceded the establishment of the DL in October 1944; the organization of the DL and the factional struggles that took place within it; and the CCP's attempts to influence this group during and immediately after the war. Subsequent relations between the CCP and the minor parties will be deferred to Chapter Nine.

The United National Construction League and the Federation of Chinese Democratic Parties

During the spring and summer of 1939, signs of a letdown in the spirit of resistance were apparent in Chungking. Military friction between the Communists and the Central Government was occurring on a scale and with a frequency that dismayed many politically active public figures. It was also during this period that the Government and the KMT were considering constitutional government. The PPC had formed the 25-member "Association for the Promotion of Constitutionalism," and in November the KMT Central Executive Committee said it would convene the National Assembly on November 12, 1940. Much discussion of all these issues was being carried on.

In the early fall, Liang Sou-ming, an independent long active in education and rural reconstruction, returned from an eight-month tour of the front and the guerrilla areas determined to try to preserve the unity that China had demonstrated until recently. Liang, Chang Chün-mai, and others formed the United National Construction League, or UNCL (*T'ung-i chien-kuo t'ung-chih hui*). On November 29, 1939, Liang received official approval for the formation of the League from Chiang Kai-shek.[39] The membership included more than 30 delegates to the PPC, among them the leaders of the China Youth Party, the National Salvation Association, the Third Party, the Vocational Education Group, and the Rural Reconstructionists. The League made no attempt to form a party organization, but tried instead to coordinate the activities and policies of the political splinter groups. Except for such influence as could be exerted by a collective voice, it made no bid for independent political influence. The leadership of Chiang Kai-shek was positively affirmed. No criticisms were included, but calls were made for constitutional rule and an extension of civil rights.[40]

When elements of the Eighth Route Army clashed with government troops in southwestern Hopei in March 1940, the UNCL offered to mediate. With the approval of the Generalissimo and the Communists, the UNCL submitted a plan for differences between the two parties to be reconciled in the PPC. Ultimately, the plan was shelved, and no permanent results were achieved. But the UNCL was encouraged by this apparently promising beginning.[41]

Nearly a year later, in the wake of the New Fourth Army Incident, the UNCL again attempted to act as peacemaker. It secured preliminary approval from both Chiang Kai-shek and Chou En-lai for an all-party committee with power to make binding decisions concerning KMT-CCP relations. Before action was taken, however, the KMT switched its support to the idea of an advisory committee within the PPC. This second fruitless effort finally led to the formation of a new political coalition.

Even before the second attempt at mediation, members of the UNCL had come to feel that a new body could better represent independent political thinking. Thus, when called upon in the New Fourth Army crisis, the leaders of the League informed the government that "they would be only too glad to mediate, but at the same time they desired to organize a 'Federation of Democratic Parties and Groups' to serve as a kind of buffer . . . and to constitute a real third force in Chinese politics."[42] But "when this proposal was presented to the Generalissimo, he immediately turned it down, refusing altogether to approve such an organization."[43] The leaders of the small parties and the independents decided nonetheless to organize the new association in secret. Disillusioned with their role as pure mediators, they were now beginning, however tentatively, to think in terms of constituting an independent force.

When it came into being, on March 25, 1941, the Federation of Chinese Democratic Parties (*Chung-kuo min-chu cheng-t'uan ta t'ung-meng*) included three minor parties, two non-party organizations, and a number of individual members. Except for the last category, one became a member of the Federation by belonging to one of the member organizations. The minor parties were the China Youth Party, the National-Socialist Party, and the Third Party; the non-party organizations were the Rural Reconstructionists and the Vocational Education Group. Many of the individual members came from the National Salvation Association, which had achieved such prominence during the year before the outbreak of the war. The Association was not organizationally represented because it had been denounced by the government as Communist-led. The founders of the Federation disagreed, but felt that inclusion of the Association might jeopardize the future standing of the new body. Furthermore, the National Salvation Association had never been very well organized. For these reasons, its leaders joined as independents, and the Association was represented in fact, if not in name.

Parties and Groups

The China Youth Party. In the period of intellectual activity that took place after World War I, a "Young China Study Association" was formed at Peiping University, with overseas Chinese student membership in Japan and France. At first non-political, it gradually moved into politics and split into a left and a right faction. Li Ta-chao, Yün Tai-ying, and the left wing in general soon went over to the infant CCP. In 1923, the rest of the group, led by Tseng Ch'i, Li Huang, and Tso Shun-sheng, formed the China Youth Party, as it was later called. Though it nominally supported an advanced social program, the Youth Party was far to the right. It supported Wu P'ei-fu during the 1920's, and was consequently distrusted by the KMT. The bulk of its strength was in Szechwan, and was based on military and landlord support. Though reluctant to discuss membership, the party was perhaps as strong as the KMT in Szechwan during the war.[44] During the 1940's, Tso Shun-sheng was the party's most active figure; for part of this time, he taught at the Central Political Institute, the KMT training school.[45]

As the KMT moved farther west and farther to the right during the early war years, the views of the two parties came closer together, particularly on the Communist issue. Active in the UNCL, the Federation, and the DL, the Youth Party occupied a favored position with respect to the Central Government. It was the only party whose representation in the PPC was not cut after the October declaration of the Federation.

The National-Socialist Party. Headed by Carsun Chang (Chang Chün-mai), Lo Lung-chi, and Chang Tung-sun, this party was a lineal descendant of Liang Ch'i-ch'ao's Political Study Group. It was formally organized in 1931, counting mainly foreign-trained scholars and educators in its top leadership. It was an articulate group, conservative but not so far right as the China Youth Party. It was never known for a mass following or for unanimity within its own ranks, but was quite influential among educated, middle-aged moderates.[i] Generally, it upheld Western-style democracy, industrial and agricultural cooperation, and a combination of planned and free economy. On paper, its organization paralleled the KMT.

The Third Party.[j] This party represented those members of the left-wing Kuomintang who had neither gone over to the Communists nor been reintegrated into the main body of the party after the split of 1927 at Wuhan. They claimed to be the legitimate inheritors of Sun's Three Principles, and upheld the so-called Three Great Policies. The group was led by Teng Yen-ta until his execution by the KMT in 1931. Some elements connected with this group were active in the Fukien Republic of 1933. An illegal, underground organization until 1938, it had as its more or less acknowledged leaders during the war years Chang Po-chün and P'eng Tse-min. Membership may have been as high as 15,000.[46]

The Rural Reconstructionists. This name was applied to those members of the Chinese Rural Reconstruction Association who took part in wartime political activities.[k] The two leaders of the group were Liang Sou-ming and James Y. C. Yen, each with his own personal following. Yen's group was less politically oriented than Liang's, though both were basically non-political. Thus the reconstructionists became "the lengthened shadow of Liang Sou-ming."[47] This was a very small group, with no interest in expanding its following.

The Vocational Education Group. This association was not specifically a political party. The Vocational Education Association had been formed in Kiangsu in 1917 by Huang Yen-p'ei to promote an American-style system of industrial-arts schools. The group,

[i] According to James Shen, Chang Chün-mai refused to comment either way when told that Gunther's *Inside Asia* had placed the party's membership at about 10,000. It is my speculative opinion that this figure is too high. Lo (Ph.D., Wisconsin) and the philosopher Chang Tung-sun were considerably to the left of Chang Chün-mai, and the party was in effect badly split.

[j] Previously, this group had been formally known as the "Liberation Action Committee of the Chinese People."

[k] The Association was a non-political body devoted to coordination of reconstruction activities and to the interchange of information and opinion among those interested in the movement. Meetings had been held in 1933 (at Tsou-p'ing, Shantung), in 1934 (at Ting-hsien), and in 1935 (at Wu-hsi).

which financed its educational work through connections with local warlords, became unpopular with the Kuomintang at the time of the Northern Expedition. In particular, Huang clashed with the rightist CC clique, though he was later on good terms with the Generalissimo.[48]

The National Salvation Association. As we have seen, the National Salvation movement had formally begun in March 1936. National Salvation organizations of all types sprang up throughout the country, most of them spontaneously but some with CCP leadership or inspiration. Though there was only sporadic organizational contact between these groups, their platforms were quite similar: armed resistance to Japan, an end to civil war, constitutional rule, and civil rights. By 1937, this had become a very loose, sprawling mass movement. In influence and "membership" it ranked behind only the KMT and CCP, and it was generally leftist in tone. It never became a party in the accepted sense; some attempts were made to create a party structure in 1939, but lack of agreement on a positive program prevented the development of any formal organization.[49] National Salvation remained a propaganda forum, issuing appeals for KMT-CCP unity on the basis of the National Salvation platform.

The Executive Committee of the Federation was headed by Huang Yen-p'ei of the Vocational Education Group and Tso Shun-sheng of the China Youth Party. Huang was later replaced by Chang Lan, an educator and the former governor of Szechwan, who had joined the Federation as an independent. Other members of the committee, many of them from the Youth Party, were Tseng Ch'i, Li Huang, Chang Chün-mai, Lo Lung-chi, Liang Sou-ming, and Chang Po-chün.[50]

The first act of the Federation was the adoption of the following program, which was not made public for several months:

1. To carry out resistance to the end. To recover all lost territory and fully reestablish the integrity and sovereignty of China. To oppose all movements for compromise with the invaders.
2. To embody the democratic spirit in political institutions,

putting an end to one-party control over the State. Pending the enforcement of a Constitution, to establish a body representing all parties and groups for the discussion of national affairs.

3. To strengthen internal unity. All current disagreements between parties and groups to be immediately adjusted.

4. To urge and assist the Kuomintang to carry out the Outline of National Resistance and Reconstruction, determinedly and fully.

5. To establish real unity and oppose local separatism, but at the same time to define and enforce the spheres of power of the Central and local governments.

6. To insist that the army belongs to the nation, and that military men must owe loyalty to the nation alone. To oppose all party organizations in the army, and to oppose the use of the army as a weapon in party strife.

7. To enforce government by law. To protect the lives, property and personal liberty of citizens of China and oppose all secret arrests and penalties unsanctioned by law.

8. To protect the legitimate expression of public opinion by guaranteeing freedom of speech, publication, assembly, and association.

9. To give effect to the abolition of one-party rule mentioned in Point 2, the following reforms should be made: (a) the government's prestige and influence should not be used to promote the power of any one party in schools and cultural organizations; (b) official personnel should be selected on the basis of the "best and ablest" as advocated by Dr. Sun Yat-sen, and the use of national political power for purposes of party recruiting should be abolished; and (c) the "New District System," whereby headmen of villages are selected by examination rather than election, should be altered.

10. With reference to the current political situation, to give attention to the following points: (a) the improvement of the food, living conditions, and pay of soldiers at the front; (b) the abolition or modification of all executive orders interfering with the expansion of production; (c) strengthening the government's supervisory organs in order to put an end to all "squeeze" and corruption in carrying out State economic measures.[51]

This document, at least as much a condemnation as a program, was much more outspoken than any previous pronouncement from any source other than the CCP.

In view of the political atmosphere in Chungking, the leaders decided to operate a propaganda center outside of China, in Hong Kong. The Hong Kong contingent began in September to publish the newspaper *Light* (*Kuang-ming pao*), with Liang Sou-ming as chief editor.[l] Meanwhile, during the summer, a difference of opinion had arisen with respect to publication of the program. The groups inside China, subject to harassment and retaliation, generally favored issuance of a watered-down version. The Hong Kong group insisted on going ahead with the original plan: to publish the program just before the September session of the PPC and decide from the Kuomintang's reaction whether or not to assume the seats assigned to constituent parties.[52] A compromise was worked out whereby the full program was published, but left unsigned, in *Light* on "Double Ten" (October 10, 1941).

The Kuomintang reaction was quick and hostile. The program was suppressed as much as possible in China, although it did become generally known. In Hong Kong, the KMT first tried to discredit the organization. Sun Fo argued in a series of speeches that the anonymous program was a sign of bad faith, if not of actual subversion. Then the British were asked to eject Federation leaders on the ground that the party existed nowhere outside Hong Kong. By the time British authorities discovered that the Federation included two of the five members of the PPC Presidium, Liang's house had been searched and other actions taken. Subsequently, the Hong Kong contingent was left alone by the British.[53] In China, Chang Chün-mai was dropped from the Presidium, and other small-party men lost their seats in the PPC.[54]

Communist reaction to the Federation was, naturally, very favorable. In October 1941, Shen Chün-ju and Chang Po-chün ap-

[l] This is the origin of the name that was resurrected for use after 1950, the *Kuang-ming jih-pao,* to designate the paper that was presumed to speak for the Democratic League, other bourgeois-democratic parties, and the non-CCP intelligentsia.

proached Chou En-lai in Chungking to ask whether the CCP would be willing to participate. After some hesitation, Chou declined, saying that the presence of the CCP would only compromise the Federation and its work. He did, however, promise support from the sidelines, and the *Hsin-hua jih-pao* reportedly provided press facilities for Federation propaganda.[55] The overseas Chinese press also hailed the program.

Since the anonymous publication of the program had proved an unwise maneuver, formal announcement was made in Chungking in November, and the Federation became a public organization. Activities in Hong Kong ended abruptly when the Japanese took the city on Christmas Day, 1941, and members of the Federation made their way back into unoccupied China. Now, when the Central Government was least tolerant, the Federation was forced to operate without legal protection, within easy reach of the powerful object of its criticism.

The China Democratic League: Formation and Factions

The years 1943 and 1944 were a period of crisis for the Central Government and the KMT. Both domestically and abroad, their failings were being criticized in a manner they could not ignore. Consequently, in the hope of improving a badly tarnished image, proposals for constitutional rule and an end to the Period of Tutelage were once again brought forward. The virtual ban on political activity was somewhat relaxed. Under these very mildly encouraging circumstances, the activities of the Federation revived. Branches were set up in Kunming, Chengtu, Kweilin, and elsewhere. Membership began to grow again, and influential figures such as Huang Yen-p'ei and Shih Liang organized independent groups for the promotion of constitutional rule.[56]

The experiences of the Federation tended to lead it away from acting merely as a sounding board for independent opinion, or as a disinterested mediator between the CCP and the KMT. By 1944, it was beginning to think of itself as a "third force," a grouping with small but possibly important political influence of its own. Some elements, however, were playing an opportunistic game, hoping to find, finally, a desirable position in either the KMT or the CCP.

These circumstances—partially relaxed restrictions, discussion of constitutional rule, and the Federation's changing conception, disinterested or not, of its own role—brought renewed interest in reorganization. In September 1944, it was decided to form a new body, though there was difficulty in agreeing on actual structure and administration. Participation by group, as in the Federation, was finally abandoned in favor of membership on an entirely individual basis. Once again, Double Ten was selected as the occasion for announcing the formation of the new group, the China Democratic League, or DL (*Chung-kuo min-chu t'ung-meng*).

The League issued no founding statement, but its leaders made it clear that this body was dedicated to the same goals as the Federation. The DL was concerned with the prevention of civil war, the nationalization of all armed forces, and the institution of a democratic government (either constitutional rule satisfactory to all parties, or some form of coalition government). In particular, it pressed for an all-party deliberative body, and for a truly representative National Assembly. Related to these basic demands were the customary statements on civil liberties, governmental reforms, etc. Much of the League's energy went into writing for periodicals and newspapers, work for which many of its members were well suited. Some newspapers and periodicals were sponsored by the League itself, some by the constituent groups, and some by independents sympathetic to the League. The League thus spoke for a large number of people—the uncommitted, educated groups, generally—but could not really represent them because there was no machinery for doing so.

From the beginning, the Central Government viewed the League with suspicion and hostility, and acts of repression were common. In October, a large student meeting in Kunming was bombed, during a speech by Lo Lung-chi, by what were generally thought to be KMT agents.[57] Publication activities were interrupted or suspended, and various other harassments (especially arrest and temporary detention) were frequent. These incidents aroused hostility and criticism, but the League made little attempt to exploit them for their popular protest value, indicating that its attitude toward a mass following was ambivalent.[58]

Helping to consolidate the League position, however, was the Stilwell crisis, which broke shortly after the League was founded. The subsequent cabinet shakeup, together with American concern for Chinese domestic affairs, made it more difficult for the government to take action against the League. Nevertheless, the League's position remained perilous. If a hard line was taken, it would not be tolerated by the KMT; yet a moderate approach would probably be ignored. Moreover, a hard line would only increase antagonism and perhaps lead to the civil war that the League was trying to prevent. This dilemma was most acute for those who were truly independent of both the KMT and the CCP. This explains some of the contradictions found in the pronouncements and political behavior of the League. It has been described as taking on "the various aspects of a genuine political party, an informal political club, and a pressure group working for certain political ends."[59]

Until V-J Day, the two main centers of DL activity were Chungking and Kunming (before its fall in November 1944, Kweilin was also an important center of liberalism). This geographic fact paralleled a deeper split. The group in Szechwan was based on such elements as the Youth Party. The Kunming group had brought to Yunnan—and above all to Southwest Associated University—much of the spirit and sentiment of the December Ninth movement in Peking. The Chungking group was in general older, more conservative, more realistic, and somewhat readier to compromise with the government. Many of its members had been in and out of public life for a long period of time, and were very familiar with the political facts of life. The Kunming group, on the other hand, was made up mostly of younger writers, teachers, and students. They tended to be more idealistic, more radical, and more anti-government. In many cases, their political experience dated only from 1935 or later and had been concerned with such seemingly clear-cut and attractive issues as patriotism, an end to civil war, opposition to Japan, civil rights, and democracy.

This divergence was heightened by the political atmosphere in the two areas. The Chungking group was directly under the eye of the Central Government, which could thereby control its activities, and could use personal relations to present its case to the members of the League. Rewards, as well as pressures, could be easily applied. In Kunming, by contrast, League members were partially beyond the reach of the capital, and the warlord governor of the province, Lung Yun, adopted a benevolent attitude toward their activities.

Within the League, the Youth Party at first occupied a dominant position. Although the Chairman, Chang Lan, was an independent, he was a native of Szechwan and had long been in contact with Youth Party leaders. Furthermore, he spent much time at his home in Chengtu; his duties then devolved upon the Secretary-General, the energetic Tso Shun-sheng. The Youth Party also controlled the League's financial committee.[60] Large memberships in Chungking and Szechwan further added to the strength of this group.

A semblance of unity was maintained until October 1945, when a series of splits took place at the sessions of the Provisional National Representative Conference. The most important result was to reduce the influence of the Youth Party. The anti-YP elements wanted to have the meeting convened as a regular National Congress. Rules of procedure would then require the reelection of the Central Committee and the reappointment of all those in top positions.[61] It was even suggested that the post of Secretary-General be abolished entirely. After a bitter debate, the Conference adopted a proposal by Chang Po-chün: the post would be retained; but in the absence of the Chairman, the Standing Committee would select one of its members to act as presiding officer.[62] It was also decided, in another compromise move, to expand the Central Committee. Cheng Chen-wen then moved that in cases where the DL's position was opposed by the YP, the latter should "not attack proposals in the current situation made from the Yunnan side."[63] Nor, he added, should the YP affirm that the position of leadership in whatever form of government China might adopt should go to the KMT and Chairman Chiang.[64] A number of other, less important, wrangles also took place at this time. Even though the YP was still strong within the League, Tso refused to consider taking up his post as Secretary-General. In December, the YP formally withdrew from the League. Liang Sou-ming, an independent acceptable to all factions, somewhat reluctantly replaced Tso as Secretary-General.

The Report on Organization delivered by Chang Po-chün at the time of the Provisional Conference provides considerable detail on the inner structure of the League.[65] During the first year of operation, most work had centered in the capital and had been carried on informally by CC members. By September 1, 1945, however, a formal Chungking Municipal Branch had been established and was beginning to function. There were 336 League members in Chungking, mostly civil servants, members of the professions, and cultural figures. Surprisingly, very few came from educational or business circles. In contrast, the Szechwan Provincial Branch as a whole counted more than 2,000 members, over half of them in Chengtu. Many of these had military connections. More than ten hsien branches had been set up.[66] The Yunnan Branch, in existence since December 1944, claimed about 200 members, the majority in educational circles. In Yunnan, the League also directed the China Democratic Youth League (*Chung-kuo min-chu ch'ing-nien t'ung-meng*), with several hundred members, mostly from Southwest Associated University and Yunnan University.[67]

The CCP and the Democratic League through October 1945

Not even the most suspicious KMT sources suggest that there was extensive CCP influence among the small parties prior to the limited revival of Federation activity in 1944. Yet the CCP was more sympathetic to the Federation than was the KMT, and relations were friendly between most Federation members and the Communists in Chungking. The CCP always considered these groups important united-front targets; a thoroughgoing early study of them was produced by Chang Chih-i, now and for many years a deputy director of the United Front Work Department.[68]

In the KMT areas, particularly among the educated, CCP policy aimed to isolate the KMT and gain support for itself on the basis of democracy, civil rights, domestic peace, and nationalism. While this kind of democracy was viewed as "bourgeois" by the CCP, these very categories were the edge of its anti-KMT weapon. It was this sort of "bourgeois" democracy for which the League stood. The KMT, although itself committed to some form of democracy, could grant League demands only at the cost of granting the CCP nationwide legality, freedom of organization, agitation, etc. The CCP therefore had the KMT in a corner. If the KMT made concessions to the League, the CCP would be the principal beneficiary. If the KMT refused to do so, the League's criticism would help isolate the KMT and destroy public confidence in it.

The effective use of the DL in this manner required that it be influenced in ways that did not compromise its image of independence and integrity. Properly handled, the DL could become a forum, a way of reaching much larger groups outside the League (especially students, teachers, professionals, and businessmen without official connections). It might be a source of skills that the CCP needed; it might be a way station for those anxious to get out of the KMT but unwilling to move as far as the CCP. The Government often charged that the CCP attempted to control the DL by infiltration; but this was seldom true (though Chou Hsin-min and Yü I-fu, both members of the CC, were later found to have been CCP members). A policy of infiltration ran the risk of compromising the League with the Government and of alienating the League itself.[69]

Much more effective in bringing the DL into line with the CCP were open contacts (individual or organizational), aid given to the League as a whole or to certain factions against others, proper coordination of propaganda and programs, and the action of the KMT and Central Government. It would be hard to overstress the effect of KMT repression and harassment in pushing much of the League to the left. There was very little possibility that the Government would heed proposals or criticism emanating from the League; but the KMT, having decided not to heed the League, was nevertheless not prepared to ignore it. The result was almost constant action to intimidate, harass, and silence those who would speak out.

Contacts between the League (or individual League members) and the CCP were handled through the permanent Representative Group (especially Tung Pi-wu, Wang Jo-fei, Hsü Ping,[m] and—when available—Chou En-lai), and by the staff of *Hsin-hua jih-pao,* headed by P'an Tzu-nien. Most of these contacts were made with the National Salvation leaders and the members of the Third Party, particularly Shen Chün-ju and Chang Po-chün. Liang Sou-ming also met frequently with the Communists. It is not clear to what extent these contacts were official DL-CCP activities, and to what extent they were unofficial or personal.

During 1944, before the DL was formed, the CCP supported the Federation and the smaller groups spawned from it in their demands for constitutional rule. The *New China Daily* published a number of pamphlets on this and other subjects for the Federation, and helped distribute them in Chengtu, Kunming, and Chungking. At the time of the League's formation in October 1944, the CCP encouraged the new membership rule, which made it easier to expand the membership of the League, and to place an occasional Party member inside the organization. The Communists also reportedly provided a subsidy of 1,000,000 yuan in a lump sum, plus 60,000 yuan per month.[70] The monthly payments were turned over to Chang Po-chün by Wang Jo-fei and Hsü Ping, and may have been part of the CCP effort—which had plenty of unsolicited support in the League—to curtail the influence of the Youth Party.

Apart from these specific acts, there was probably little direct Communist influence on the content of the League program. Undoubtedly the Communists in Chungking tried to convince League members of the justice of their views, but so did the KMT. It was necessary for the CCP to use caution, because the League still contained many non-Communists and anti-Communists. Since the League was arguing for democratic reforms, the CCP appears to have tried to gear its own propaganda program to that of the League, rather than to set forth a line for the League to follow. This

[m] Hsü Ping, whose real name is Hsing Hsi-p'ing, is presently the Director of the UFWD.

was reasonably effective, for after the Provisional Conference, those most hostile to the KMT (Salvationists and Third Party) dominated the most important committees—finance, organization, and propaganda.

This relationship between the League and the CCP, loose but effective, became gradually tighter in the postwar period, until finally what remained of the League fully accepted CCP leadership, thereby becoming an ally of the Party in the anti-KMT united front.

Chapter 9

The Civil War

THE END of the war with Japan came so suddenly that neither side was able to make immediate use of all the opportunities it presented. It also removed the enemy who had been the original cause of the united front, and who had kept the power struggle between the KMT and the CCP in nominal suspension. Now that struggle became primary and open. During the four years that followed, the contest for supremacy in China passed through three stages, ending with the complete victory of the Chinese Communist Party over the Kuomintang. First came a period of negotiation and maneuver, which lasted until early summer 1946, following the breakdown of the agreements reached at the Political Consultative Conference. During this period, though the KMT appeared much stronger than the CCP, it had trouble extending its influence over North China and Manchuria. Second was the phase of KMT military initiative and overextension, which lasted until the CCP Manchurian offensives of May 1947. Behind these hollow military advances, however, the KMT was succumbing to internal decay and loss of support. Third was the period of CCP initiative and KMT collapse, ending with the Nationalist retreat from the mainland and the establishment of the People's Republic of China in October 1949.

Despite the rapidity of KMT collapse in the last years of the civil war, a Communist victory was by no means a foregone conclusion in 1945 and 1946. In most areas, the KMT was significantly stronger than the CCP: it had a monopoly on international recognition, including that of Russia; its armed forces were better equipped and much bigger than the Communist armies; it controlled the larger and richer part of China; and it benefited from extensive United States aid and support. As one effort, among others, to change this balance of power, the CCP employed a variety of united-front approaches to gain support and isolate the KMT.

If it is argued that in 1936 and 1937 the united front was forced upon the CCP by external circumstances (and I have challenged this view), unquestionably the continued use of this strategy after the war was the CCP's own decision. In 1949, at the moment of CCP victory, Mao reiterated the importance of the united front as one of the three principal elements in the Party's success. This approach was also an integral part of *On Coalition Government* (1945), the policy statement with which the CCP entered the postwar world.

Here Mao set forth a willingness, as a minimum program, to enter into a coalition government with the KMT on three conditions: the CCP's freedom of action must not be compromised, there must exist the opportunity for legal and open competition throughout China, and it must be understood that the CCP's maximum program remained the achievement of socialism. On these conditions, the CCP would accept as allies those who accepted all or part of the program of "new democracy" and did not threaten Communist leadership. Meanwhile, the liberated areas and the Communist-led armies were the guarantee of the Party's continued independence; this was the CCP's power base if events in China should turn toward civil war.

With V-J Day, the postwar maneuvering began. The main issues were full nationalization of the armed forces, extension of government authority over all regions and local governments in the country, and the constitutional reform and liberalization of the Central Government. The KMT required concessions from the CCP on the first two before it would consent to consider the third; the CCP would agree to the first two only after the third had been carried out to its satisfaction. During this period, two important series of negotiations took place. The first, under General Hurley's auspices, was carried on between Chiang Kai-shek and Mao Tse-tung in August and September 1945. The second, arranged by General Marshall, was the Political Consultative Conference (PCC), convened in January 1946. Both achieved impressive results on paper, but neither party limited its action in the light of these results, or had much confidence in the other's good faith.[1]

Chiang Kai-shek was determined to extend his political and military control over the whole of China. He saw political rivals as petitioners for a share in the government, subject to whatever restrictions the KMT might impose. The CCP spoke and acted as a sovereign power, entitled to full equality with the KMT on the basis of democracy, its war record, and its formidable military power. The CCP sought a political solution where it was weak, while simultaneously consolidating and expanding its hold on territories where it was able to do so—by taking over former enemy areas, disarming Japanese and puppet troops, enlisting new recruits, setting up organs of local government, etc. The Communists were very cautious about concessions that would weaken their military strength or bring the regions they governed under centralized control. As Mao put it in a confidential circular: "We are prepared to make such concessions as are necessary and as do not damage the fundamental interests of the people. Without such concessions, we cannot explode the Kuomintang's civil war plot, cannot gain the political initiative, cannot win the sympathy of world public opinion and the middle-of-the-roaders within the country, and cannot obtain in exchange legal status for our Party and a state of peace. But there are limits to such concessions."[2]

The CCP's appreciation of its own strengths and weaknesses was contained in a secret document dated August 30, 1945, shortly after the signing of the Sino-Soviet Friendship Treaty (August 14) and Mao's flight to Chungking with Patrick Hurley (August 28).[3] Its author said that civil war was likely, but that it might still be possible "on the basis of KMT-CCP cooperation, to achieve peaceful development."[4] Peace was possible for three reasons. First, the Chinese people did not want civil war and were responding to the CCP's call for democracy and peace. Second, the Allies, especially the United States and Russia, did not want civil war in China; and third, Chiang had many problems and might be willing under certain circumstances to recognize the position of the CCP. Meanwhile, he pointed out, the CCP also had many problems, among which were difficulties in taking over urban centers, Chiang's linkup with puppet troops and his monopolization of surrendering Japanese forces, and the fact that "the Soviet Union, because of the obligation to carry out the terms of the [Sino-Soviet] treaty, cannot help us directly."[5] Hu complained that "we do not understand actual Russian policy."[6]

Thus the CCP was not at this time irrevocably committed to civil war. The Communists' propaganda campaign and public image depended heavily on their apparent reasonableness and dedication to peace, just as it had once depended on a good war record and apparent dedication to unity. Furthermore, if the clock was running against the KMT, the CCP had much to gain by putting off the final split, and by trying to force the Kuomintang into accepting the onus for the break. Meanwhile, a favorable bargain might be struck at the negotiation table.

A Party spokesman discussed these points in December 1945, when open conflict seemed very close. This, he said, was not a period of war, but a transitional period of "national democratic united front" in opposition to civil war—with the understanding that "outsiders" be excluded from the liberated areas, that these areas be expanded, and that the sympathy of the masses be won.[7] He pointed out that although American imperialists were aiding the KMT, the Americans did not want civil war; in fact, he said, the CCP had won considerable sympathy with the American public and some parts of the government. Therefore, the CCP should not directly oppose the United States but should seem to welcome its mediation and let the KMT force the issue.[8]

Amid growing tension and hostility, General Marshall was able to arrange for the convocation of the Political Consultative Conference (PCC), composed of KMT, CCP, and minor-party delegates, which met from January 13 to 31, 1946. The hopeful results achieved by the PCC seemed to dispel the gloomy atmosphere in which it had convened. A nationwide cease-fire was arranged, and agreements were reached (in principle) on government organization, a program of national reconstruction, military problems, a

National Assembly, and a draft constitution. These steps were supplemented by the creation of an Executive Headquarters in Peiping to enforce the cease-fire with three-man truce teams. On February 25, a supplemental agreement was signed that appeared to solve (in principle) the thorny question of military organization.

But these partial accords were taking place against a background of continued maneuvering and polarization of opinion. By the time the PCC had completed its deliberations, the KMT and CCP positions were very clearly defined. Chiang Kai-shek put Manchuria outside the jurisdiction of the truce teams; the CCP continued its expansion. The meeting of the Kuomintang Central Executive Committee in early March, dominated by those opposed to the PCC, so altered and repudiated the agreements that they became a virtual dead letter. In response, the CCP occupied the important Manchurian city of Ch'angch'un on April 18, 1946. Communists moved into the partial vacuum left in northern Manchuria by the withdrawal of Russian forces. Thereafter, the decisions of the PCC were ignored, or used as propaganda, but no longer served as a serious basis for possible coalition. The evidence suggests that by March or April both sides "were committed to the assumption that their differences would be settled on the field of battle."[9] From now on, negotiations would be geared to the needs of the armed struggle.

Once again, the CCP's united-front formulations provide an accurate barometer for this shift in attitude. Earlier, the CCP's propaganda had been keyed to "peace, democracy, and unity." These popular goals were not disavowed, but from the summer of 1946, the Party called with increasing frequency for "an anti-feudal united front," "a New Democratic united front," and finally "an anti-Chiang united front." KMT intelligence itself noted this shift in emphasis and commented on it.[10] Its significance is that a new enemy was being explicitly defined, and the united front was being employed to isolate this enemy so that it might be destroyed. In this sense, explicit use of the vocabulary of the united front was evidence that war had been declared. The CCP's work of persuasion was as continuous as its effort to improve its territorial and military positions. We therefore resume the account of the CCP's attempts to influence public opinion and the intelligentsia through the Democratic League and other minor political groupings.

The Minor Parties and the CCP

The most important of the minor parties toward which the CCP directed its action was the Democratic League, mostly because of the DL's nature rather than its size. Its tradition of independence, its dedication to liberal causes, and its range of personal connections with students, academic circles, businessmen, journalists, etc. gave it a prestige and an influence far beyond its rather small membership.

But the League was not the only minor political group. Scores of new associations, parties, and federations sprang up immediately after the war, most of them miniscule in size and insignificant in influence.[a] A few were more important; these were mostly the followings of figures already prominent in the DL. Huang Yen-p'ei, supported by Chang Nai-ch'i, organized the National Construction Association (NCA) in Chungking in August 1945; it held its first congress in December with 136 members present.[11] Much of the membership was drawn from the old Vocational Education Group, and the NCA had considerable influence with the business class. Its General Committee moved to Shanghai in 1946. The Chiu-san Society (named in commemoration of the date of the formal Japanese surrender) was led by the sociologist Hsü Te-heng, and by P'an Shu (brother of the Communists P'an Han-nien and P'an Tzu-nien). It grew out of a non-political group formed in November 1944, the Democracy and Science Forum (*Min-chu k'o-hsüeh tso-t'an hui*). In August 1946, the Society's headquarters moved from Chungking to Peiping, where many of its members had university positions. A somewhat similar body—small, composed mostly of scholars and educators, but with considerable prestige—was centered in Shanghai; this was the Association for the Promotion of Democracy (APD), led by the well-known educator Ma Hsü-lun. These or-

[a] One source describes 105 such organizations, ranging from the DL to the League of Those Disgusted with Party Conflict (*Yen tang-cheng t'ung-meng*). *Cf.* Chung-lien ch'u-pan-she, *Chung-kuo tang-p'ai.*

ganizations served to spread the influence of the DL. They also offered their leaders a platform from which they might speak and act independently of the League. Later, when the League was dissolved by the KMT, these minor groupings took on some of the functions that the League had performed.

Our earlier discussion of the Democratic League terminated with a description of the strife-torn Extraordinary Congress of October 1945, at which the influence of the Youth Party was severely curtailed. Tso Shun-sheng resigned from his position as Secretary-General and was replaced by Liang Sou-ming. These events were taking place in the broader context of Chiang-Mao negotiations, competition and sporadic fighting in North China, the resignation of General Hurley, and the appointment of George C. Marshall as President Truman's Special Representative. Shortly thereafter, the KMT announced its intention to convoke the PCC and to allocate the delegates to this Conference. At this point the KMT intervened in the DL's internal quarrel, offering the Youth Party a disproportionate number of seats in the PCC if it would dissociate itself from the League. The YP formally withdrew from the DL in December.

On October 19, 1945, a meeting took place between Teng Ch'u-min for the DL and Wang Jo-fei and Hsü Ping for the Communists. An exchange of materials was agreed on : one copy of all political or military intelligence collected by the DL, as well as material relating to culture, education, industry, or commerce, was to be supplied to the offices of the *New China Daily*. In return, the CCP agreed to supply the League organ, *Democratic Weekly,* with materials on domestic and international politics, and to expand the *Daily*'s printing service to handle League propaganda.[12] Thus, besides improving its intelligence net, the CCP gained an excellent platform from which to publicize views compatible with its own.

We come now to the difficult question of whether or not formal collaborative agreement was reached between the DL and the CCP. When the DL was outlawed in 1947, pro-Government newspapers carried an account purporting to be the text of such an agreement. At the time, it was discounted as another piece of unscrupulous political propaganda. But classified sources compiled as early as summer 1946 discuss the alleged agreement in detail. These materials were not propaganda, and are therefore worthy of closer attention. All accounts of the agreement are quite similar, but only one suggests how the information was obtained. "Last year, during the opening of the PCC (probably during the first ten days of January), Lo Lung-chi, in the Reception Room of DL Headquarters at 300 Kuo-fu Road, spoke with a certain reporter about DL-CCP relations (this reporter was the high DL cadre, Ch'en Ming-ho). According to Lo's statements, the DL and the CCP had recently concluded a 'cooperative agreement.' "[13] The agreement, reportedly signed in November 1945 by Chang Po-chün and Chang Shen-fu, is usually quoted as follows:

> The Chinese Communist Party and the Democratic League, in order to overthrow the one-party dictatorship of the Kuomintang and to realize a democratically governed new China, will fight together hand in hand. The DL will give as much support as possible to all measures taken by the CCP in the Liberated Areas, and will expand their influence. The two parties agree to abide by the following terms: (1) neither side will cooperate independently with the KMT; in case of negotiations, each side will notify the other, and after obtaining agreement, may then proceed to reach a decision with the Kuomintang; (2) in any subsequent conferences whatsoever, the DL will have the duty of supporting all proposals of the CCP that do not violate the principles of the Democratic League; (3) no elements in the Democratic League are restricted in any way by the proposals of the CCP, but when there is complete disagreement, this may not be publicly made known; (4) the DL may set up branches in the Liberated Areas, to be recognized and aided by the CCP, and will exchange intelligence with local CCP branches.
>
> Appended: it is further agreed that the CCP will increase its monthly subsidy to the DL to 200,000 yuan.[14]

One source contained an additional clause in which each side agreed not to try to infiltrate the other.[15]

As quoted, this agreement is broad but by no means unconditional. Given the general climate and the imminent meeting of the

PCC, it might serve as preparatory maneuvering to counter the dominant position of the Kuomintang. It should be pointed out that there is no demand here for the overthrow of the KMT as such, but instead a call for the end of tutelage. League members were not bound to follow this agreement; if they moved with the CCP, they did so voluntarily. Nor is it claimed that the Chairman of the League, Chang Lan, approved this agreement (or even knew of it). At this time, Chang Po-chün was still head of the CCP Organization Department, while Chang Shen-fu was head of the Culture Committee. Lo Lung-chi was in charge of the DL's propaganda. Thus it is by no means clear that the alleged agreement was an official League position. It may have been a personal or factional step taken by some parts of the League on their own.

The significance of the agreement—assuming its existence—was its indication of the widening grounds on which many non-Communists were prepared to voluntarily move closer to the Communist position. When all parties assented to the proposals made later in the PCC, the League and other independents were pleased with their own part in finding a solution that seemed to recognize many of their views. Hope was aroused by the PCC agreements, but most of the League had moved closer to the Communists; they had felt it necessary to support the CCP position on most issues to prevent the KMT from dominating the entire conference. Now they were waiting to see how the agreements would be carried out.

Meanwhile, the League was undergoing important changes. Very few of the League members in Chungking were natives of the area. As soon as the government returned to Nanking, they left Chungking, either scattering to return to their former homes or moving back to the capital. In May 1946, therefore, Nanking became the League headquarters. Moreover, an estimated three-fourths of the Szechwan group had been associated with the Youth Party; thus membership in the province dropped from about 2,500 to a few hundred as soon as the YP pulled out of the League.

In a move that had important effects on the League, the Central Government asserted its influence over the province of Yunnan. By December 1945, Lung Yun had been transferred out of the province.

League activities were disrupted, and matters quickly led to a student strike at year's end. For League activists, Kunming changed from a haven to a very dangerous place. It remained, however, an important center until the summer of 1946. Gradually the wartime centers of the League quieted down; they were replaced by Nanking, Shanghai, Canton–Hong Kong, and to a lesser extent, Peiping and Sian. A Malayan Branch was established in Singapore in April 1946. The League, though never very large, doubtless succeeded in increasing its membership from a low of about 1,000–2,000 in early 1946.

The KMT's view that from early in 1946 the League was simply a front for the CCP was a considerable distortion of the actual situation. There were at this time many League members of genuinely independent convictions, whose political activity in the face of growing personal danger was evidence of their sincerity and integrity. Yet the tendentious KMT accounts are substantially correct regarding the *fact* of increasingly frequent similarity between many elements of the League and the CCP, in respect to both political platform and political action. What these sources fail to make clear is, first, the effect of KMT and Government action in driving the two together; second, the fact that most collaborative action was taken by individuals and factions in the League, and was not felt to be binding on those who disagreed; and third, that to a very great extent, League members who favored collaboration with the CCP did not think that they were sacrificing their independence and integrity.

At the same time, the harassment and intimidation of the League continued. Carsun Chang was accused of fomenting a student riot in Kunming, then prevented from flying down to investigate. The Chungking residences of Huang Yen-p'ei, Chang Shen-fu, and Shih Liang were ransacked by the police, as were the headquarters of the League itself.[16] The League organs, various incarnations of *Min-chu* (or *Min-chu chou-k'an*), were suppressed on several occasions during 1946. Above all, it was the callous, almost nonchalant, assassination of Li Kung-p'u and Wen I-to in the streets of Kunming during the summer of 1946 that crystallized anti-KMT sentiment.

The murder of Wen I-to, who was held in admiration and affection for his scholarly attainments and enthusiastic idealism, was a particularly profound shock. Liang Sou-ming, as Secretary-General of the League, made a detailed study of the case and concluded that the General Headquarters of the Yunnan Garrison had been primarily responsible for the killings. But the behavior of the Central Government in dealing with the case, notably its secrecy and its apparent desire to shield the Yunnan headquarters, constituted in Liang's view strong prima facie evidence of—at least—complicity after the fact. There was also an implicit conclusion that the KMT bore responsibility for an atmosphere in which actions like these could be undertaken with the expectation of top-level support.[17]

Many members of the League felt that the CCP stood near to their own democratic convictions. The KMT, they argued, had forsaken Sun's principles, and had by this time come dangerously close to discrediting itself in theory and in practice. It could find a place in the China of the future by granting a truly liberal constitution, genuinely nationalizing the army, instituting reforms, and admitting all parties and groups to a share in political power. If it could do this, they thought, domestic peace might ensue. Yet many saw this abdication of power as a step the KMT was very unlikely to take voluntarily. In this analysis, the only hope of checking the KMT's ambitions lay in joint action by the opposition—the League and the CCP.

Since the CCP's united-front approach indicated that it shared the DL position, many League members felt that their cooperation with the CCP was a step taken independently and in the interests of democracy. Combined with the picture of CCP administrative efficiency and honesty, and with the belief that the CCP had forsaken classic Marxism-Leninism, this greatly broadened the basis for cooperation. This position was expressed by Tseng Chao-lun, a man of considerable prestige in intellectual and educational circles, and a lineal descendant of Tseng Kuo-fan. He wrote in the summer of 1946 that the DL "does not and will not believe in Marxism. It has little or no use for extreme measures as a means of bringing about political reforms." However, he went on,

> Communism, with all the possible criticism that might be piled upon it, is at least very much better than fascism. It is fundamentally different in quality. . . . Without the cooperation of the Chinese Communist Party, it would be impossible to emancipate the Chinese people from the yoke of the Gestapo service and give them the minimum of freedom. . . .
>
> Another reason why we need not be afraid of the Chinese Communist Party is that, while they believe that Communism would be the ultimate outcome of world order, they have no intention of introducing Communism . . . into China at the present stage, nor for a generation to come.[18]

Even someone so conservative as Carsun Chang was prepared to say, "So long as their [the CCP] demand was limited to a coalition government, I thought that it would be wrong to refuse to work with them."[19]

The view that League collaboration with the CCP did not imply a loss of integrity or independence is seen in the League's position concerning the formation of the State Council. The PCC had called for this, but nothing had been done. In August 1946, General Marshall, representatives of the League, and others pushed for the organization of the State Council in an effort to return the struggle from the battlefield to the conference table. The State Council was to have been the principal agency through which government reorganization would take place. Therefore, control of this body was vitally important to all contenders. The main issues revolved around allocation of seats and veto power in the Council.[20] Both the League and the CCP insisted that their combined votes be sufficient to constitute a veto. The government claimed that this showed how the League was working with the CCP.

Liang Sou-ming denied that this was the case, explaining (with a certain disingenuousness) that the League's position was essential to the cessation of civil war: only if the CCP were sure that its interests were protected would it consent to negotiate seriously; otherwise it would continue to fight. The integrity of the DL guaranteed that neither the KMT nor the CCP would be able to trample upon the other. Yet this was a defense of explicit cooperation between the League and the CCP.[21]

During the year following the end of the war, most League members returned to the eastern provinces and to the major cities of China. Many were finding life very difficult under circumstances of political harassment, incipient civil war, and inflation. Considerable numbers were either unemployed or working at whatever ill-paid and uninteresting jobs they could find. Now the CCP supported its propaganda appeal with a concrete offer of help. After conferring with Lo Lung-chi, Chang Po-chün, and others in Shanghai, Chou En-lai authorized the CCP Representative Group in Nanking to make the following offer:

> We have received a copy of the record of Mr. Chou En-lai's discussions with your League. In Nanking and Shanghai, unemployed members of your League number more than 300. Those of them with the capacity for service in such fields as culture, education, commerce, and industry may be registered with this Group in order to facilitate finding work for them. This Group has accordingly assigned Comrade Hua Ch'iang as the person in Nanking responsible for registration. He is located at the office of the *New China Daily,* 360 Chung-shan Road. Please notify unemployed members of your League that whoever wishes to go to the Liberated Areas to work should, beginning September 26, 1946, go to the assigned place to register, bearing a certificate from your League.[22]

A number of League members accepted this offer. Others were publicized by the CCP as having done so, though in fact they did not actually proceed to the Communist-controlled areas.

On October 11, the KMT (whose troops were in the process of occupying Communist-held Kalgan) announced its intention to convoke the National Assembly a month hence for the purpose of adopting a constitution and ending the Period of Tutelage. This step was taken unilaterally and without fulfilling any of the preliminaries outlined by the PCC. Minor-party leaders were just then in Shanghai, trying to persuade Chou En-lai to return to Nanking for further negotiations. In the upshot, neither they nor he went back to the capital. The reaction of most of the League was one of outrage and anger. Charges of fascist dictatorship were met with allegations of Communist domination. At this point, a section of the National-Socialist Party headed by Carsun Chang, which had wavered for several months between the two major parties, decided to participate in the Assembly. The League's Central Committee, firmly in the hands of the intransigently anti-KMT group, refused to submit a slate of nominees, thereby openly boycotting the Assembly. Carsun Chang's group prepared its own independent list, and joined the YP in collaboration with the KMT. The DL's refusal to take part in the November deliberations was definitive, placing it in a position of irrevocable opposition to the KMT and the government machinery the KMT was about to create.

The CCP Representative Group was withdrawn from Nanking in February 1947, an act tantamount on both sides to a formal declaration of the war that had been in progress for some months. As the Communists pulled out, they turned over all their property in Nanking and Shanghai to the Democratic League for its use. There may also have been an agreement at this time to permit CCP elements to use the DL as a cover organization, and to use the regional DL structure as a part of the CCP communication network.[23] The League, which now had no middle ground left to it, was for a time permitted to exist on a kind of sufferance. This was partly because of American interest in the group and partly because the KMT did not wish to damage its image any further by making fresh martyrs to liberalism. As late as January 1947, General Marshall, unaware of how completely split the League was, had written to President Truman: "The salvation of the situation, as I see it, would be the assumption of leadership by the liberals in the government and in the minor parties, a splendid group of men, but who as yet lack the political power to exercise a controlling influence. Successful action on their part under the leadership of Generalissimo Chiang Kai-shek would, I believe, lead to unity through good government."[24]

The Government's accusations against the League became more

frequent, if not more specific. Throughout the summer and fall, the League felt that its days were numbered. Finally, on the night of October 27, 1947, and apparently over the objections of some KMT elements, the decision was taken to outlaw the League as accessory to the "Communist bandits." A directive was so issued by the Ministry of the Interior the following morning, which further alleged anti-Government military action by some League members—Lo Pin-chi in Manchuria, K'ung Ts'ung-chou in the Northwest, and Li Yin-feng in Szechwan.[25]

Negotiations with League leaders, Huang Yen-p'ei in particular, resulted in an agreement that if League headquarters would officially declare itself dissolved, no arrests or other punitive action would be taken. After some days of negotiation, this was done on November 5. During and shortly after these negotiations, many League leaders departed for Hong Kong, where in January 1949 there was convened the "Third Plenary Session" of the Central Committee. This rump League declared itself fully reconstituted, thus repudiating the action of the previous fall. Its resolutions amounted to full and complete acknowledgement of Communist leadership.[b] It had now fully discarded its impartiality, coming to believe, with the KMT and the CCP themselves, that true impartiality was impossible in 1947–48.

From this time on, Hong Kong became the center of minor-party activity, not only for the Democratic League and the groups associated with it, but also for a number of clique "parties" made up of KMT dissidents. Economic conditions were difficult for those without funds or relatives in the colony; prices were higher than in Shanghai, and opportunities for employment were fewer. P'eng Tse-min, head of the local DL branch, helped to establish a hostel in which members could stay for periods of up to two months.[26]

[b] These are summarized in Hua-shang jih-pao tzu-liao-shih, Part *Chia,* p. 15. They called for: (1) the complete overthrow of the dictatorial and traitorous reactionary faction of the KMT; (2) the implementation of the agrarian revolution and the liquidation of the feudalistic representatives of the landlords and local bullies; (3) the condemnation of America's support for Chiang and its policy of intervention in Chinese domestic politics; and (4) the cooperation of all democratic groups in the formation of a strong democratic united front.

The principal groups outside the Democratic League were the factions making up the so-called Revolutionary Committee of the Kuomintang (RCKMT), which was formally organized in January 1948.[27] Its leading figures were Mme. Sun Yat-sen (Soong Ch'ing-ling), Li Chi-shen, Ts'ai T'ing-k'ai, T'an P'ing-shan, Ho Hsiang-ning (Mme. Liao Chung-k'ai), and Liu Ya-tzu. This association, which grew out of factional dissension in the KMT, first began to form in 1940 or 1941, when Li Chi-shen, Feng Yü-hsiang, and others began to meet secretly to promote "organizational democracy within the party and constitutional democracy throughout the country."[28] Together with Madame Sun and others they formed the Society of Kuomintang Democratic Comrades. After the war, Ts'ai T'ing-k'ai and Li Chi-shen organized another group called the Kuomintang Democratic Promotion Society, made up mainly of politicians and military leaders from Kwangtung and Kwangsi, many of whom had been Ts'ai's associates in the Nineteenth Route Army or had participated in the Fukien Republic. Meanwhile, Ch'en Ming-shu and others were forming yet another clique, known as the San-min chu-i Comrades' Association. These groups amalgamated to form the RCKMT, while still retaining their old organization.

Neither the RCKMT nor its constituent groups were political parties in the accepted sense; they had an even smaller following than the DL and its component groups. But from the standpoint of the CCP's united-front work, they had some importance. First, their connections inside the KMT were good. Since many of them were military leaders, their influence might well sway the allegiance of some of Chiang's officers. And the organization was a convenient shelter for those wishing to leave the KMT. Second, many of the RCKMT leaders had considerable influence in the provinces—particularly the provinces of southern China, Kwangtung, Kwangsi, and Yunnan. There were persistent rumors that these areas might revolt against the Nanking Government and set up separatist, non-Communist regimes headed by some of these same men. Furthermore, Li, Ts'ai, and others were trying—not very successfully—to collect some sort of military force in the hinterland.[29]

All of these groups were united by their opposition to Chiang Kai-shek. All were considered by the CCP to be important united-front targets. In March 1947, just after KMT forces occupied Yenan, the CCP issued a secret directive entitled "The Program of Underground Struggle," calling for a "democratic, anti-totalitarian, anti-civil-war united front." Designated for special attention as "four main groups" were the DL, the Association for the Promotion of Democracy, the San-min chu-i Comrades' Association, and the National Construction Association.[30] A number of UFWD workers were sent to Hong Kong; perhaps the best known among them was one operating under the pseudonym Fang Fang, long active in south China and in overseas Chinese affairs. Propaganda was available through the Hong Kong edition of *The Masses* and the newspaper *Chen-pao*. Chou Hsin-min, a Party member, was the DL's Secretary-General.

On May 1, 1948, the Chinese Communist Party issued a May Day call for allies:

> Laboring people of the entire country, unite; ally with the intelligentsia, liberal bourgeoisie, all democratic parties and groups, social luminaries and other patriotic elements; consolidate and expand the united front against imperialists, feudal, and bureaucratic capitalist forces; fight together to destroy Kuomintang reactionaries and build a new China. All democratic parties and groups, people's organizations, and social luminaries, speedily convene a Political Consultative Conference, discuss and carry out the convoking of a People's Representative Assembly to establish a Democratic Coalition Government.[31]

Four days later, minor-party leaders telegraphed Mao Tse-tung, "We herein express our response and support to your call, and hope by its realization to meet our national renaissance." The following groups signed this telegram: the RCKMT, the DL, the Peasants' and Workers' Democratic Party (formerly Third Party), the National Salvation Association, the Association for the Promotion of Democracy, the San-min chu-i Comrades' Association, the Kuomintang Democratic Promotion Society, and the Chih-kung Tang.[c] A few months later, most of the leaders of these groups accepted the CCP's invitation to go to Harbin to await the takeover of Peiping and ultimately the convocation of the bodies that would approve the establishment of the People's Republic of China.

The united-front appeal to the Democratic League and other minor parties was both ideological and material. On the ideological level were nationalism, democracy, and opposition to Chiang Kai-shek. "Democracy" was defined loosely in "New Democratic" form, stressing features most attractive to League members. The material appeal was made in the form of subsidies and services, and in the form of active solicitude for the welfare of League members. Equally important, the CCP knew how to appeal to the desire of these men for a sense of worth, contribution, and participation in the Chinese future. It was just this desire that the KMT so consistently flouted by disregarding their suggestions, impugning their motives, and threatening their personal safety.

If the minor parties moved increasingly toward the Communists, it is necessary to ask of what benefit this was to the CCP. Although their memberships were small, their talents were impressive, and in very short supply among the Communists. Moreover, in a land where personal connections have great political significance, their members had widespread contacts with various circles that the CCP might otherwise have found it difficult to approach. Many businessmen would listen to Chang Nai-ch'i or Huang Yen-p'ei; teachers and students to Lo Lung-chi and Chang Tung-sun; military figures to Li Chi-shen or Ts'ai T'ing-k'ai; cultural leaders to Sung Ch'ing-ling or Kuo Mo-jo. It is clear, therefore, that the DL performed what the CCP calls a "bridge" (*ch'iao-liang*) function—a way of reaching a large and otherwise inaccessible group through the action of a strategically placed intermediate group. One observer who had spent much time in the Liberated Areas put the case in precisely these terms: "To find a bridge over to the people in Chiang Kai-shek's areas was difficult. . . . During the early part of the war, the

[c] Barnett, p. 83. The Chih-kung Tang was active mainly among overseas Chinese.

party found few intellectuals as allies. . . . Nevertheless, it was the revolt of many of these intellectuals that hammered the final nail into Chiang Kai-shek's coffin."[32]

The Last Stages of Civil War

In concentrating our attention on the Democratic League we have neglected other areas that are at least equally important. For example, student activities passed into increasingly radical hands. By the latter months of 1946, the student movement was strongly anti-KMT and anti-American. This was symbolized for many by events in Peiping, where, on December 24, an American Marine was accused of raping a young Pei-ta co-ed.[d] A protest against the United States was quickly instigated, perhaps by the CCP, and found a wide response. As so often in the past, the protest was headed by students but spread beyond student circles. The United States was attacked for the behavior of many of its servicemen, and for its support of the discredited KMT, in which the students no longer had faith.

In the following year, the student movement swelled to even larger proportions. One observer called it the "greatest in China's history" in terms of numbers involved.[33] In May and June, the demonstrations took the form of a united front "against civil war, against hunger, against oppression"—surely the most generalized common enemy in the history of this technique.[34]

The decline and collapse of the KMT was hastened by widespread defection and surrender from the armed units it commanded. In the last stages of the civil war, this process was so rapid that it could be attributed only to nearly complete loss of both military discipline and the will to resist. To this extent, the techniques of friendly army work developed during the war were not a primary cause of the increasing military isolation of the KMT. But there seems to be no doubt that these techniques, which had often been considered a part

[d] Despite ambiguous evidence, the accused and another Marine alleged to be his accomplice were convicted by an American court-martial. Later their sentences were set aside.

of the united-front approach, were extremely effective in promoting the desertion of whole units and individuals. Perhaps the key tactic was a promise of merciless destruction if resistance were continued, contrasted with an offer of generous treatment in return for surrender. The CCP declared, "Our army will not kill or humiliate any of Chiang Kai-shek's army officers and men who lay down their arms, but will accept them into our service if they are willing to remain with us, or send them home if they wish to leave. As for those troops of Chiang Kai-shek who rise in revolt and join our army and those who work for our army openly or in secret, they shall be rewarded."[35]

Another way in which the united front might be employed was through personal contact between groups it was trying to influence and UFWD workers. We have already seen this in the case of the minor parties. Another example comes from Shanghai during the last stages of the civil war. With the fall of the city coming ever nearer, many businessmen prepared to flee, taking with them most of their capital and resources. Had this turned into a general exodus, Shanghai's economy would have been crippled. In order to counter this tendency, reported a Chinese businessman, "Groups of underground 'United Front Workers' were hurriedly dispatched to contact the panic-stricken would-be refugees."[36] Men experienced in this kind of united-front operation, notably Hsü Ti-hsin, were extremely active. Businessmen were assured of generous treatment, protection of their property, and the opportunity to do business. Copies of Mao's "The Present Situation and Our Tasks" were distributed to publicize the CCP's intended policy toward the "national bourgeoisie." Robert Loh observed, "The pamphlet was remarkably effective. It acted as a tranquilizer on the nervous industrialists and traders. It allayed their suspicion and fear of the Communists; and left them with the feeling: 'Well, nothing could be worse than life under the Nationalists.' Many stayed on."[37]

When possible, all of these avenues were used at the same time. A. Doak Barnett's account of the siege and takeover of Peiping (December 1948–January 1949) describes the employment of military pressure and threat, generous offers, minor-party representatives, student groups, and UFWD functionaries.[e] The Communists' initial goal was to prevent the Nationalist commander, Fu Tso-yi, from making a determined resistance, thus wrecking the city ("the beautiful and priceless vase" that Fu held in his hands, as one observer put it).[38] Next they wanted the acquiescence and participation of the residents in the takeover of the city and in its continued functioning. Lastly, they expected to make the city their new capital.

The military threat, the warning that the Communists had it in their power to take the city by storm or by siege, came when Peiping was surrounded and cut off from outside support in December operations. The point was driven home by the seizure of Tientsin, which was completed by mid-January. At the same time, the Communists were making their customary generous offer.

> With Peiping, Tientsin, and Tangku completely surrounded, your way of retreat has been completely cut off. . . . There is no outside help. If you intend to break through, think of the lessons of Kalgan and Hsuchow. There is only one course for you: follow the example of Cheng Tung-kuo in Changchun—that is surrender en bloc. . . . We will treat you generously, as we did General Cheng Tung-kuo. The lives of you and your families will be completely protected. As for Fu Tso-i, although he has been listed as a war criminal, we will give him another chance to repent. . . . If you agree, send negotiators to see us. . . . Our offensive will soon be launched, so you must make a decision immediately—otherwise don't say we didn't warn you.[39]

More specifically, the Communists put forth an eight-point program that pledged protection of life and property, non-confiscation of private industrial and commercial holdings, maintenance of school and hospital services, and respect for foreigners; the program also stated that bureaucratic capital, utilities, and public-service industries would be taken over by the People's Liberation Army, but that

[e] Barnett, pp. 315ff. This is an invaluable contemporary account of political events and the general atmosphere in the city. A much more personal and impressionistic account of the same period is given by Derk Bodde, *Peking Diary: A Year of Revolution.*

private shares would be honored; other points dealt with demobilized soldiers, war criminals, etc.[40]

Even before the city was taken over, the CCP made preparations for its government through the creation of a Military Control Commission. Preliminary plans were drawn up, with the participation of students and faculty from Tsinghua University, located in the Communist-controlled suburbs.[41] The chairman of this commission was Yeh Chien-ying, and his choice for prospective Vice-mayor of the city was an experienced united-front operator, Hsü Ping (Hsing Hsi-p'ing), a member of an old and wealthy Peiping family.[f]

Minor-party leaders were in the forefront in speaking for the peaceful disposition of the city. In this they reflected the widespread feeling that a fight should be avoided if at all possible. Liang Sou-ming, formerly Secretary-General of the DL, spoke from retirement to suggest that Peiping be made an open city. One of the more important links between the headquarters of Fu Tso-yi and Yeh Chien-ying was Chang Tung-sun. Chang, a noted philosopher on the faculty of Yenching University and formerly a member of Carsun Chang's National-Socialist Party, had been the head of the Peiping branch of the Democratic League prior to its suppression. Fu Tso-yi sent Chang to initiate negotiations with the Communists. These negotiations continued sporadically, under Chang and others, until the final terms of surrender were worked out. On January 31, 1949, the city of Peiping was peacefully "liberated."[g]

The takeover of Peiping was enormously important, not only because of its significance as one of China's largest, oldest, and most symbolic cities, but also because (as Barnett points out) it was the first major city to come under Communist control by peaceful nego-

[f] Yeh himself had had extensive experience in the Party's external relations. He had been one of the Communists sent from Pao-an at the time of the Sian Incident. He had also represented the Party in the Peiping Executive Headquarters created under Marshall's auspices. The CCP was choosing its personnel so as to reassure the population of Peiping of its intention to meet reason with reason and moderation.

[g] Fu's troops were evacuated and later incorporated in the Communist armies. Between the 22nd and the 31st, the Communists agreed to a "grace period" in which those who wanted to leave for the KMT areas, and could arrange transportation, would not be prevented from doing so. Barnett, pp. 332–34.

tiation, thereby setting a pattern that might be followed elsewhere. If others in China saw that the Communist "liberation" was orderly, calm, and nearly bloodless, they would be much more receptive to propaganda like that preceding Fu Tso-yi's surrender.

Student groups, which had been patiently cultivated for years, now appeared as "invaluable allies of the Communists in the take-over period. . . . It probably is not going too far to say that the Communists would have had a difficult time getting along without them."[42] Barnett's account shows how they tirelessly carried on propaganda services, acted as minor political functionaries, made surveys, re-educated teachers, etc. In some cases, he indicates, the students wished to move faster than the Party would permit, and had to be restrained. Furthermore, the Communists appealed to some students to enroll in North China People's Revolutionary University for political workers, and to others to join a corps of political workers being sent to the South, where fighting was currently going on. The response to these calls was excellent.

On February 20, Peiping became the capital of the North China People's Government, headed by Tung Pi-wu. Before the end of the month, minor-party leaders arrived from Hong Kong. Included were Li Chi-shen, Shen Chün-ju, Chang Po-chün, Ma Hsü-lun, and others.[43] These events signified the success of CCP policy. As already suggested, this success was in part the inverse of KMT failures. But loss of faith in the KMT did not mean that that faith would automatically be transferred to the CCP. Although a "wait-and-see" attitude was common, the Communists succeeded in enlisting much positive backing; this success was the result of many policies, a number of which the CCP regarded directly or indirectly as parts of its united-front strategy: winning over (or neutralizing) the majority, isolating the minority, and defeating enemies one by one.

Chapter 10

The United Front from 1949 to 1954

AT THE MOMENT of victory, Mao Tse-tung stressed again the value of the "three main weapons with which we have defeated the enemy"—namely, "a well-disciplined Party armed with the theory of Marxism-Leninism, an army under the leadership of such a Party, and a united front of all revolutionary classes and all revolutionary groups under the leadership of such a Party. Relying on them we have won basic victory."[1] Now the tasks were, internally, to "form a domestic united front under the leadership of the working class, and advance from this to the establishment of a state which is a people's democratic dictatorship"; and externally, to "unite in a common struggle with those nations of the world which treat us as equals . . . and form an international united front."[2]

The CCP was shifting its attention from the struggle for supremacy to the tasks of creating a powerful nation-state led by the Party. The united front was one element of continuity linking the years of national and civil war with those of socialist construction; hence its function was changing from the isolation of an enemy to the integration of the people in support of the new regime. The united-front approach had become an almost instinctive element of the Party's mentality: "Everybody is our friend, except the imperialists, the feudalists, the Kuomintang reactionaries and their accomplices. . . . This united front is so broad . . . [and] so solid that it possesses the resolute will and the inexhaustible capacity to defeat every enemy and overcome every difficulty."[3]

SETTING UP THE UNITED FRONT

The line that the CCP intended to follow was set forth in *On the People's Democratic Dictatorship* and in the Common Program passed by the Chinese People's Political Consultative Conference (CPPCC). In the first, Mao decisively, almost savagely, rejected the categories of Western democracy, even those in *On Coalition Government*. Instead, he portrayed a four-class coalition, exercising a joint dictatorship over its enemies. Members of the coalition were "the people"; they were led by the working class (i.e., the CCP), on the basis of the unbreakable alliance of the workers and peasants. These two were the exploited laboring classes and therefore shared a common political outlook. The other two classes included in "the people" were the urban petty bourgeoisie and the national bourgeoisie. With the workers and peasants constituting 80–90 per cent of the population and in control of the apparatus of the state, there was, Mao said, "no need to fear rebellion by the national bourgeoisie."[4]

The same conception lay behind the Common Program of the CPPCC, the "organizational form of the people's democratic united front." In its first plenary sessions, held in September 1949, the CPPCC ratified the Organic Law and the Common Program. Until 1954, these documents functioned as a provisional constitution. The CPPCC therefore acted as a constituent assembly and served as the nation's highest representative body until the convocation of the National People's Congress (NPC) created by the 1954 constitution. Altogether, 11 minor political parties and groups sent 106 delegates (out of a total of 585 voting and 77 non-voting representatives); there were also 10 "democratic personages" not affiliated with any group and 75 specially invited persons. This was almost exactly one-third (191 out of 585), and it reminds one strongly of the three-thirds system. These minor political parties were those that had existed before the establishment of the People's Republic. The lineup of minor-party delegates in the first CPPCC was as follows:[5]

Revolutionary Committee of the KMT	16
China Democratic League	16
China Democratic National Construction Association (NCA)	12
Chinese Peasants' and Workers' Democratic Party (PWDP)	10
Chinese People's National Salvation Association	10
San-min chu-i Comrades' Association	10
China KMT Democratic Promotion League	8

China Association for Promoting Democracy (APD)	8
Chih-kung Tang	6
Chiu-san Society	5
Taiwan Democratic Self-government League (T'ai-meng)	5
Non-party	10

Non-Communists, mostly members of minor parties, were appointed to high posts in the government. Though the hollowness of such positions soon became clear, it was not immediately apparent. Three of six vice-chairmen of the Chinese People's Government were non-Communists, as were two of four Deputy Premiers of the State Administrative Council (SAC). Non-Communists were given the portfolios of the following ministries (in all cases a CCP member was vice-minister): Light Industry, Post and Telegraph, Communications, Agriculture, Forestry and Land Reclamation, Water Conservation, and Culture and Education. Non-Party men were appointed to lower positions in all other ministries, to the Supreme Court, to the People's Revolutionary Military Council, etc. These delegates and officials were not elected, but were picked or confirmed by the CCP. It was their job to assist in the creation of a state structure that had been determined prior to the convocation of the CPPCC. All minor parties had already accepted the principle of CCP leadership; now they accepted its implementation. This was the beginning of a new relationship between the minor parties and the CCP, the start of a new structure for the united front.

Simultaneously with the incorporation of minor parties into the state structure, United Front Work Departments expanded throughout China. Each of the six major administrative regions into which China was initially divided had its Party Committee, under which was the United Front Work Department. By this time, Li Wei-han had been the Director of the Central UFWD for some time.[a] Li was seconded by Hsü Ping (Hsing Hsi-p'ing), whom we

[a] A KMT source dates his tenure from sometime in 1946 (*Fei-wei jen-shih tzu-liao*). The earliest confirmed information available to the United States Department of State is September 1949 (*Directory of Chinese Communist Officials*, 1963 ed.). Born in 1896, Li is a native of Hunan and a veteran of the Long March, but has apparently never been in Mao's inner circle. He was in France with Chou En-lai, returning to China in 1923. He was a member of the Sixth CEC and of

have already met, and by Liao Ch'eng-chih.[b] Interestingly, Liao was a member of the Seventh Central Committee, thus outranking Li Wei-han in the Party hierarchy.

Temporarily, minor-party groupings were frozen. In 1949 and early 1950, while its headquarters and leading members moved to Peking, the CCP considered the number, composition, and functions of the bourgeois-democratic parties (here abbreviated BDP). Until these decisions were made, the minor parties were forbidden to recruit new members or make any other changes, although certain duties were assigned to them.[c] Thus, by holding the BDP in suspension, the CCP "did not institutionalize the united front until military domination of continental China was virtually completed. Thus there could be no question of organized opposition to basic Communist policies, no opportunity for a liberal third type of united front."[6]

Consolidation of the minor parties into at most three separate organizations was apparently considered at one point in late 1949, the others to be absorbed by the DL, the RCKMT, and the National Construction Association (NCA).[7] For reasons that are not clear, this plan was abandoned. Eight minor parties finally emerged. The National Salvation Association dissolved on December 18, 1949, ostensibly because its historic mission was completed.[8] The passing of this famous association was given no publicity. It had never been

---

the Politburo under Li Li-san, a position he lost at the Fourth Plenum. During the 1930's and the war, he held a variety of high posts in the Party and in the Shen-Kan-Ning Border Region. But he was not a regular or alternate member of the Seventh Central Committee (he recovered his membership in the Eighth CC).

[b] Liao is the son of Liao Chung-k'ai, the left-KMT member assassinated in 1925. His mother, Ho Hsiang-ning, has long been associated with left-wing and united-front causes; she has been a prominent member of the RCKMT, and is presently (1966) its Chairman. Liao, who spent some of the 1920's and most of the prewar 1930's in jail, has been prominent chiefly in overseas Chinese work and in Sino-Japanese relations.

[c] They were to weed out undesirable members, such as landlords, KMT reactionaries and their agents, and imperialist spies. The minor parties were in the forefront in denouncing the State Department's *White Paper* as a document proving American imperialism in China. They also protested against Japanese rearmament, the UN intervention in Korea, and the neutralization of the Formosa Strait.

a political party in the accepted sense, but had instead been the loose confederation of participants in a virtually spontaneous mass nationalistic movement. Perhaps this very tradition was thought potentially dangerous: a broad and loosely defined popular organization, which carried the suggestion that patriotism could find a focus outside the CCP. Most of its leading members already belonged to other groups, particularly the DL or the RCKMT; now the rest joined one or another party. Meanwhile, the San-min chu-i Comrades' Association and the China KMT Democratic Promotion League merged with the RCKMT to bring the total down to the present eight. Of the eight, the most important—none of them were very large—were the RCKMT, DL, and NCA. Ranking behind these in size and in influence were the PWDP, the APD, the Chiu-san Society, the Chih-kung Tang, and the Taiwan Democratic Self-government League (T'ai-meng). These eight groups held a series of meetings with the UFWD during November and December 1950, as the next step in the formation of the new united front. All of the minor parties reaffirmed their acceptance of CCP leadership and their allegiance to the Organic Law and Common Program. Most of them also adopted revised constitutions patterned after that of the CCP.

In general, the BDP were permitted to retain present members (providing they had not committed crimes against the people, or been classed as reactionaries, bureaucratic capitalists, etc.). But for the purposes of future recruitment and activity, each of the BDP was now assigned specific groups among which it was to work, and for the education and transformation of which it was largely responsible. This was called "the principle of division of labor within the united front." It also fragmented non-Party elements, ensuring that they could not form a bloc of their own. Certain restrictions applied to all the BDP. They were not permitted to recruit in small cities or villages, or among the rural population. The armed forces, organs of military administration, public security forces, military schools, intelligence organizations, revolutionary universities, and diplomatic establishments were all specifically excluded.[9] None of the BDP were permitted to approach any of the national minorities.

The BDP were assigned the following groups:

RCKMT. "Related masses" (*so lien-hsi ti ch'un-chung*), which included prior members or members of the two other antecedent groups that had been merged with the RCKMT; those in government agencies who in the past had served the KMT or the National Government, but who now had good records; former KMT members who wished to make the necessary acceptances; elements classified as democratic-revolutionary, mainly military leaders who had had contacts with the KMT on an individual basis.[10] Among the most important leaders of the RCKMT were Li Chi-shen, Ch'en Ming-shu, Chang Chih-chung, Ho Hsiang-ning, Lung Yun, Liu Ya-tzu, and Fu Tso-i. In the late 1950's, the Party internal organization included, aside from the customary Organization and Propaganda Departments, a Social Contacts Work Committee headed by Shao Li-tzu, and a Work Committee for the Peaceful Liberation of Taiwan under Chang Chih-chung.[11]

DL. Target groups assigned to the DL were petty-bourgeois intellectuals, especially cultural and educational workers (faculty members in universities, middle schools, and primary schools), university students, technical personnel, professional people, government personnel, businessmen, and patriotic democrats among overseas Chinese. "Bad" elements, or those belonging to classes to be liquidated, were not to be admitted; if already members, they were to be expelled. "Members should be recruited at key points and not in widespread areas . . . i.e., political, economic, and cultural centers."[12] Leaders were Chang Lan, Shen Chün-ju, Lo Lung-chi, Ho Hsiang-ning, Shih Liang, Chang Tung-sun, and Chou Ching-wen.

NCA. The national bourgeoisie in general was the class assigned this party: industrialists and large merchants, with medium and small industrialists and shopowners forming the "mass base." Special emphasis was given to activists in industrial and commercial federations, chambers of commerce, etc. "All local branches of the Association already established should, according to local conditions, recruit members on the principle of increasing membership 100 per cent to 200 per cent in one year."[13] Apart from the customary departments, the NCA created an Industrial Reconstruction Guidance Department to help the industrialists control and transform themselves.

APD. This party was assigned industrial and commercial elements, progressive intellectuals, and professional men. Nuclei should be cultural, educational, scientific, and technical personnel. A tendency toward "development for development's sake" should be eradicated.[14]

PWDP. No less descriptive name could be found than Peasants' and Workers' Democratic Party. Needless to say, not one peasant or worker is or ever will be a member. Recruitment was to take place among the urban petty bourgeoisie, especially public functionaries, school teachers, technicians, small industrialists, and merchants.[15] For some reason, this group has considerable membership among doctors of both Chinese and Western medicine, and among public health officials. Although in general there is only a small amount of overlap in the membership of the minor parties, the PWDP stated it would welcome members of other parties, including CCP members "to strengthen the leadership in our party."[16] Chang Po-chün, himself a prominent member of the DL until the Hundred Flowers, was backed up in the PWDP by his long-time associate P'eng Tse-min.

Chiu-san Society. This group worked with progressive educational, cultural, and scientific workers. "The relationship between the Society headquarters together with its branches and the CCP Central UFWD should be strengthened in order to step up further the attempt to learn from the C.P. of China."[17]

T'ai-meng. This group was to recruit among Taiwanese, and to some extent among Fukienese with relatives in Taiwan; it was set up in November 1947 by Hsieh Hsüeh-hung, a woman who had participated in the February 28th uprising in Taiwan. At first aiming at Taiwanese independence, this was the least important of the BDP under the Communists. Taiwanese opposition to Chiang Kai-shek and the KMT is largely opposition to rule by mainlanders. In an earlier period, Taiwanese who had made their careers under the KMT were stigmatized as self-seeking turncoats. The same stigma attaches to those working for the CCP. So far as a BDP united-front appeal has been beamed at Taiwan, it has been more the work of the RCKMT (aimed at top KMT leaders) than any effort of the T'ai-meng to reach the masses of Taiwanese.

The size of the BDP is difficult to determine, since the regime has never published this information; and the various minor parties have never publicly discussed their membership in absolute figures, but have spoken only of growth percentages. A careful and conscientious effort to determine the actual figures has been made by James D. Seymour, in a thesis dealing with the BDP. Correlating a great deal of scattered information, he finally estimates the total membership in 1950 at 20,000 to 40,000, with the majority concentrated in the DL, the NCA, and the RCKMT.[18] This is a very small number, but if we accept Chou En-lai's statement that in early 1956 there were "roughly 100,000 higher intellectuals" in China, then it appears that the BDP were quite strategically located with respect to this very important group.[19]

The relationship of these small parties to their assigned groups is described as a "bridge function" (*ch'iao-liang tso-yung*). In other words, the BDP act as spokesmen for, avenues to, and sources of information about their "related masses." The BDP help control and transform these related masses. Since the BDP are under the gun of the UFWD, they can be made accountable for the tasks assigned to them. They can satisfy their UFWD overseers only by getting the desired results among the target groups. Thus, happily or not, the BDP act as a device for spreading the influences and pressures that the Party wishes to employ.

If the BDP did not exist, it would be more difficult, or impossible, for the Party to reach certain groups or strata. This is particularly important in China, with its traditionally compartmented social organization. The CCP understood the importance of having the right connections and knowing the right people, and the BDP provided an avenue of approach where otherwise there might have been only a closed door or a closed mind. This may be simply a matter of straightforward influence or persuasion: student demonstrations touch off mass movements, and a handful of teachers may put the students in the streets; a well-known businessman may persuade others to invest in the New China; a journalist may destroy old loyalties and create a need for new ones. But exercise of this function does not require real willingness on the part of the "bridge"—though of course the CCP wants genuine enthusiasm. The BDP, therefore, serve as satellite task forces for the Party, charged with specific tasks that vary with the needs of the moment.

The control exercised over the BDP by the UFWD has always been close and continuous. The detail with which early surveillance and supervision took place in Peking in late 1949 is described by a former Communist security official:

> Every day they [agents of the UFWD and other Party departments] collect and send in large amounts of intelligence [on people] ranging from the leaders of the various parties, such as Li Chi-shen and Huang Yen-p'ei, down to small fry in cultural circles living in little inns outside the Ch'ien-men [main gate]; no one is exempted from surveillance, investigation, and report.
>
> The Social Contact Section has a long-term contract with the Peking Hotel [former Grand Hotel de Pékin] and engages as necessary the Liu-kuo Hotel [former Grand Hotel des Wagons-Lits, in the Legation Quarter] and the China Travel Service. In addition, several smaller inns are kept on long-term contract, while the Ts'ui-ming Chuang [a famous restaurant] is also used regularly. Upon arrival, guests find that everything is well provided for in all these hotels, and in the beginning are likely to feel completely at ease; but as they gradually come to feel that there are people watching them, they cannot but become disturbed.[20]

One feature of the united-front security structure was the network of "reception centers" (*chao-tai-so*), which combined the functions of liaison office, hostel, clubroom, banquet hall, and control point. Many Party and government agencies maintained these reception centers, as did social and cultural organizations. But according to this former security official, the "most important among these are the Public Security Reception Centers, corresponding to 'quasi-detention points,' and the Reception Centers of the UFWD Social Contacts Section, dealing with 'outsiders' [*wai-jen*]."[21]

The security and intelligence functions of the UFWD are confirmed in a detailed article on united-front operations in Canton in 1953.[d] It reported that the UFWD under the South China Regional

[d] "The 'United Front' Enterprise in Canton," RHKCP 14/54 (Jan. 21, 1954). The article originally appeared in the pro-Nationalist Hong Kong newspaper

Party Bureau was headed by Feng Pai-chü, who had recently replaced Fang Fang (later to become a Vice-Director of the Central UFWD). Five united-front reception centers were reported in existence in Canton proper, with four more in other cities in the province of Kwangtung. Their functions included surveillance and reporting, control of minor-party operations, and thought reform.[22]

The day-to-day operations of the BDP were also closely supervised. Chou Ching-wen writes,

> Whenever a minor party wanted to hold a meeting, it had to ask for instructions concerning the major topics and the contents of the discussion. The resolutions or statements passed at a meeting also had to have the approval of the UFWD before they could be announced. The list of candidates in any election of these minor parties likewise had to be approved by the department. The presence of Li Wei-han . . . at any meeting of the minor parties, for the purpose of making a speech and giving instructions, was supposed to be a great honor. Local branches of the minor parties must also invite the local head of the UFWD to their meetings. In addition, UFWD agents were always present to report on the daily activities of members. Sometimes, officials from the UFWD would come to the conference themselves to gather first-hand information. The minor parties also had to ask . . . about applications for membership to the parties.[23]

According to the report from Canton, the functions of UFWD officials in liaison with the BDP were to determine the inclinations and observe the activities of BDP members; to attend their meetings and functions; to convey to the BDP the instructions or suggestions of the Party; to transmit BDP reports to the Party; to supervise the ideological reform of BDP members; and to pass on applications for membership, etc.[24]

The Party also exercised financial control over the BDP.[25] Chou Ching-wen tells of submitting budgets and accounts to the Ministry of Finance until 1952, then to local government agencies.[26] But he

---

Hsin-wen t'ien-ti, Dec. 26, 1953. It is probably biased, but agrees quite well with such information as we possess.

is wrong in saying that all contributions were, ostensibly, to come from BDP members: the DL's Fourth Congress, in December 1949, passed a resolution that funds could also come from the government and (unspecified) other sources.[27] This should cause no surprise. The CCP had subsidized the DL for years, and had provided aid for many of the groups in Hong Kong during the Civil War. If the minor parties had had to depend solely on the resources of their none too affluent members, activities would have been greatly curtailed, if not suspended altogether.

A final element of control is provided by CCP members who are also members of the minor parties. Semi-official KMT sources claim that a formal minimum of 2 per cent has been established, with actual figures running up to 50 per cent.[28] The latter figure, at least, is far too high. A survey of other KMT-compiled data gives average figures well under 5 per cent.[e] The possibility of secret members exists, but these cannot be very numerous. All of these CCP members seem to be at intermediate levels, where they are probably used as a check on the activities and attitudes of the BDP.

It is evident that the Party never had any intention of allowing the bourgeois-democratic parties to function as they might in a bourgeois democracy. And it is equally clear that the BDP themselves understood and accepted this condition. Yet, like San-min chu-i propaganda during the war, the public statements of both the Party and the BDP might be viewed by outsiders in terms of their own conceptions of "democracy," "political party," etc.

At first, it was the hope of both the Party and the BDP that the latter would play an active role in the development of a new China. There was an initial period, lasting perhaps into 1952, when this seemed possible. The full and undeniable independence of China, the feeling that China was beginning to move forward after decades of weakness and corruption, the tasks of reconstruction, the attack

[e] *Fei-wei jen-shih tzu-liao*. Despite the very large number of persons (over 2,300) whose biographies and posts (past and present) are given here, ordinary BDP or CCP members are not usually included. Therefore, these percentages may not be truly representative.

on many of the undeniable abuses of Republican China, the Korean War—all combined to create an enthusiasm that for a time overcame BDP misgivings. But before long, it became clear that the BDP leaders had envisioned a larger role in the shaping of policy than the Party was willing to grant them. The Party wanted imaginative and dedicated implementation of policies it would determine for itself, and the BDP were considered instruments to this end. With this structure, it was not long before the BDP lost much of their spontaneity and initiative. As instruments, they were less effective than before, but the Party could still use them.

Aspects of United-Front Work

The tasks to which the united front has been set are many and various. "So rich has the content of China's people's democratic united front become that it is related to every aspect of work in our country and the activities of all the democratic parties and groups and people's organizations."[29] Li Wei-han was not claiming here that all work depended on this policy, but rather that a united-front approach has been part of a whole range of activities, much wider in scope than in previous years.

Many of these applications of the united front have been made the patriotic duty of all Chinese. By identifying the united front with nationalism, and by making itself the leader of that united front, the Party seeks to reinforce its claim that only by serving socialism can the people exhibit their patriotism.

> The unprecedentedly broad and deep development of the people's democratic united front is expressed in most concentrated form in the present great patriotic tide. . . . This movement has profound content: the patriotism of the Chinese people today is by no means an abstract thing. Its content is opposition to imperialist aggression and feudal oppression, it is upholding the fruits of the Chinese revolution, it is upholding New Democracy, it is upholding progress and opposing backwardness; it is upholding the working people, it is upholding the internationalist alliance of China with Russia, the people's democracies, and the working

> peoples of the entire world; it is struggling for the future of socialism.[30]

Therefore, non-Communists are put in a position where they can prove their love of country only by their support of the CCP. While many, perhaps most, of the intellectuals may not wish to accept this position, the Party's monopoly of power prevents any unauthorized expression of patriotism. Everyone must belong to some organization, so that even the alternative of withdrawal is largely denied. This bears in very real and human terms upon the individual. Mu Fu-sheng, in one of the most perceptive personal accounts to come out of mainland China, writes that the "Chinese Communists seem to count a genuine patriot half a comrade."[31] He then goes on to describe the difficult choice that genuine patriotism creates for non-Communist intellectuals:

> For the intellectuals under the Communist regime the choice, if they have it, is between working for a Government with which they disagree but which is the only place where they can do some good for the country in technical capacities, and leaving or staying away from the country. There is no question at all of helping the country remove what is undesirable in the Government. Boycott, even if practicable, will not shake the Communists. This choice the Communists present as one between patriotism and selfishness, because those who leave or stay away can neither change the Government nor serve the country. . . . In China today many intellectuals serve patriotism under a penalty. The Communists want patriots for the sake of Communism, but these are patriots in spite of Communism.[32]

Examples from the early years of the regime are numerous. One was the "patriotic pact," begun in November 1950, following Chinese intervention in the Korean War. The patriotic pact could be made by any individual or group, ranging from a gambler's pledge to quit gaming to an Industrial Shock Brigade's dedication to higher production.[33] During the Resist-America Aid-Korea campaign (one of the principal "patriotic" movements during the period of reconstruction), a directive included the following as part of that campaign: takeover and disposal of American-subsidized relief institutions; organization of religious and welfare circles to undertake study of current events and business methods; mobilization of various circles to join in the May Day parade.[34] Examples could easily be multiplied, but the point is that determination of the content of patriotism was fully in the Party's hands. Lack of an immediately obvious connection between a given act and patriotic behavior did not stop the Party from asserting such a connection. Meanwhile, the bourgeoisie and intellectuals, unacceptable on class grounds, could gain approval by embracing this predetermined content.

Some years later, Chou En-lai invoked the united front with respect to the composition of the CPPCC, liberation of Taiwan, and socialist transformation of commerce and industry. At the same time, he said that the bourgeois-democratic parties were largely responsible for the mobilization of the intellectuals.[35] In short, it is clear that the united front is not limited to any particular area, but can be applied with great flexibility to a wide variety of specific situations.

Party and Non-Party

One specific problem to which the united-front approach was applied during the early years of the regime was the relation between Party members and non-Party personnel in government agencies. This was an old problem. During the Sino-Japanese War and the Civil War, Communist victory depended heavily on good relations between Party and non-Party cadres, and with the non-Party population in general. But by early 1951, when the CCP was reconstructing the damage of more than a decade of war, setting up a nationwide administration, governing cities larger than many Party members had ever seen before, fighting the Korean War, and mopping up the last remnants of opposition, the dimensions of this problem were unprecedented.

In most areas, the proportion of non-Party functionaries was very high. In Shanghai, even after the "three-anti" movement, over 70 per cent of the officials were non-Party.[36] In the Northwest Military and Administrative Region, during the period 1949–51, civilian Party members numbered about 50,000 or 0.22 per cent of the population: "Out of these, only a small portion can be assigned as cadres for various kinds of work, and the number of old cadres that can be assigned as leading personnel is even smaller."[37] In many cases, the Party found it necessary to confirm virtually an entire staff in its pre-liberation functions. Clearly, the effective use of scarce administrative skills required that working relations be as good as possible.

During the first year of the People's Republic, this question received only sporadic attention. A highly fluid domestic situation, the desire to establish Party control over the government, and the job of screening out the most obvious and determined anti-Communists all required that the task of adjusting these relations be temporarily deferred. By the spring and early summer of 1951, however, the Party was ready to apply itself to this task. A movement was touched off by a report made by Li Wei-han before the First National Conference of Secretaries-General. The report, entitled "Strengthen Further the United Front in Government Agencies," defined the united front in organs of government as the relation between Party and non-Party.[38] This was justified as a kind of inter-group, or inter-class, collaboration; in practice, it was natural that this problem be handled by the Non-Party Cadres Section of the UFWD. Li insisted that Party members make good use of non-Party personnel, that they carefully evaluate their abilities and delegate responsibility and authority on that basis. This required clear understanding of policy, and agreement on specific measures. Here the Party should take the lead. Every Party member had a responsibility in this area, which could not be left to upper echelons.

Papers and periodicals across the country printed the report and discussed it at length. Hundreds of meetings were held. In Chungking, representatives of the minor parties made suggestions concerning elimination of local bandits, promotion of rural-urban trade, and adjustment of labor-capital relations. They also said that local

Party cadres had certain shortcomings: they lacked experience running a large city, and were often inefficient, haughty, or guilty of "commandism."[39] A much longer and more thoughtful consideration of the question was published in the Party's organ for central China.[40] First, it was admitted that many Party cadres did not respect the abilities of non-Party officials, and sometimes even refused to follow orders issued by non-Party superiors. Second, there was the question of division of responsibility and authority when Party and non-Party occupied the top two positions in a given agency. If the Party comrade was in the number-one position, he should guard against the tendency to do everything himself. Instead, he should delegate appropriate tasks to his second, together with the necessary authority to get the job done. He should listen to advice, provide guidance, and give due credit for accomplishment. More interesting, however, was the reverse situation—though it may be questioned how often such restraint was exercised.

> If the non-Party comrade has primary responsibility and the Party member occupies the secondary position, he should first of all recognize that the non-Party man is in charge, and that he is to assist him. . . . Should there arise a difference of opinion in principle between the non-Party and Party men, the responsible Party member should earnestly set forth his own opinion so that both sides can arrive at complete unanimity. If his opinion is not accepted by the other side, he can only reserve his opinion, waiting for the appropriate time to bring it up again, or bring it up in other ways. He cannot constrain others to accept his own opinion. In actual daily work, he should fully respect the non-Party man's opinion, and should, especially through his own exemplary conduct, educate middle- and lower-level Party cadres to respect and obey the leadership of non-Party comrades.[41]

These general statements were followed up by a six-point directive from the General Administrative Committee (GAC). Specific Party officials were made responsible for this work, personnel departments were assigned certain united-front duties, united-front symposia were to be held, and periodic reports were required.[42]

What emerges from all this is an obviously sincere desire on the part of the leading Party elements to effect a policy consensus with persons of ability outside the Party. Such a consensus rested ultimately on a united-front frame of mind: no strict class viewpoint would consider a genuine and voluntary collaboration possible. But the Chinese Communists viewed the majority of the bourgeoisie as having the potential for voluntary and enthusiastic acceptance of the state program under the leadership of the Party. It was the job of the Party to find ways to tap that voluntary enthusiasm; it was up to the non-Party official not only to do his work, but to feel a sense of dedication.

Yet despite the Party's conviction that it had a definite responsibility for the proper utilization of non-Party elements, the problem was very difficult—and the higher the level, the more difficult. At lower levels, where operations are almost entirely in implementation of concrete policies, or largely technical in nature, this approach may be possible, provided it does not lead to general disregard of the Party. But at higher levels, where formation of policy, or its interpretation, is involved, the matter is more difficult. The crux is that it is impossible to lead and follow at the same time. Both sides know where the real power lies. Decisions taken by non-Party officials must at some point, either before issuance or prior to execution, be reviewed and approved by the Party. But then non-Party authority, in any autonomous sense, has vanished.

Agrarian Reform

An excellent example of the united front's flexibility is provided by the agrarian reform movement. Here there were no doctrinal pretensions, but rather an effective technique for social analysis and action.

In 1947, Mao wrote: "Although the proportion of landlords and rich peasants in the rural population varies from place to place, it is generally only about 8 per cent (in terms of households), while their holdings usually amount to 70 or 80 per cent of all the land. Therefore the targets of our land reform are very few, while the people in the villages who can and should take part in the united front for land reform are many—more than 90 per cent (in terms of households)."[43] This policy, set forth in October 1947, marked both rich peasants and landlords as the classes to be eliminated. This was the most radical land reform policy in the post-soviet period. "During the winter of 1947–48, the poor peasants were encouraged to give no quarter to the landlords and rich peasants; as a result a number of the latter were subject to harsh treatment. Even the properties of some middle peasants were infringed upon in what were later labeled 'ultra-leftist errors.' "[44]

The swing back toward moderation began in January 1948. Less than a month later, it was directed that the land law of 1947 was to be applied differently in different regions. In areas liberated prior to Japan's defeat, land was not to be redistributed. In areas liberated between September 1945 and August 1947, where poor peasants were a majority and middle peasants a minority, the land law was to be applied as stated. But in newly liberated areas, reform was to be applied at first only to landlords, not to rich peasants.[45] The percentage remained the same: "The total scope of attack should generally not exceed 8 per cent of the households or 10 per cent of the population."[46]

After the formation of the People's Republic and the enactment of the Agrarian Reform Law of June 28, 1950, the rich peasants were considered a part of the united front. The enemy was restricted to the landlords alone. Although the CCP now had greater freedom than ever before to mark off its enemies in any way it saw fit, the size of the enemy was cut down. The reason for this, and its effectiveness, is shown clearly in a report on land reform near Peking. Cadres were directed not to touch 60,000 *mou* (1 *mou* equals about one-sixth of an acre) owned by rich peasants in the area. This was

> beneficial to isolation of landlords. Prior to liberation, the psychology of fear on the part of rich peasants and landlords was the same. Rich peasants in general considered themselves definitely to be the object of agrarian reform; a similar view was taken by peasants in general. But as soon as classes were differentiated during the agrarian reform and as soon as rich peasants realized that our policy towards them was not the same as towards the

> landlords, they began to separate themselves from landlords and their feelings tended to stabilize.[47]

A more general discussion of the Agrarian Reform Law made it clear that the poor peasants were to unite with middle peasants, neutralizing rich peasants by allowing them to retain their property on good behavior (i.e., if they did not oppose land reform; if they did so, they were to be treated like the enemy, the landlords).[48] It was stated that rich peasants constituted about 6 per cent of the rural population, and landlords about 4 per cent. Thus the agrarian united front at this time was to include at least 95 per cent of the rural population.[49] Middle peasants, about 20 per cent of the total, were reliable allies, and unity with them was considered vital. Errors like those committed in some of the older liberated areas in 1947–48 would simply drive middle peasants to the side of the landlords and rich peasants, to the great detriment, and possible defeat, of the movement. To assure that this did not happen, it was desirable that middle peasants be represented in Peasant Associations, up to a total of 50 per cent.[50] But middle peasants might be hesitant and had to be won over by criticism and self-criticism, and by actual participation in the reform movement. Rich peasants, though a part of the united front, were to be excluded from Peasant Associations, at least until the conclusion of land reform, lest they dilute them and influence them in the direction of the landlords. Later, when the landlords had been eliminated, they might be admitted.[51]

Thus both rich and middle peasants were included in the united front. Definite and important distinctions were drawn between them, but both were offered incentives for cooperating and faced with threats if they did not. By participating in the movement, or by occupying a neutral position, they were made to feel they were part of an irresistible tide composed of the vast majority of the population. By contrast, if they opposed land reform, they stood almost alone against the fury and violence that the agrarian revolution loosed upon its enemies. This approach successfully fragmented and paralyzed much of the potential resistance that the movement might have met in the countryside had it been less discriminating in its selection of enemies. This approach also provided guidelines for cadres, for poor peasants, and for other activists who might question why some well-to-do elements were spared. It had been proved repeatedly that once the fires of radicalism were kindled in the villages, they burned with great heat. Such had been the situation Mao saw in Hunan in late 1926. The errors in the older liberated areas were the result of excessive radicalism that drove large segments of the rural population into opposition. Hence the united front was also a way to prevent the excesses of overenthusiasm from endangering the success of a movement.

Although the rich peasant was included in the agrarian united front at this point, his eventual elimination had been planned from the very beginning. The liquidation of the landlord class meant that the rich peasants occupied the end of the scale, and were the next target to be dealt with (see below, pp. 238–39).

The Wu-fan Campaign

When the CCP came to power in 1949 and 1950, it took over a thoroughly deranged and demoralized economy. Nor did the CCP have the personnel, education, or experience to run by itself those elements of a modern financial and industrial system that still survived or could be put back into operation. Therefore, the skills of the national bourgeoisie were vitally needed.

The national bourgeoisie, which in the 1920's had meant those Chinese businessmen or industrialists suffering from the competition of privileged foreign enterprise, now referred to members of this group who were willing to cooperate with the CCP. In most cases, these men had suffered badly under the last years of KMT rule, and the CCP had directed appeal after appeal to them. *On the New Democracy* had stated that the Chinese revolution was ultimately a socialist, not a bourgeois, revolution, but that "It will neither confiscate other capitalist private property [aside from large banks, heavy industry, transport, communications, etc., in the public sector even under the KMT] nor forbid the development of capitalist production that 'cannot manipulate the people's livelihood,' for China's economy is still very backward."[52] As the CCP grew in power, this policy was reiterated, as in a classic statement from *On Coalition Government*: "Those people are mistaken who think that the Chinese Communists are against the development of individual initiative, the development of private capital and the protection of private property. Foreign and feudal oppression cruelly fetters the development of the Chinese people's individual initiative, hinders the development of private capital, and destroys the property of the broad masses of the people. The task of the New Democracy we advocate is precisely to remove such fetters and stop such destruction."[53] The Common Program, adopted in 1949, stated, "The basic principle for economic construction of the People's Republic of China is to attain the goal of developing production . . . through the policy of taking into account both public and private interests and benefits to both labor and capital."[54]

Within this framework, to be sure, the Party exerted as much control as possible. Control of currency and the establishment of large state trading companies "whose orders and contracts might be vital to a private company's survival,"[55] were perhaps the most important of the measures undertaken in 1949 and early 1950. This process was formalized in June 1950 by "adjustment of public and private relationships" in which the government was supplier of raw materials and purchaser of finished goods for many firms. During this same early period, labor-management relations were controlled by the Workers' and Employers' Consultative Conference, a form of compulsory arbitration. During 1950, furthermore, private firms were called upon to make full reports on all aspects of their operations: financial status, operating procedures, production schedules, inventory, plant, sales, etc. On the basis of these reports, Provisional Regulations for Private Enterprises were promulgated. Businesses were required to submit at regular intervals their plans for production and sales, to be put into effect after government approval. Earnings and profits were to be distributed in various ways specified in the regulations.[56]

Finally, businessmen were beginning to be pushed into the sort of mass participation that is such a notable characteristic of the CCP regime. In Tientsin, on a bitterly cold November 30, 1950, over 42,000 local industrialists, businessmen, technicians, managers, etc., thronged the Sports Stadium in a great patriotic demonstration against "American aggression" in Korea. They pledged that they would stand firmly at their posts and work to increase production, would support the People's Government in its efforts to stabilize retail prices, and would oppose hoarding and speculation.[57] A similar rally was held in Peking on December 9th, the anniversary of the great student demonstration in 1935. In Shanghai on December 15 some 150,000 are reported to have turned out, and many other cities held similar functions.[58]

However onerous and irritating all this might have been to the business community, it was probably less difficult to do business then than it had been under the KMT. Moreover, the businessman had only to look at the rural areas to see that the treatment accorded him was infinitely better than that received by the landlords. Regulations, like one adopted by the Central-South Military-Administrative Committee, prevented any widespread disruption of the urban economy: "No struggle of the village type may be initiated either in cities and towns with concentrated industry, or in market towns with a little industry and trade. No such struggle shall be permitted whether or not it is demanded by local poor or by peasants of nearby villages."[59]

Meanwhile, before the work of reconstruction had been completed or any degree of direct government control over the private sector of the economy had been achieved, the Korean War broke out. The emergency economic policies then adopted brought considerable prosperity to the business community:

> A governmental purchasing spree began in all of the big cities of the coastal provinces. From military raincoats and rubber shoes to medicines, everything went into the governmental stock pile. The government raised its purchasing prices in an effort to boost production. Quality didn't matter much. Speed was the essential. Unprecedented prosperity prevailed throughout the latter half of 1950 and all through 1951. Old factories were working overtime, new ones were springing up everywhere. Many artisans set up shop at home, gradually turning themselves into a new capitalist

> class. Shanghai saw the birth of untold thousands of these upstart wartime millionaires.
>
> Smuggling became an honourable profession as the government worked desperately to secure raw materials from overseas. "This is smuggling for the revolution," Chen Yi, Shanghai's mayor, said. The smugglers' profits were enormous, but the government turned its head.[60]

But a year later, the Party was ready to turn the "struggle" side of the united front against the national bourgeoisie. The Korean War had become a war of attrition and stalemate. The initial stages of reconstruction were complete. Agrarian reform was beginning to slow down, and the government was established and operating at all levels.

The "three-anti" (*san-fan*) and "five-anti" (*wu-fan*) campaigns were clearly political and social, rather than economic, in purpose. They were designed to push government and Party control into areas of the economy and bureaucracy where it had not yet been firmly and directly exercised. The Wu-fan campaign served to intimidate the business community, to indicate what they could expect if they did not thoroughly accept "working-class leadership." Finally, the campaign was placed in the context of the united front.

The San-fan Wu-fan campaign was perhaps the shortest of all the "five major campaigns" (land reform, Resist-America Aid-Korea, suppression of counterrevolutionaries, San-fan Wu-fan, and thought reform). It began in the last month or two of 1951, gained momentum through the spring of 1952, then diminished in intensity and straggled to an end by midsummer. Only land reform and suppression of counterrevolutionaries were more harrowing for those involved. Ostensibly the Wu-fan campaign was directed against vaguely defined crimes—bribery, tax evasion, fraud, theft of government property, and economic espionage. The last of these "referred to the act of discovering the government intention, for example, to buy up certain commodities and then using that knowledge to make excessive profit. A number of businessmen had profiteered in this fashion during the Korean War."[61] It soon became clear that the scope of these crimes was so broad that any irregularity, real or presumed, could be fitted into one or another of the categories. The movement began with the dispatch of "five-anti teams" by the government to larger private enterprises.[62] These corresponded in function to the land-reform cadres sent into the villages to make preliminary investigations, set up the necessary organizations, and supervise the movement. Three forms of struggle were used, though not clearly distinguished: through employees and "tiger-hunting" teams; through denunciation by other members of the bourgeoisie; and through denunciation by family members of the accused.

Most widely used was the first. Groups of "tiger hunters" (the merchants and industrialists were the reluctant tigers) were organized as accusation teams. They denounced their employer for professional and personal crimes, organized mass meetings at which he was further accused and made to confess, and kept him under constant surveillance. This last was probably intended initially to keep pressure applied around the clock, but it often served to prevent the harassed and desperate man from committing suicide.[f]

The struggle broke up any possible unanimity in the business community. Business associates and competitors were forced to inform on one another, sometimes in very ingenious ways:

> At the very beginning of the [Five-anti] campaign, several really unscrupulous businessmen in each branch of industry and commerce were apprehended. After these men had confessed, they were told that their crimes deserved "more than one death" but that their actual fate would depend upon the contributions they individually made to the campaign. . . . Moreover, because they knew well their own branch of business and the other men in it, they were the most capable of devising crimes to which the others were pressed to confess.[63]

---

[f] Loh, *Businessmen,* p. 42. The situation was perhaps not quite so serious as Loh suggests: he comments that leaping from upper-story windows was "thoughtless of the welfare of passersby in the street below. A number were killed during the Five-anti's movement under a rain of plummeting businessmen."

Many imagined that the tiger-hunting movement aimed at the destruction of the bourgeoisie. This impression was strengthened by the ferocity with which the movement was pushed in its early and middle stages. In March 1952, Chang P'ing-hua, a Party member, reviewed the progress made to date in Wuhan. He was reported as follows: "Chang urged ferocity and opposed hesitancy in the current struggle, criticizing the compromising attitude toward the enemy. He considered it undesirable not to put the 'tigers' under rigid control. He revealed that many of them remain perfectly free, playing billiards or poker, or even insult cadres and masses at meetings, or deface our slogans, while in some cases they have escaped or committed suicide."[64] Li Hsien-nien "warned against procrastination in work . . . saying that it was not right to fear 'violation of human rights' regarding the enemy and that 'tiger hunting' must be thoroughly conducted."[65] Laborers and other employees were told that the conduct of the movement depended on their active participation: "Workers, employees, and shop assistants! You are the main force of the Five-anti united front. You should stand firmly on the side of the working class and draw a clear line of demarcation against the capitalists. Since you have long been associated with the bourgeoisie, you must be conversant with the internal conditions of the bourgeois class, whose attempts to evade the Five-anti campaign will be totally frustrated once you speak out."[66]

Despite all this, the bourgeoisie was not "the enemy" in a strict united-front sense—that is, it was not intended that the bourgeoisie be eliminated. Ch'en Yi, mayor of Shanghai (the center of the movement), made this point:

> The measures adopted by the People's Government are in no way an indication that it has changed its policy toward the bourgeois class or that the people's democratic dictatorship has turned into an alliance of three classes. . . . The government policy of uniting with the bourgeois class remains unchanged, and the people's democratic dictatorship is still a regime represented by the people's democratic united front formed by the working class, the peasant class, the petty-bourgeois class, the bourgeois class, and

> other patriotic democratic elements. . . . The Five-anti struggle is different from the agrarian reform movement, and the bourgeois class will not be eliminated in this struggle as the landlords were in agrarian reform.[67]

This was, instead, a way of drawing lines for the movement—both for the bourgeoisie and for the Party. As the struggle phase of the movement achieved its immediate goals, these guidelines were laid down more specifically. A model was provided by an act with the lengthy title "Standards and Measures Set by the Peking Municipal Government for Dealing with Industrial and Commercial Establishments Classified into Various Categories in the Five-anti Movement." According to this measure, also applied in Shanghai and elsewhere, five categories were established: (1) law-abiding establishments, about 15 per cent; (2) basically law-abiding establishments, about 50 per cent; (3) establishments guilty of fairly serious violations of the law, about 30 per cent; (4) establishments guilty of serious or complete violations of the law, about 5 per cent; and (5) a few establishments guilty of "appalling crimes that must be punished to assuage the indignation of the masses."[68] Now, it was said, severity must be tempered with mercy. Those in category 3 whose illegal profits exceeded 10 million yuan but who "have thoroughly confessed to their offenses, sincerely repent, and actively report others" were to be placed in category 2.[69] Even those guilty of "appalling crimes" might receive a "mitigated penalty" if they repented and turned state's evidence.

The most frequent form of punishment (aside from the inevitable public confession) was the imposition of fines, though imprisonment and execution were sometimes used because of their exemplary effects. The Party and the government could make the fines confiscatory, punitive, or simply demonstrative. The amount of money collected was considerable; indeed, one purpose may have been to partially deflate the economy. The total may have reached or exceeded $1 billion.[70] Government control was greatly increased, since many businesses passed into the public sector through inability to pay the fines levied or continue operation after paying. The remainder were thoroughly cowed, ready now to accept "voluntarily" a much greater degree of control by the Party and government. The number of those subjected to judicial or quasi-judicial punishment seems to conform quite closely to the guidelines indicated above. In the *People's Daily* (Oct. 1, 1952), it was reported that 76 per cent of 450,000 merchants and industrialists in seven cities were found guilty of one or more offenses. The *Southern Daily* (*Nan-fang jih-pao,* June 8, 1952) recorded a higher percentage, 90 per cent of 160,000.

But these figures are misleading because nearly every city dweller, in one way or another, was affected by San-fan Wu-fan. Every businessman, industrialist, or commercial operator felt the blow, whether or not he was finally subjected to some sort of formal punishment. Certainly it lay within the power of the Party to prolong the movement, or to eliminate the business class. It did not do so because it felt that the continued operation of the private sector of the economy was still necessary. But this decision was conditioned and justified by the united-front analysis of Chinese society and by the use of united-front tactics. Thus, in terms of united-front theory, the Party sought a new and higher unity on the basis of class struggle.

A new organizational form was indeed created to serve the disrupted business community. This was the All-China Federation of Industry and Commerce. Formed in June 1952, it was a much larger and more comprehensive body than the NCA. One of its principal functions was to supervise the integration of private enterprise with a planned economy. This role was laid out in considerable detail in October 1953, when the National Congress of Industry and Commerce (presided over by Li Wei-han) stressed that the private sector was to be gradually transformed. It was emphasized that cooperative private operators would find good positions in the new economy, and would not be eliminated.

There are remarkable parallels in these examples of the use of the united-front approach. Where a segment of the population was divided into various categories, as in land reform and the San-fan Wu-fan campaign, the size of these categories is almost exactly the same. The "enemy" comprises 5 or 6 per cent; about 65 per cent is more or less firmly on the side of the movement (up through the poor and lower-middle peasants in land reform; up through basically law-abiding establishments in the Wu-fan campaign). The remainder is a wavering, intermediate group, which should either be conditionally won over or be neutralized. The consistency of these percentages, and the frequency with which they recur, very strongly suggest that they are being deliberately applied, and do not necessarily grow out of actual conditions.

Another characteristic is the flexibility of this tripartite division into friend, waverer, and enemy. All three parts are always present, and the definition of who falls into which part is in Party hands. Much greater flexibility is possible when the enemy can be defined operationally rather than in absolute terms. If one has only eternal friends and eternal enemies, it is hard not to be dogmatic and rigid.

Once an enemy has been defeated, a realignment takes place, and a new principal target is marked out so that "enemies can be defeated one by one." When Japan was the enemy, CCP collaboration with the KMT was necessary and justified. With Japan's defeat, the KMT became the primary object of attack. First the landlords, then the rich peasants, were marked for elimination. One should not fight the Japanese and the KMT at the same time, nor attempt to eliminate at one stroke both the landlords and the rich peasants.

This may seem a rather trivial formalization of action that could have been taken anyway. It is true that none of it is *necessarily* required, but there can be little doubt that this is the way the CCP *has* viewed many situations and that it is on this basis that the Party has acted. The need for doctrinal sanction, so powerfully felt by Communists everywhere, is thereby satisfied: neither the rightism of permanent compromise nor the leftism of doing everything at once. Finally, the Party has used the united-front approach so as to elicit (or force) majority support—and has then taken the apparent fact of majority support as evidence of its own legitimacy.

Chapter 11

The United Front since 1954

The United Front under the Constitution

The adoption of the Constitution on September 20, 1954, meant that the People's Republic had reached higher levels of organization and institutional permanence than during its first five years. This progress rested on the fact that the CCP had widened its control over Chinese society; structurally speaking, it had replaced the old leading elements with its own cadres or with Party-directed specialists. It had exchanged the system of regional military-administrative areas for a well-controlled provincial structure. UFWD were attached to each of the Party committees at the provincial level, and were also set up in all major—and some minor—cities where there was scope for united-front activities. With its hands on the levers and switches of a highly centralized apparatus, the Party was ready to step up its transformation of Chinese society.

With the First Five-Year Plan, and the early stages of the transformation of capitalist industry and commerce, the Constitution marked the beginning of the "period of the general line for the transition to socialism." In effect, these events signified the end of the New Democracy, i.e., the end of the revolution's bourgeois-democratic phase. But even though the united front had been a specific feature of an earlier and less advanced stage of development, it was not discarded as a once useful tactic that had now been outgrown. The Preamble to the Constitution said, "The united front will continue to play its part in mobilizing and rallying the whole people in common struggle to fulfill the fundamental task of the State during the transition, and to oppose enemies within and without."[1] This is a rather perfunctory statement, but mention of the united front in the Preamble to the principal document of state shows its continuing presence in the minds of the top Party leaders.

A contrast between theoretical importance and practical decline in significance was characteristic up to the beginning of 1956, when the Party tried to recover the élan of the united front's earlier days. The BDP and the intellectuals were given much more prestige and were assigned (at least ostensibly) a much more important role in supervision and criticism of the Party. The result, finally, was the traumatic failure of the Hundred Flowers movement. After this unsuccessful effort to make the united front operational in its old terms, the divergence between theory and practice became wider and wider. For while the practical significance of the united front as an element of domestic policy has now shrunk almost to the vanishing point, its theoretical position has been continually raised and made more abstract.

With the adoption of the Constitution, the Common Program and the Organic Law were superseded, and the National People's Congress (NPC) replaced the CPPCC as the theoretical source of sovereignty and the highest legislative body in the state. The CPPCC, which might have been abolished, was retained as a forum, but without any clearly defined constitutional function. Liu Shao-ch'i, in discussing the draft constitution, remarked that some people had thought that the status and tasks of the CPPCC should be spelled out in the Preamble, but "the Committee for Drafting the Constitution considers there is no need to make such an addition to it."[2] Liu went on to say

> The Chinese People's Political Consultative Conference is the organizational form of our people's democratic united front. It exercised its functions and powers on behalf of the National People's Congress and will, of course, no longer be required to exercise them in the future. It will, however, continue to play its part in the political life of our country as the organization of the united front. Since it is a united-front organization, the parties, groups, and organizations in the united front will, in consultation, themselves work out all the provisions concerning it.[3]

In December 1954, the CPPCC adopted a new "constitution" of its own, "Regulations Governing the Chinese People's Political Consultative Conference."

Thus the CPPCC was no longer an instrument of state power, or a part of the formal state structure. But its membership was very large (the Third National Committee numbered over 1,000), and it was elaborately organized. As might be expected from Liu's remarks, it was closely supervised by the UFWD. Li Wei-han was one of 14 vice-chairmen under the chairmanship of Chou En-lai (eight of them were CCP members). Hsü Ping (Hsing Hsi-p'ing), then a deputy director of the UFWD under Li, was the Secretary-General of the CPPCC. Although it had no organizational ties to the NPC, many of its members were also delegates to the Congress, so that in fact the two bodies overlapped.

The CPPCC serves the CCP and the Government as a broadly organized directorate for mass organizations and non-government, non-Party structures that otherwise have little lateral contact with each other. Here their representatives receive and transmit to local levels the directives and policy decisions that affect their members. The National Committee, Standing Committee, and permanent subcommittees provide coordination of plans that involve several of the constituent organizations. In addition, the CPPCC is required to register mass support for the Government, the NPC, and the CCP. In some measure, it is permitted or required to keep higher levels informed of feelings or suggestions on the part of its members. Therefore the CPPCC's main role is in coordination and implementation—allocation of effort, assignment of tasks, and supervision of accomplishment. Because nearly everyone is represented, and because the Party leads, the CPPCC is, spontaneously or not, "the organizational form of the people's democratic united front." Meanwhile, the position of the CPPCC outside the Constitution was a partial "de-institutionalization" of the united front.

As a part of the advance to a higher level of social organization, the Constitution effected a certain rearrangement of the class structure of "the people" composing the united front. Article 8 stated that the "policy of the State towards rich-peasant economy is to restrict and gradually eliminate it."[4] This included both the "old" rich peasants who had survived agrarian reform and the "new" rich peasants who had achieved that status after 1951. The reason for this step, which was a necessary preparation for the collectivization of land ownership, was explained in these terms: "China's rich peasant economy has many feudal qualities. . . . From start to finish, it has no really positive function of benefit to national planning and the people's livelihood."[5] The rich peasants were to be educated in patriotism and law-abiding conduct, for "elimination" in this context did not mean execution and was not used in the same sense as in the land-reform movement.[6] Liu Shao-ch'i observed that there would inevitably be struggle, but that "it will not be necessary to start a special movement, as was the case in land reform, to eliminate the rich peasants."[7]

The policy toward the national bourgeoisie continued to be different from the handling of the rural elements. Article 10 of the Constitution stated: "The policy of the state toward capitalist industry and commerce is to use, restrict and transform them. The State makes use of the positive qualities of capitalist industry and commerce which are beneficial to national welfare and people's livelihood, encourages and guides their transformation into various forms of state-capitalist economy, gradually replacing capitalist ownership with ownership by the whole people."[8]

The work of gradually eliminating the private sector of the economy was placed squarely within the context of the united front, and was one of the smoother operations carried on by the Party and its satellites. In 1954 the State Council, under the Constitution, replaced the GAC. Under the State Council were eight general offices charged with various administrative functions. The Eighth General Office was responsible for united-front work, particularly with reference to the national bourgeoisie. It was headed by Li Wei-han, who was seconded by Hsü Ti-hsin, Chang Chih-i, and Sun Ch'i-meng.[a] Hsü Ti-hsin, an economist, has probably had more experience than any other member of the UFWD in working with businessmen: he was also a director of the Central Administration of

[a] "Directory of National Positions in the Chinese Communist Party, Government, and Armed Forces," *CB,* 513 (July 16, 1958). Hsü Ti-hsin, who was instrumental in working with Shanghai businessmen just before the takeover, was known to be a vice-director of the UFWD by early 1956, but may have assumed this position earlier. Chang (vice-director, UFWD, by April 1955) had long been associated with united-front and nationalities work in the Central-South region. He later became one of the principal spokesmen of united-front theory.

Industry and Commerce, a vice-chairman of the Federation of Industry and Commerce, and a member of the Central Committee of the NCA. Sun Ch'i-meng, not a Party member, is one of the leaders of the NCA, and also a vice-chairman of the Federation of Industry and Commerce.

Most of the transformation took place during 1955 and 1956, largely by means of the joint state-private firm in which the state became the senior stockholder. From there, it was only a step to full state control. Without trying to trace the details of the movement, we can observe the characteristic united-front and "bridge" functions that the members of various organizations were required to play, and how useful they were to the regime:

> By this time, early 1956, Charlie Chan [*sic*] was chairman and I was the Deputy Chairman, of the "Working Committee of Young Businessmen." The "young businessmen" numbered about 18,000 and were affiliated with a Communist front organization, the "Democratic Youth Association of Shanghai." The "progressive" young businessmen, therefore, became the activists in the campaign to socialize the country's nominally private enterprise. As the leaders of this group, Charlie and I worked out a system of "shock-attack teams" which were to facilitate the transformation. Our team became the model which was duplicated by the hundreds in Shanghai during the next few days and by the thousands throughout the rest of the country. . . . We worked closely with the Federation of Industry and Commerce. We notified the businessmen of the special immediate meetings. We helped the cadres explain the campaign, especially to the less well-educated businessmen. We put pressure on the few who were reluctant to give up their enterprises. We aided the businessmen in making out their applications for the Joint State-Private status.
>
> And, most of all, we cooperated with the propaganda cadres and the press to publicize the campaign.[9]

Thus, in the words of a prominent theorist, "The democratic united front has become the principal method for the liquidation of the capitalist class."[10]

During 1955 and 1956, there was a serious reconsideration of the united front as a whole, and of the functions to be exercised by the groups and individuals composing it. At about the same time, the UFWD was somewhat enlarged. Although we cannot be sure in all cases when appointments were made, new deputy directors under Li Wei-han included Yü I-fu (a Manchurian who had once been secretary to Chang Hsüeh-liang's brother), Chang Chih-i, P'ing Chieh-san (from Hopei, a former head of the North China Regional UFWD), Wang Feng (a prominent Mongol), and the economist Hsü Ti-hsin.[11] This expansion was probably the result of the campaign for the transformation of private industry and commerce; it may also have signified a closer link between united-front work and nationalities work, but the membership overlap between the Nationalities Work Commission (a government body) and the UFWD does not appear to be large at either the central or regional level. On the other hand, Liao Ch'eng-chih is no longer listed as a deputy director, perhaps indicating that overseas Chinese work is no longer a principal concern of the UFWD.

The Hundred Flowers and the Theory of Contradictions

The BDP, like the UFWD that controlled them, continued without important change until the early months of 1956, following Chou En-lai's speech concerning policy toward the intellectuals. In February, the UFWD sponsored the Fifth National Conference on United Front Work. "Here the tasks and policies . . . were discussed, and it was decided to make an overall examination of united front work."[12] This was an early step in the movement that led to the Hundred Flowers, deriving theoretical justification from the fact that the social and economic base of the bourgeoisie and the intellectuals had been stripped away (most of the transfer of private industry and commerce to joint public-private management had taken place in 1955).

Li Wei-han recognized that despite the functions assigned them, the BDP were not thought very important: "Some say, 'In the Communist Party there are those who do not take the democratic parties and groups seriously. In the democratic parties and groups themselves there are also those who do not take the democratic parties and groups seriously.' That, I believe, is not merely a matter of the viewpoint of certain people but is a reflection of views prevailing in the society at large."[13] But now the BDP were to have a wider sphere of operation, a greater responsibility within the framework of socialism. Criticism from non-Party intellectuals and ex-capitalists was sought. Party members were told to carry out this policy and not to neglect united-front individuals and organizations. In sum, because of changes in the situation inside China, the class struggle was now to be carried on by persuasion.[14]

The Party cannot abdicate its control functions, and it does not really trust the intellectuals and political figures who compose the BDP. But it needs the skills and training of these persons, for knowledge is scarce in China; it wishes them to participate with dedication and positive desire. Beyond this, the Party wants to be able to trust the intellectual both politically and professionally because it has a great need to believe that it can inspire enthusiasm and commitment. But it cannot really bring itself to share authority and responsibility. Here is a contradiction in which thesis and antithesis have produced no synthesis capable of mediating between monopolization and delegation of authority. Nevertheless, the summer of 1956 saw an attempt to find a solution. The policy of "long-term coexistence, mutual supervision" (*ch'ang-ch'i kung-ts'un, hu-hsiang chien-tu*) was the new role of the minor parties. Hence, despite the transformation of the BDP's substructure, the Party was committing itself to keep them in existence, and to allow them to try an expanded role in commenting on the performance of the CCP.

The first public mention of the new policy came in June 1956, and the expansion of the BDP, which had already started, was stepped up. Their total membership probably tripled, to about 100,000 by the end of 1956.[15] Probably the Democratic League was the largest, with a maximum membership of about 35,000.[b] The National Con-

[b] *KMJP,* Oct. 21, 1957. It was reported here, in the midst of the anti-rightist drive, that 2,199 rightists, 6 per cent of the DL, had been exposed. This gives a DL membership of approximately 36,600. These figures also agree with the estimate of Chou Ching-wen concerning the size of the DL when he left China at the end of 1956 (personal interview with the author, July 11, 1962).

struction Association had about 25,000 members, and the RCKMT approximately 15,000.[16] The other BDP were much smaller: Chang Po-chün's reactionary megalomania was later proved in the eyes of the Party when he was quoted as saying he hoped the Peasants' and Workers' Democratic Party could reach 10,000 members.[17]

In the following months, there was a tremendous amount of publicity concerning "long-term coexistence, mutual supervision." Forums were held throughout the nation, minor parties held conferences and discussion meetings, and representatives of the regional UFWD discussed the policy as it related to their own areas. Some criticisms were made, by the UFWD as exemplary self-criticism, and by the BDP. For example, Chang Kuo-fan, of the DL's Tientsin chapter, said that the BDP should really represent their constituencies, not simply carry out the policies of the CCP. He also thought the DL should do more mass work.[18]

Some of this public discussion dealt with the reasons for the continued existence of the BDP. Why, asked one observer, should the BDP be retained at all? His answer was a complete inversion of Marxism: aside from the NCA, the class base of most of the BDP was never very strong or clear—only a minority of their members had been exploiters. The further transformation of the memberships of the BDP was therefore no reason to terminate these parties now, any more than their weak class basis had been a reason for refusing to recognize them in the past. But, he continued, if they had no independent program anymore, why keep them around? Because, although their original democratic platforms had been fulfilled even without an independent program, their existence was required. So long as there were Party and non-Party, advanced and backward, the BDP should remain in existence and perform the following functions: supervising, through advice and criticism, the implementation of policy; acting as agencies of the CCP, the Government, and the people for propaganda and education; and serving as a bridge to their related masses.[19] The mobilization of the minor parties was also a part of the Party rectification movement, which was then beginning.

But despite all this publicity, the BDP, like the intellectuals in general, remained cautious. The events leading up to Mao's speech of February 27, 1957, *On the Proper Handling of Contradictions Within the People,* need not be recounted here. But even this did not produce the desired participation. It was not until the UFWD organized a series of 13 forums during May and early June, with the specific purpose of eliciting the true views of the BDP leaders, that the dikes of caution and reserve were breached.

The criticisms, which were voiced freely from early May until June 8, covered a very broad and basic spectrum.[c] But running through the vast majority of them was the complaint that the Party had dominated all aspects of life in China to far too great an extent. Although some of the critics indicted the Party, and even challenged the value of Communism itself, many others were more limited—and more poignant—in their remarks. One can detect in many of the criticisms a longing for the spirit that had existed in 1949, when these people thought that they might have not only a truly meaningful role to play in the building of a new China but also a part in determining what that role should be.

A prominent PWDP member asserted, "In leading the masses to carry through the revolution in the past, the Party stood among the masses; after the liberation, it felt the position had changed and, instead of standing among the masses, it stood on the back of the masses and ruled the masses. . . . Government cadres should differ in duties, not in status."[20] Lo Lung-chi, who, along with Chang Po-chün, was one of the principal targets of the anti-rightist drive that followed, said that if the democratic parties and groups hoped to exist together with the Communist Party in the long run, three problems should be tackled: how to develop these organizations, how to give them a part in policy-making conferences, and how to strengthen the role of their basic-level components.[21] Chang Po-chün was quoted as saying, "I admired very much the Polish democratic parties after the October [1956] Incident because they managed to take action. I felt that in the past the CCP exercised too tight

[c] The Hundred Flowers movement gave rise to an extensive literature. Perhaps the best survey of the range and variety of criticism is found in Roderick MacFarquhar, *The Hundred Flowers Campaign and the Chinese Intellectuals* (New York: Praeger, 1960).

a control over the democratic parties. This was particularly so with local organizations. Cadres were chosen by the Party on their behalf, much to my dissatisfaction."[22] During the same brief moment of relaxation, the Chiu-san Society informed local chapters that "in the membership expansion work, it will not be necessary to refer everything to the [local CCP] committees for decision."[23]

The Party leaders had not anticipated this kind of response. Proponents of the Hundred Flowers, including Mao himself, had persuaded themselves that genuine acceptance of the Party, patriotism, and removal of the BDP's class basis would, naturally, produce constructive comment and criticism. Once the Party realized what had happened, it moved to stem the tide of bitterness it had loosed. The BDP "should not reflect the bourgeois inclinations and demands of these people. That is to say, they should not represent those interests . . . that go against the laws of historical development."[24] Both doctrinally and organizationally, the BDP had gone wrong:

> It has been proved by the facts that once they deviate from the Communist Party leadership, the democratic parties are bound to lose their bearings, go in the direction opposed to socialism, and lose the confidence of the people and the possibility for long-term coexistence. To rely on the leftists, unite and teach the middle-of-the-roaders to turn to the left, isolate and disintegrate the rightists, and serve socialism truly under the leadership of the Communist Party—this is the only correct line and the only outlet for the democratic parties. Only thus can there be long-term coexistence and mutual supervision.[25]

The policy was retained in name, but the attempted synthesis had proved itself a failure.

The Divergence between Theory and Practice

The rectification and anti-rightist movement following the Hundred Flowers lasted into the summer of 1958, then gradually began to diminish. By the end of 1958, and through the following two years, most of those designated "rightists" were removed from this category, and freed from the disabilities it entailed.[d] In 1959 and 1960, in fact, a restricted version of the Hundred Flowers (still known by that flawed title) was cautiously revived.[26] The outstanding characteristic of this "movement" is its attempt to divorce politics from other aspects of the life and activity of the intellectuals, and to allow a greater latitude in the latter than in the former. This is fundamentally different from the approach employed in the 1957 Hundred Flowers movement, which was based on the assumption that both aspects could develop in harmony and with mutual reinforcement. The new approach is an admission that the intellectual cannot be successfully made both red and expert. But his participation is still needed, and this is an attempt to utilize his professional knowledge while leaving political matters to the Party. To some extent, then, this policy is an admission of defeat—the development of a genuine sense of dedication among the intellectuals has apparently failed on the crucial issue of support for and faith in the leadership of the Chinese Communist Party. That nearly all intellectuals are performing important tasks determined ultimately by the Party, that they must and do work hard, and that they still feel pride of nation need not be questioned. But the CCP wanted far more than this, and has apparently failed to get it.

Meanwhile, the apparatus of the united front (the UFWD, the BDP, and the CPPCC) continues to function, but at present there is hardly any pretense that it has important tasks to perform. These agencies and groups are rarely mentioned in the Chinese press; and when they are, the notices are perfunctory and vague. Several of the BDP held general meetings in October 1960.[27] Hsien meetings in Hopei and Kiangsu during March 1962 had unspecified united-front problems on their agendas.[28] In June 1965, the Kwangtung provincial UFWD held an informal meeting, attended by local CPPCC and minor-party delegates. They were addressed by T'ao Chu, but otherwise there is no indication of what was discussed.[29]

There is no way of knowing how large the BDP are at present, but one might speculate that their recruitment rate is offset by their

[d] *PR*, 26–58 (Aug. 26, 1958), p. 4. On January 3, 1960, after many rightists had already been reinstated, a wholesale lot of 26,000 was removed from the list.

mortality rate. Since the BDP rarely recruit younger people, their "related masses," too, are doubtless declining in vigor, usefulness, and numbers.[e]

The BDP and the UFWD were given little credit, publicly at least, when Li Tsung-jen, former Acting President of the Republic of China and a long-time exile in the United States, returned to the mainland in July 1965. UFWD and BDP functionaries were well down the list of those who welcomed and feted Li upon his return.[30] This was the occasion for a number of public appeals to "KMT personnel in Taiwan" in which Hsü Ping, Ts'ai T'ing-k'ai (RCKMT), and others affirmed that "all patriots, both forerunners and latecomers, belong to the same family . . . freedom of movement is guaranteed both to and from the motherland." Courteous treatment was promised.[31] But the united front, as such, was not mentioned. Little has been heard from Li Tsung-jen since.

The structure of the central and regional UFWD remains much as in the past, though Li Wei-han was purged from his post as Director in March 1965. He was replaced by the 64-year-old Hsü Ping.[32] The cause of Li's ouster is not known, but it has been suggested that it may have been in connection with the Socialist Education Campaign.[33] It is also possible that Li had been under a cloud since the Hundred Flowers fiasco. In any case, prior to his removal, he had already lost his positions as Vice-Chairman of the CPPCC and member of the Standing Committee of the National People's Congress. He was elected as an NPC delegate from Sinkiang, and has been reportedly involved in minorities work.[34] A few new men have been appointed to the UFWD: Hsüeh Tzu-cheng (a Szechwanese who studied for a time in Russia; vice-mayor of Peking, 1955–57); Liu Ch'un (Kiangsi; extensive nationalities work, especially in Inner Mongolia); Fang Fang (Kwangtung; active in military, underground, and united-front work in the Fukien-Kwangtung areas; many posts in Canton municipal government and prominent in overseas Chinese work); Chin Ch'eng (Hopei; previous

[e] During the Hundred Flowers period, Lo Lung-chi had said that the BDP were allowed to recruit only among "old-style" intellectuals (*NCNA*, May 10, 1957).

work was in propaganda and a variety of miscellaneous government posts); Liu Shu-chou (active mainly in Shanghai, where he was Director of the Shanghai Municipal UFWD); Li Chin-te (virtually no information).[35]

Very few of these men hold significant positions outside the UFWD, the NPC, and the CPPCC (with the exception of Hsü Ping, who ranks as 49th alternate in the Eighth Central Committee). Liu Ch'un is a member of the Nationalities Work Commission, and Fang Fang is a member of the Overseas Chinese Commission (it is interesting to note that the heads of these two government commissions, Ulanfu and Liao Ch'eng-chih respectively, are both much higher in the Party structure than the head of the Central Committee's UFWD). Thus it would appear that from a career standpoint, the UFWD is a dead end. Throughout its history, only one person who has been associated with the UFWD—K'o Ch'ing-shih, who died in 1965—has reached, or seemed likely to reach, the very top echelons of the Party. In K'o's case, his association with the UFWD was brief and was almost certainly not the cause of his rapid rise in the early 1960's. As for Ch'en Shao-yü and Li Wei-han, they had both already passed the zenith of their career when they became associated with the UFWD. Thus it seems that though united-front work may be important, united-front workers are not. Perhaps the Party feels they may have been contaminated by those with whom they have come in contact.

This decline in the practical use of the united front, however, is not paralleled by an equivalent decline in united-front theory—except in the sense that the process of ideological abstraction and historical placement empties the united front of much of its specific content. In 1956, during the first stages of the Hundred Flowers movement, and more clearly after Mao's address of February 27, 1957, the united front was placed in a fuller and more rigorous theoretical setting. Instead of remaining simply an outgrowth of certain Chinese peculiarities, the united front was raised to a new level of theoretical abstraction by the theory of contradictions. Much of this had been anticipated earlier, but it was now given systematic statement.

Mao's theory argues that at any moment, in nature or in society, there exist many contradictions, not just a simple thesis and antithesis. But in each realm of existence there is always a principal contradiction, not only more important than the other contradictions, but also different in kind. All lesser contradictions may be repressed, and their resolutions postponed; but this cannot be done with the principal contradiction, which must be resolved through the force of transformation. The principal contradiction cannot be resolved easily or without struggle; therefore, it sooner or later becomes an "antagonistic" contradiction—in contrast to "non-antagonistic" contradictions, which can be peacefully solved or suspended, at least temporarily. After this principal contradiction has been resolved, a new one arises to take its place, and it, in turn, must be resolved through struggle and violence. For example, the contradiction between capitalism and socialism exists even before the contradiction between capitalism and feudalism has been fully overcome. The first cannot come to the fore so long as feudalism still exists; in fact, feudalism's antagonistic opposition to both the capitalist and the worker will prevent the sharpening of the conflict between them.

In China, the principal "contradiction" was imperialist exploitation, particularly direct Japanese aggression. Mao is credited with understanding that Japanese aggression transformed the class and party contradictions in China, forcing them into a subordinate and non-antagonistic status. The result was, according to this theory, the determination of the CCP to form a united front against the Japanese, even including such former enemies as Chiang Kai-shek and the KMT. The antagonistic contradiction with Japan required not only the suspension of civil war and class struggle, but also a positive effort to gain the support or neutrality of elements that might otherwise have gone over to the enemy. The defeat of Japan, far from bringing an end to struggle, meant that a new contest—between the CCP with its supporters, and the KMT—became the principal and antagonistic contradiction. Internationally, the United States represented to the CCP the source of antagonistic contradiction, for its support of the KMT and for its containment of international Communism.

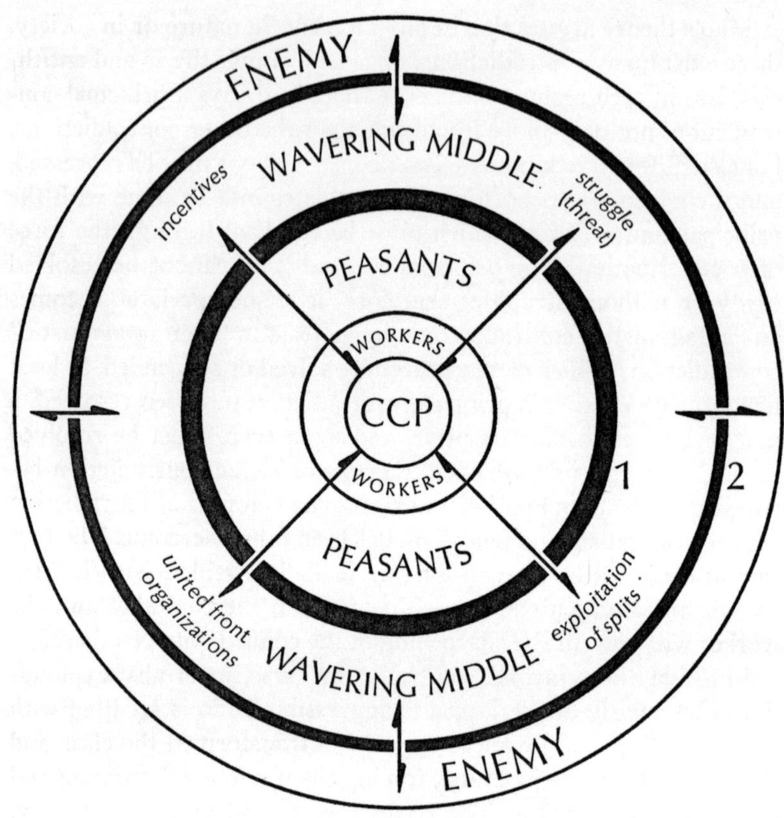

Representation of the CCP's Concept of the United Front as Part of the Theory of Contradictions

The numeral 1 indicates the boundary of the basic worker-peasant alliance, led by the CCP; 2 indicates the outer limit of "the people," i.e., the outer limit of the united front and the limit within which contradictions are non-antagonistic. The arrows indicate pressures or influences acting upon the middle group; notice that the middle group can either stay on the side of "the people" or go over to "the enemy." The identity of those in the outer two circles (middle and enemy) will change according to circumstances; all parts of this structure are always present; the enemy should not comprise more than 10 per cent of the population, preferably less.

After the establishment of the People's Republic, the principal contradiction in China was the feudalism of the landlords, followed by that of the bourgeoisie. But because the national bourgeoisie, like other Chinese, had suffered imperialist exploitation, its outlook was not inevitably capitalist. The national bourgeoisie, in spite of its class, had a revolutionary side. Therefore, the contradiction between the laboring classes (workers, peasants) and the bourgeoisie, though potentially antagonistic, could be resolved non-antagonistically, so long as the bourgeoisie exhibited its revolutionary and not its capitalist side.

In short, the composition of a united front is determined by the nature of the enemy, and includes all those whose contradictions can be treated "non-antagonistically." Another way of putting it is that the united front consists of all those considered to belong to "the people." Mao's speech in February 1957, growing out of a historical experience in which the Party had exercised leadership over diverse segments of the population, affirmed that "within the people" there were contradictions, but that they were all non-antagonistic and could therefore be resolved without an uncompromising struggle "between the enemy and ourselves."

Nevertheless, all components of the "united front of the whole Chinese people" are not on an equal footing. Instead the Party thinks of a series of concentric circles, which can be illustrated graphically. The wavering middle group (classically, the bourgeoisie) can go either way because of its dual nature: over to the enemy and antagonistic contradiction, or over to the side of the people. As in the war against Japan and in the agrarian reform movement CCP alliance with the middle may be crucially important. But leadership is always exercised by the Party on the basis of the unbreakable worker-peasant alliance. However far this approach departs from reality, it provides a flexible instrument for the analysis of society. It recognizes the existence of social conflict within a socialist state, yet places it at a level below overt and violent class struggle.

Mao set forth this theory of antagonistic and non-antagonistic contradictions prior to the outburst of criticism in 1957; a nearly unbroken stream of writings concerning the theoretical and historical place of the united front continued from that time to about 1962. It was, therefore, *after* the Hundred Flowers and the anti-rightist drive, when united-front practice seemed fatally compromised, that the most extensive, thoroughgoing, and detailed statements of united-front theory were written.[36]

The writings of Chang Chih-i, particularly his major work, *A Tentative Discussion of the Chinese People's Democratic United Front,* are cast explicitly in terms of Mao's theory of antagonistic and non-antagonistic contradictions within the people. He discusses the history of the united front from 1920 onward; but as he moves past 1949, he becomes gradually less specific and more abstract. Looking past the present to the future, he asks and answers the following question: "Does it violate Marxism-Leninism to use the method of the people's democratic united front—that is, to use this special weapon of class warfare, peaceful transformation, to realize the socialist revolution—in order to achieve the goal of complete liquidation of the exploiting classes? . . . This special form of the class struggle is not only entirely compatible with the principles of Marxism-Leninism, but is a creative development."[37]

The same line was taken by Li Wei-han. The most extensive of his treatises, "The Struggle for Proletarian Leadership in the Period of the New-Democratic Revolution in China," is almost entirely historical, though it is cast in the form of illustrations of general principles. But when he discusses the tasks of the united front in the present, he seems less sure of himself:

> Some think that the united front is unnecessary if we want to carry on the proletarian dictatorship and build socialism. They don't understand that we have a long history of maintaining a united front with the national bourgeoisie, the democratic parties, and other patriots. In the socialist stage, despite their negative side of trying to take the capitalist road, the national bourgeoisie are willing to remain in the united front and accept socialist transformation. *Therefore, we have no reason not to continue to co-operate with them.* Besides, the national bourgeoisie is a class which possesses relatively rich knowledge and culture and a relatively large number of intellectuals and specialists. The working

> class should continue to maintain the united front with the national bourgeoisie, because the united front will play an important role in educating and reforming them and because their knowledge can be made use of to serve socialism, while the enemy can be isolated to the maximum and the anti-imperialist forces can be strengthened.[38]

It is this task, the individual remolding of the self, that Li defines as the function of the united front in the present. "When self-education and self-remolding is well carried out, the united front is enabled to forge ahead, consolidate itself further, and shoulder the revolutionary tasks . . . still more satisfactorily."[39] Moreover, "One can foresee that China's people's democratic united front will continue to be strengthened and keep on developing until classes disappear and Great Harmony reigns."[40]

Internationally, the concept of the united front has been proclaimed, but has been much more difficult to act upon; it has, however, created a kind of symmetry between Chinese experience and the world as a whole. Until the Sino-Soviet split put an end to it, the Chinese often expressed this symmetry by equating the socialist world, led by the Soviet Union, with the solid core alliance; the capitalist-imperialist nations with the enemy; and the Afro-Asian world with the intermediate forces. This view perhaps reached its height at the time of the Bandung Conference. But the world was too complicated, or too unresponsive, for this sort of united front, and the growing rifts in the core alliance meant that it was not really an appropriate way of seeing the world revolution.

More recently, and especially in Lin Piao's famous speech, the symmetry has been reestablished by seeing the world as an enormous China, with China and other anti-revisionist socialist states corresponding to the base areas in the interior; the capitalist-imperialist nations as the modernized but decadent cities of the coast, which control and exploit parts of the hinterland; and everywhere "the people," comprising 90 per cent of the population, waiting for their liberation. Eventually, the revolution will take the course in the world that it took in China proper. More and more "base areas" will be created by wars of national liberation; the rulers of the United States and its allies will be more and more isolated, both from without and from within. Finally, the countryside will overwhelm the cities.

It is within the model of wars of national liberation that the united front today has its principal theoretical application on the international level. This model, the Chinese believe, is that developed by Mao and successfully tested in the Chinese revolution. It is based on the same tripartite strategy that we have seen so often before: the weapons of armed struggle and the united front, wielded by a militant Marxist-Leninist party.[41]

Conclusion

During the course of its development, the united front has grown from tactic to strategy to ideology. In all stages of its evolution, it has had some influence on the way Chinese Communist leaders view their experience and attempt to apply its lessons. But many observers have noted the decline in recent years of the united front as applied to concrete problems. Possibly, Peking could argue that now, with the period of the New Democracy long since replaced by the period of transition to socialism, the united front (a characteristic feature of the revolution's bourgeois-democratic stage) no longer has any function. There is no question that the CCP could dismantle the organizational structure of the united front at any time. If it has not chosen to do so, I think we must ask why.

On a practical level, in so totally structured a society, if the CCP abolished the UFWD, the BDP, and the CPPCC, other organizations would be required. The Party would certainly not permit their members to remain unorganized and hence outside the system. Since these bodies do exist, and have a history and a tradition of sorts, the Party might just as well use them. The argument that the minor parties are permitted to exist as deceptive window dressing to fool people into thinking that China is a democracy can have no validity. It might once have had some force; but since the early 1950's, the CCP has been more forthright in this area than the deception argument implies, and normal human beings are not quite so easily misled. Therefore, the real explanation for continuing the united front must lie elsewhere than in the maintenance of a good international image, or in an attempt to fool the people.

The real reasons for continuing the united front probably have more to do with the self-image of the Party leaders and their sense of justification than with any immediate practical problem that the united front may help to solve. First, there is the matter of nationalism, with which the united front is inextricably connected. We have seen that the Party uses the united front as one form of expression of its patriotism; by asserting that the united front includes all patriotic Chinese, and by insisting that the Party leads the united front, it equates support of the Party with nationalism. The leaders of the CCP are themselves influenced by the image they project for others. They, too, feel the claim of nationalism. The continuation of the united front, with its strong nationalistic connotation, thus reassures them at the same time that it proclaims their patriotism to others.

One part of this sense of nationalism is the Party's view of its place in Chinese history. It sees this history as unique, though governed generally by Marxist laws of social development. China's "historical peculiarities" have required the creative application of the universal truths of Marxism-Leninism to the concrete problems of the Chinese revolution. In modern times, the most important of these historical peculiarities has been the effect of imperialism, differentiating China and the colonial areas from Russia and the West. Therefore, the united front is seen as one manifestation of China's individuality, and of the relevance of her experience for all parts of the world that have been affected by imperialism.

The united front is not only a part of the past history of the revolutionary movement in China but also part of that process in the present and the future: "The democratic method, the method of unity-criticism or struggle-unity, is the method of handling contradictions among the people; it is also the method of the united front. Through the people's democratic united front, we are able to adopt various ways to unite with the people of the various democratic classes on a very wide basis; we are also able to help people carry on self-education and self-remolding in many ways."[1]

The CCP has thought in united-front terms for so long, and it has applied this kind of analysis to various situations so frequently, that the approach has become a habitual, almost instinctive, cast of mind. It even penetrates light conversation, as when Mao Tse-tung was telling Edgar Snow about his early life: "There were two 'parties' in the family. One was my father, the Ruling Power. The Opposition was made up of myself, my mother, my brother, and sometimes even the laborer. In the 'United Front' of the Opposition, however, there was a difference of opinion. My mother advocated a policy of indirect attack. She criticized any overt display of emotion and attempts at open rebellion against the Ruling Power. She said it was not the Chinese way."[2] Chou En-lai was more explicit when he wrote: "In the course of social development, people often generally fall in their thinking and standpoint into three categories—the progressive, the intermediate, and the backward—and often divide themselves into leftists, those in the middle, and the rightists. This is not an artificial classification. It is determined by the objective law of social development and the objective law of development of man's thinking."[3]

Another evidence of this phenomenon is the persistent statement that the enemy—whatever enemy is being described at the moment—always represents no more than 6 to 10 per cent of the total population. This is sometimes meant to be descriptive—for example, when Mao and Lin Piao state that 90 per cent of the world's peoples oppose American imperialism, or that in colonial wars of national liberation, the united front can and should comprise 90 per cent of the population. Sometimes it is used prescriptively, as in the land-reform and Wu-fan campaigns. In his 1956 report, Chou En-lai classified the intellectuals as active (40%), fairly active (40%), backward (10%), and reactionary (10%).[4] This is once again the left-middle-right/enemy breakdown that is the hallmark of the united-front frame of mind. Most recently, in the "Communiqué of the 11th Plenary Session of the Eighth Central Committee," this view of the distribution of society appeared in both the "domestic" and "international" sections. Domestic: "Give enthusiastic support to the revolutionary Left, take care to strive to unite with all those who can be united, and concentrate our forces to strike at the handful of anti-Party, anti-socialist bourgeois Rightists." International: "In order to isolate U.S. imperialism to the maximum and deal blows to it, the broadest possible international united front must be established against U.S. imperialism and its lackeys. The Soviet revisionist leading group . . . has been conducting splittist, disruptive, and subversive activities. . . . They cannot of course be included in this united front."[5]

Mao Tse-tung sees himself (and the Party he has sought to create) as the leader who sets the goals and lays down the main lines of policy. The rest of the population, excepting only a small minority of enemies, participates voluntarily because it is genuinely and enthusiastically committed to the goals that the Party has set. Countless statements in these terms show how strong and how necessary to Mao is his self-image as the leader of the great unity of the Chinese people. The contrary condition, "isolation from the masses," is more than just the separation of the leaders from the led; it implies a loss of legitimacy and a drying up of the revolutionary spirit, which can come only from the creative enthusiasm of the masses.

Thus the significance of continued affirmation of the united front now lies primarily in its symbolic value to the Party itself, and much less in the organizational relation of Party to non-Party. Historically, the united front justified CCP leadership of the revolutionary process; in the present it links this history with the concept of the non-antagonistic unity of the Chinese people and their movement under the Party toward a Communist society.

The united front may have become largely irrelevant to concrete problems within China. It may have become somewhat formalized and dogmatic at the theoretical level. Even with respect to wars of national liberation, it is as much metaphorical as operational. But to call an end to the united front after all these years would suggest that the vision of unity is only a shattered illusion, and that the Party does not have the capacity to rally the masses around itself. Despite what may be growing doubts as he nears the end of his life, this is an admission that Mao Tse-tung cannot make to himself. He must continue to believe that he can distinguish his masses of true friends and rally them to strike at his handful of enemies. As long as Mao's conception of the Chinese revolution endures, the united front will remain a part of the CCP's view of modern Chinese history, of its place in that history, and of its self-image as the leader of China's—and the world's—peoples.

Appendixes

The Expansion of United Front Work

[A directive issued by the Secretariat of the CCP Central Committee on August 5, 1940. My translation of a secret, inner-Party document.]

I. In accordance with the decision of July 7th, it is necessary to broadly expand united front work. In friendly armies, enlargement of the work of making friendships is necessary to win over the 2 million members of these friendly armies to continued resistance to Japan. In the making of friendships, there have been absolutely no achievements. You must accept a severe reprimand from the Party, and you must examine your work on the basis of this decision.

II. During the past three years, some local party bureaus and military forces have basically neglected this work. Especially since the Kuomintang began carrying out its anti-Communist policy, many cadres —even including some leading cadres—have come to feel that the Kuomintang and the Central Armies are all diehards, and that our line is one of opposition, struggle, and preparation for a split. They have not investigated the inner workings of the Kuomintang and the Central Armies, or their actual conditions; they have not investigated the attitudes and actions of various social strata, or the prior social relationships of the cadres themselves (in order to utilize these relationships to expand the work of making friendships). They have investigated neither the conditions of propaganda work nor the organization of the united front. They have not exercised guidance over the organs of the united front (United Front Bureaus or Liaison Bureaus) and working personnel, nor have they examined them and kept them up to the mark. Everyone feels there is nothing to be done, including the basic failure to even set up this kind of organ. Some people regard the numerous directives of the Central Committee that call for the strengthening of the united front as prattle, gobbledygook that makes little sense. They just wait for the war to end, or have lost hope and sit pessimistically with folded hands and empty heads.

All of these conditions exist to a serious degree in our Party and in our Eighth Route and New Fourth Armies. As a consequence, a great many local reports to the Central Committee contain only war reports or reports on other work, but very rarely, if ever, a report on united front work. At this time, the Central Committee strongly calls this to your attention. Wherever the mistaken phenomena described above exist, you must, within the Party, carry out self-criticism, generalize the experience and lessons of the past three years, advance the areas of achievement, and rectify the areas of error. The Central Committee is presently waiting for a general report from you on united front work—especially emphasizing work with respect to friendly armies—to be issued, via telegraphic transmission, within a month of receiving this directive.

III. Investigation of the problem of policies toward friendly parties, friendly armies, and the various classes and strata is a central problem for cadres at all levels, especially at middle and higher levels. If there are to be correct policies, there must be a correct understanding that will enable us and our cadres to reflect correctly the concrete facts of the various friendly parties and armies, and of the various classes. In actual situations to date, a great many cadres have had no correct comprehension of true conditions in the various parties, groups, armies, and circles of the contemporary united front, or of what their intentions, policies, directions, and methods may be at any given moment and in any given matter. Some are always in a fog, neither hearing nor asking; some are slipshod and lax, not seeking full details. Basically, the minds of these comrades have not been transformed to think politically and tactically.

If we do not clear up this situation, we will not be able to deal with the great international and domestic changes that will come in the future. Consequently, we must change this situation; we must intensify the tactical education of the cadres. And the principal method for this kind of tactical education is to guide the cadres in a discriminating investigation of the concrete conditions of the various parties, groups, armies, and circles, and of their intentions, policies, methods, and directions at any given time and in any given matter.

IV. Great international and domestic changes will come in the future, and our whole Party must be prepared, spiritually and organizationally. The correct policy of the united front is the guarantee of attaining victory. In 19 years of struggle, our Party has made a magnificent record. But it has also made serious errors. In the Period of the Great Revolution, there was Ch'en Tu-hsiu's error of rightist opportunism, which was all coalition and denied struggle. In the Period of the Agrarian Revolution, there was the error of Li Li-san's leftist opportunism in the Soviet and White areas, which was all upheaval and denied coalition with certain possible elements outside of the workers and peasants. As a result of these two errors, the Great Revolution failed, and the Agrarian Revolution suffered heavy losses. We are now in the third period, and we must generalize our past experience in order to avoid the errors of the first two periods. Tactically, with regard to the various parties, groups, armies, and circles, we only oppose the small minority who at present are directly attacking us, and ally with the vast majority of middle and progressive elements, thereby crushing one by one those obstinately capitulationist and anti-Communist groups. Therefore, to utilize contradictions to win over the majority in order to oppose the minority, and to crush them one by one, is a correct tactical line of Leninism-Stalinism.

The Organization and Work of United Front Bureaus

[A directive issued by the United Front Work Department of the Central Committee on November 2, 1940. My translation of a secret, inner-Party document.]

Because the organization and work of United Front Departments is a new problem in the Party, we do not have historical traditions and sufficient accumulated experience for reference. Therefore, though the whole Party has already been doing united front work for several years, at present many local Party bureaus still have incorrect or unclear ideas about the questions of organization and work of United Front Departments, which leads to unsoundness in united-front organization, and to weakness in work. The United Front Work Department of the Central Committee specially issues the following directive.

I

In connection with the question of United Front Departments and United Front Committees: According to materials presently available, many localities simply have individual comrades concurrently responsible for united front work; or else, although there may be a United Front Department and responsible persons, there is no sound united-front organization. In some areas it is even true that the Party Committee pays no attention to questions of united front work. In view of these undesirable phenomena, it has been specifically decided that:

A. From the Central Committee down through Provincial Committees or Regional Committees, United Front Departments must be established. In general, the United Front Department can be divided into the following sections: (1) Party-Group Section, which will be responsible for carrying on united front work among various parties and groups, local gentry, well-known cultural figures, etc.; (2) Friendly Armies Section, which will be responsible for carrying on united front work among the regular army and local armed forces; (3) United Front Cadre Section, which will be responsible for the Party members and non-Party cadres who carry on and handle united front work. But in an environment requiring secrecy, sections may be dispensed with; and under the United Front Department the establishment of Functional Operatives may be considered. In regions where there are no friendly armies, Friendly Army Sections or Friendly Army Operatives naturally will not be established.

B. Hsien Committees and Municipal Committees will decide whether or not to set up United Front Departments or United Front Functional Operatives in accordance with the working environment and with the target groups among which they are located.

C. In order to discuss and investigate problems of united-front policy, a United Front Problems Committee may be set up in addition to the United Front Department. Aside from the main responsible persons in the United Front Department, it should include and bring into participation responsible comrades from cultural, youth, and women's [activities]. In areas where we have armies and political power, army and government personnel must participate. In a secret environment, United Front Committees certainly cannot be set up. When various problems of united-front policy are encountered, they must be raised in the Party Committee for discussion and decision.

D. Whether or not a United Front Committee is organized, all responsible persons in the local United Front Department must regularly confer with the Secretary of the Party Committee on problems of united front work, and carry on work according to his directives. Important united-front problems must be raised with the Party Committee for discussion and decision.

II

In connection with the question of cadres in united front work: Many local Party Committees do not pay attention to seeking out and cultivating cadres for united front work, and in some regions even united front work itself is lightly regarded. To have cadres of poor quality doing united front work is incorrect. From now on, attention must be paid to the following points concerning the question of united front cadres:

A. As a result of the complex and important nature of united front work, it is necessary to be very careful in the selection and cultivation of united front cadres. The local Organization Department must constantly see to it that Party members with comparatively good social connections in the middle and upper strata are, so far as possible, requested to do united front work. United front cadres should have the following characteristics: a loyal and steadfast political viewpoint, an alert and decisive line, full and definite social experience, a diligent and simple life, a persevering and indomitable style of work, and an earnest and modest attitude in dealings with others.

B. In order to develop united front work widely, it is necessary, apart from Party-member cadres, to systematically and constantly seek out non-Party members who are politically genuinely sympathetic to serving our Party, to cultivate them patiently, and to employ them correctly.

C. In order to carry out secret work, united front Party and non-Party cadres must adopt a control system going beyond a given level; i.e., at the hsien level, important cadres carrying on friendly party, friendly army, or cultural work will revert to the control of the Provincial United Front Department; provincial level will revert to the control of the Central Committee or the Central Committee Branch United Front Departments. And particularly important persons connected with the united front in friendly parties and friendly armies should directly revert to the control of the responsible person in the Central Committee United Front Department. Under conditions of secrecy, control methods should strictly adhere to the following principles: (1) the separation of cadres engaged in overt and covert work; (2) the separation of Party and non-Party cadres; (3) the separation of upper levels from lower levels; (4) at each level, in connection with overt or covert united front work of Party members or non-Party members, apart from those who know each other very well, a control method of individual contacts and deliberations should be adopted, not a method of well-attended conferences; when questions are resolved, one should not let others know who is in contact with the Party; (5) Party-member united front cadres engaged solely in carrying on united front work will usually not participate in ordinary cell life; their party relations and united front work are moved up and controlled at higher levels.

III

In connection with the target groups and the scope of united front work (according to past experience, some regions limited united front work within a very narrow scope; some regions [omission in original] do not clearly recognize the targets of united front work): Hereafter it must be realized that the main targets of united front work ought to be each party and group (the Kuomintang, the Third Party, the National-Socialist Party, the National Salvation Association, the Vocational Education Society, the Livelihood Education Society, the Rural Education Society), every locally powerful clique, and every kind of friendly army. Contact with and winning over representative political and economic figures from all strata in each locality; contact with and winning over groups and leading figures in all circles (cultural, educational, news, women's affairs, youth, foreign affairs, business, science, religion, technical, social, secret groups, etc.) in each locality; contact with and winning over the gentry and members of each government agency (including *lien-pao* and *pao-chia*) in each locality—all these are targets of united front work and fall within its scope.

IV

In connection with the question of the methods of united front work (according to past experience in many places with methods of united front work, there exist a great many serious weak spots; hereafter these must be conscientiously rectified):

A. In the past there was a lack of conscientious investigation and deep understanding of the targets of united front work. We have to carry out a general analysis and have a general understanding of each party, group, stratum, friendly army, etc.; and we must carry out a many-sided, deep, and detailed investigation of the figures actually representative of each party, group, stratum, friendly army, agency, circle, and body. A detailed investigation and separate written record is to be made of these persons: name, age, native place, financial activities, history, changes in thought, political activities, habits, character, peculiarities, social relationships, etc. Without this kind of investigation and record, united front work will become empty and unrealistic.

B. In the past, initiative was often lacking in united front work. It was simply passive waiting, or a work style that said, "If they don't seek me out, I won't seek them out." Hereafter, initiative must be taken at all times and in all places to realize a work style that says, "If they don't seek me out, I must seek them out."

C. In the past, united front work often lacked regular planning: hence the phenomenon of looking for someone to help when something came up, but of paying no attention when nothing was happening. Hereafter, plans must be made for the regular seeking out of subjects with whom to build friendships.

D. In the past, the usual slant was toward political contacts; very rarely was conscientious work done to make friends, to the point of being extremely distant and unable to really work together. Hereafter, we must use all possible social connections (relatives and family, fellow townsmen, classmates, colleagues, etc.) and customs (sending presents, celebrating festivals, sharing adversities, mutual aid, etc.), not only to form political friendships with the subjects, but also to become personal friends with them, so that they will be completely frank and open with us.

E. In the past, our way of isolating diehard elements was simply to strike out mercilessly at all these elements. Hereafter, we must realize that the best way to isolate diehard elements is not merely to strike at the minority, but also to adopt various means of making contacts with various different diehard elements, thus involving them, fragmenting them, and winning them over.

F. In the past, the methods of winning over middle elements leaned heavily upon our political propaganda and our own requirements. Very rarely did we pay attention to the social position of the middle elements and to their immediate interests; we even caused some people to get the feeling they were being used. From now on, we must seriously and attentively protect the social position and concerns of the middle elements, share their adversities with them, and win them over to prolonged cooperation with us.

G. In the past, we have been earnestly helpful and protective toward the progressive forces under our direct leadership. From now on, we must be even more conscientious and sincere in the development of all kinds of progressive forces, taking their concerns as our common concerns, and their victories and defeats as our own victories and defeats.

H. In the past, our trust in non-Party cadres was insufficient, and we were not good at working with them. Hereafter we must respect their political positions, trust them to undertake certain jobs, not viewing them in the same way we do Party cadres, and, when working with them, create an atmosphere of mutual help and solicitude.

V

In connection with the question of reports on united front work: With the exception of some Party bureaus, very rarely have there been special reports relating to united front work [several illegible characters]. Every Central Committee Branch and directly subordinate Provincial Committee will either prepare such a report within a month or radio the Central Committee. The Central Committee United Front Work Department charges each Central Committee Branch hereafter to report on united front work to the Central Committee every six months. The conditions for advancing united front work in the present situation demand that the whole Party strengthen united front work. Consequently, to generalize the experience and lessons of united-front organization and united front work has profound political significance for the future development of united front work. After this directive is received in each locality, it is hoped that it will immediately be discussed in detail, and that the results of the discussion and the means of implementation will be reported to higher levels.

On Policy

[This is an internal Party directive written on behalf of the Central Committee of the Chinese Communist Party and issued on December 25, 1940. Minor stylistic changes have been made in spelling and punctuation; otherwise, the text follows the translation of *SW,* II, 441–40.]

IN THE PRESENT anti-Communist upsurge, the policy we adopt has a decisive significance. But many of our cadres still do not realize that there is a great difference between the Party's present policy and its policy during the Agrarian Revolution. It must be understood that throughout the Anti-Japanese War, whatever the circumstances, the Party's policy of an Anti-Japanese National United Front will never change; and that many policies pursued during the ten years of the Agrarian Revolution should no longer be applied uncritically. In particular, we must adopt none of the many ultra-Left policies of the latter period of the Agrarian Revolution, which are not only totally inapplicable today in the Anti-Japanese War, but were erroneous even at that time and resulted from the failure to realize the two basic features of the Chinese revolution—its being a bourgeois-democratic revolution in a semi-colonial country and its protracted nature. Such policies included: the notion that the struggle between the Kuomintang's fifth campaign of "encirclement and annihilation" and our countercampaign against it was to be a decisive engagement between what is known as the revolutionary line and the counterrevolutionary line; the economic elimination of the bourgeoisie (the ultra-Left labor policy and tax policy) and of the rich peasants (allotting poor land to them); the physical elimination of the landlords (allotting no land to them); the persecution of the intellectuals; the "Left" deviation in cleaning up the counterrevolutionaries; the Communists' complete monopoly of government work; the inculcation of Communism in citizenship training; the ultra-Left military policy (seizure of big cities and rejection of guerrilla warfare); the adventurist policy in the work in the White areas; and the organizational policy of victimization within the Party. These ultra-Left policies, the very opposite of the Right opportunism under the leadership of Ch'en Tu-hsiu in the latter period of the First Great Revolution, are manifestations of the mistakes of "Left" opportunism. In the latter period of the First Great Revolution, the policy was one of all alliance and no struggle; whereas in the latter period of the Agrarian Revolution, it was all struggle and no alliance (except with the basic section of the peasantry). These are striking examples illustrating the two extremist policies. And both these extremist policies caused very serious losses to the Party and the revolution.

The present policy of the Anti-Japanese National United Front is neither one of all alliance and no struggle nor one of all struggle and no alliance, but is a policy which integrates alliance and struggle. Specifically speaking, it means the following:

(1) All the anti-Japanese people unite (or all the anti-Japanese workers, peasants, soldiers, intellectuals, and businessmen unite) to form an Anti-Japanese National United Front.

(2) The policy of independence and autonomy in the united front—there must be at one and the same time unity and independence.

(3) In military strategy, an independent and autonomous guerrilla war is to be carried out under a unified strategy; guerrilla warfare is basic, but mobile warfare should not be neglected when conditions are favorable.

(4) In the struggle against the anti-Communist diehards, we must take advantage of their contradictions in order to win over the majority, oppose the minority, and crush the enemies separately; it is a line of justifiability, expediency, and restraint.

(5) The policy in the enemy-occupied areas and in the Kuomintang-controlled areas is, on the one hand, to develop united front work to the greatest possible extent and, on the other, to conceal our crack forces; it is, in the matter of organization and of struggle, a policy of concealing our crack forces, lying long under cover, accumulating our strength, and biding our time.

(6) The basic policy as regards the class relations at home is to develop the progressive forces, win over the middle-of-the-road forces, and isolate the forces of the anti-Communist diehards.

(7) A revolutionary dual policy toward the anti-Communist diehards, i.e., a policy of uniting with them insofar as they are still willing to resist Japan, and of isolating them insofar as they are determined to oppose Communism. In their resistance to Japan, the diehards are again of a dual character: we adopt a policy of uniting with them insofar as they are still willing to resist Japan, and a policy of struggling against them and isolating them insofar as they vacillate (as in their secret dealings with the Japanese invaders and their lack of activity in opposing Wang Ching-wei and other collaborators). In their anti-Communism the diehards also reveal their dual character, and our policy should be one of a dual character too; i.e., insofar as they are still unwilling to bring about a final breakup of the Kuomintang-Commu-

nist cooperation, we adopt a policy of uniting with them, and insofar as they pursue a high-handed policy and make military offensives against our Party and the people, we adopt a policy of struggling against them and isolating them. Such people of a dual character are to be distinguished from collaborators and the pro-Japanese elements.

(8) Even among the collaborators and the pro-Japanese elements there are people of a dual character, toward whom we should also adopt a revolutionary dual policy. That is, insofar as they are pro-Japanese, we adopt a policy of dealing blows to them and isolating them; insofar as they are vacillating, we adopt a policy of drawing them nearer to us and winning them over. Such people of a dual character are to be distinguished from the determined collaborators like Wang Ching-wei, Wang I-t'ang, and Shih Yu-san.

(9) We must, on the one hand, distinguish the pro-Japanese section of the big landlords and the big bourgeoisie, which is opposed to resistance to Japan, from the pro-British and pro-American section of the big landlords and the big bourgeoisie, which stands for resistance to Japan; and we must, on the other hand, distinguish the big landlords and the big bourgeoisie who, being of a dual character, stand for resistance but vacillate and stand for solidarity but are anti-Communist, from the national bourgeoisie, the middle and small landlords, and the enlightened gentry whose dual character is less pronounced. We should formulate our policies on the basis of these distinctions. The diverse policies mentioned above are all based on the differences arising from the class relations.

(10) The same is true of our way of dealing with imperialism. Though the Communist Party is against all imperialists, yet we must, on the one hand, distinguish Japanese imperialism, which is invading China, from other imperialist powers which are not invading China; and, on the other, distinguish German and Italian imperialism, which has formed an alliance with Japan and recognized "Manchukuo," from British and American imperialism, which stands in opposition to Japan. Furthermore, we must distinguish the Britain and the United States of the past, which adopted a Munich policy for the Far East and undermined our resistance, from the Britain and the United States of today, which have abandoned such a policy and changed to the position of supporting China in her resistance to Japan. Our tactical principle remains one of exploiting the contradictions among them in order to win over the majority, oppose the minority, and crush the enemies separately. In foreign policy, we differ from the Kuomintang. The Kuomintang alleges, "There is only one enemy, while all the others are friends"; apparently treating all countries other than Japan on an equal basis, it is really pro-British and pro-American. But we should draw certain

distinctions: first, there is the distinction between the Soviet Union and the capitalist countries; secondly, there is the distinction between Britain and the United States, on the one hand, and Germany and Italy, on the other; thirdly, there is the distinction between the people of Britain and the United States, on the one hand, and the imperialist governments of Britain and the United States, on the other; and fourthly, there is the distinction between the Anglo-American policy during the Far East Munich period and that of the present period. We should formulate our policies on the basis of these distinctions. Our basic line, contrary to the Kuomintang's, is to utilize foreign aid to the fullest possible extent while upholding the principle of independent resistance and regeneration through our own efforts; and not, as the Kuomintang does, to rely upon foreign aid or sell our birthright to any imperialist bloc by giving up that principle.

The one-sided views of many cadres in the Party on tactical questions and the resulting deviations, now to the left and now to the right, cannot be overcome unless these cadres are enabled to have a comprehensive and unified understanding of the changes and developments in the Party's policy, past and present. The main danger in the Party at present is still the mischief done by a "Left" stand. In the Kuomintang-controlled areas, many fail to carry out seriously the policy of concealing our crack forces, lying long under cover, accumulating our strength, and biding our time because they do not take the Kuomintang's anti-Communist policy seriously; at the same time, there are many others who fail to carry out the policy of developing united front work, because, regarding the Kuomintang as utterly rotten, they are at a loss what to do. A similar state of affairs exists in the Japanese-occupied areas.

In the Kuomintang-controlled areas and in the various anti-Japanese base areas, some people, caring only about alliance and not about struggle and overestimating the Kuomintang's determination to resist Japan, have blurred the difference in principle between the Kuomintang and the Communist Party, denied the policy of independence and autonomy within the united front, become accommodating to the big landlords, the big bourgeoisie, and the Kuomintang, and, docilely letting themselves be bound hand and foot, have not dared freely to expand the anti-Japanese revolutionary forces and wage a resolute struggle against the Kuomintang's policy of opposing and containing Communism; such Right viewpoints, which once existed to a serious degree, are now basically overcome. However, since the winter of 1939, "Left" deviations have appeared in many quarters as a result of the Kuomintang's anti-Communist friction and the struggles we waged in self-defense. Rectified to a certain extent, these deviations have not yet been thoroughly eliminated and still manifest themselves in various specific policies in a number of places. It is therefore necessary to study and clarify various specific policies.

The Central Committee has time and again issued directives regarding various specific policies; only a few points are given here by way of a summary.

The organization of political power. We must resolutely put into practice the "tripartite system"—Communists should make up only one-third of the personnel in the organs of political power, so as to draw a large number of non-Communists to participate in them. In places like northern Kiangsu, where we are just beginning to establish organs of the anti-Japanese democratic political power, the number of Communists may even be less than one-third of the total. Whether in government organs or in people's representative bodies, the representatives of the petty bourgeoisie, the national bourgeoisie, and the enlightened gentry who are not actively anti-Communist must be induced to take part; and those Kuomintang members who are not anti-Communist must also be allowed to take part. We may also allow a small number of right-wingers to sit in the people's representative bodies. We must definitely avoid the monopolization of everything by our Party. We seek only to destroy the dictatorship of the big comprador bourgeoisie and the big landlord class, and not to replace it with a one-party dictatorship of the Communist Party.

Labor policy. The workers' enthusiasm in fighting Japan can be aroused only when their living conditions are improved. But we must by all means avoid "Left" deviations; we should not go to extremes in increasing wages and reducing working hours. Under China's present conditions, the eight-hour working day cannot yet be universally introduced, and in certain branches of production a ten-hour working day should still be permitted. In other branches of production, the working day is to be fixed according to the circumstances. Once a contract is drawn up between capital and labor, the workers must observe labor discipline and must allow the capitalists to make some profit. Otherwise factories will be closed down, and this would be detrimental not only to resistance to Japan but also to the workers themselves. In the matter of raising the wages and improving the living conditions of the workers in the rural areas, we must especially not make excessive demands on their behalf, or the peasants would protest, the workers would lose their jobs, and production would decline.

Agrarian policy. We must explain to our Party members and the peasants that it is not yet the time to carry out a thorough agrarian revolution, and that the whole set of measures taken during the Agrarian Revolution are inapplicable under present circumstances. Under the present policy, it ought to be laid down that, on the one hand, the landlords should reduce rent and interest, so that the basic sections of the peasant masses can be aroused to resist Japan actively; and, on the other, the reduction must not be excessive. The general principle as regards land rent is to carry out a 25 per cent reduction; if and when the masses demand an increase of the percentage, we may allow 60 or 70 per cent of the crop to go to the tenant farmer while allowing the rest to the landlords, but we must not exceed this limit. The rate of interest must not be reduced to the point of making credit transactions in the community impossible. On the other hand, we should lay it down that the peasants are to pay rent and interest, and that the landlords still retain their ownership of land and other property. The reduction of interest should not be such as to make it impossible for the peasants to obtain loans, nor the settlement of accounts be such as to enable the peasants to get back their mortgaged land gratis.

Tax policy. The rate of taxation must be fixed according to income. All people with an income—except the poorest, who ought to be declared exempt—in other words, more than 80 per cent of the inhabitants, including workers and peasants, must shoulder the burden of the taxes of the state, a burden which should not be laid exclusively on the landlords and the capitalists. The practice of securing provisions for the army by means of detaining people and imposing fines must be forbidden. As to the methods of taxation, before we have decided on new and more suitable ones, we may make use of the old methods of the Kuomintang with appropriate amendments.

Anti-espionage policy. We must resolutely suppress inveterate collaborators and anti-Communist elements; otherwise we cannot safeguard the anti-Japanese revolutionary forces. But we must not sentence too many people to death, and should take care not to incriminate any innocent person. We must be lenient in dealing with those reactionaries who are wavering and those who act under coercion. In the treatment of criminals, we must resolutely abolish torture and attach weight to evidence rather than uncritically believing depositions. In dealing with captives from the enemy troops, the puppet troops, or the anti-Communist troops, except those who are bitterly hated by the people and deserve nothing less than capital punishment and whose death sentence is approved by higher authorities, we must adopt the policy of setting all of them free. We should win over to our army as many as possible of such captives as have been compelled to join the reactionary forces and are more or less revolutionary; as to the rest, we should release them, and if they are captured again, set them free again; we should not insult them, search them for their personal effects, or exact confessions, but treat all of them sincerely and kindly. We should adopt this policy toward them no matter how reactionary they are. This is very effective in isolating the reactionary camp. We should give renegades, the most flagrant ones excepted, a chance to reform themselves on condition that they stop opposing Communism; if they can turn over a new leaf and rejoin the revolution, we shall accept them but not readmit them into the Party. We must not identify the ordinary intelligence personnel of the Kuomintang with Japanese spies and Chinese collaborators, but must draw an essential distinction between them and handle them accordingly. We should put an end to the state of confusion in which any office or organization is free to make arrests, and we must lay it down that, for the establishment of anti-Japanese revolutionary order, only a judicial or a public security organ of the government is empowered to make arrests, and an armed unit may do so only during combat.

The rights of the people. We must lay it down that all landlords and capitalists not opposed to resistance to Japan are to enjoy the same right of personal inviolability, and the right to vote, and the same freedom of speech, of assembly, of association, of thought, and of belief as the workers and peasants; for the government only interferes with those who organize sabotage or stage uprisings in our base areas, but gives protection to all others and does not interfere with them.

Economic policy. We must positively develop industry and agriculture, and promote trade. We must induce those capitalists outside our base areas who are willing to come here and start industries. We should encourage private enterprises and regard state-operated enterprises only as a part of the sum total of enterprises. All this is for the sake of achieving self-sufficiency. The destruction of any useful enterprise should be avoided. Both tariff policy and monetary policy should fit in with our basic policy of developing agriculture, industry, and commerce, and not run counter to it. To achieve self-sufficiency, we must organize the economy in the various base areas conscientiously and with minute care, rather than in a crude and sketchy way—that is the main link in maintaining such base areas over a long period of time.

Cultural and educational policy. This should center on promoting and propagating among the great masses of the people national self-esteem, as well as the knowledge and tactics for resisting Japan. We should allow bourgeois liberal educators, cultural workers, newspapermen, scholars, and technological experts to come to our base areas and cooperate with us, to start schools and newspapers, and to participate in our work. We should draw into our schools all intellectuals who show any activity in resisting Japan, give them a short-term training, and assign them to work in the army or government, or among civilians; we must throw off all reserve in drawing them in, assigning them work, and promoting them. We should not be overcautious, or afraid that reactionaries may sneak in. Some such persons will inevitably creep in, but there will be ample time to get rid of them in the course of their study and work. In every base area we must set up printing shops, publish books and newspapers, and organize distribution and transport agencies. In each base area we must, as far as possible, open large-scale schools for training cadres—the larger and the more numerous the better.

Military policy. We must expand the Eighth Route Army and the New Fourth Army in every possible way, because these are the Chinese people's most reliable armed forces in maintaining the national resistance to Japan. Toward the Kuomintang troops, we must continue to adopt the policy of "we will never attack unless attacked," and develop to the utmost the work of making friends with them. We must do our best to draw those Kuomintang or non-Party army officers who are sympathetic with us into the Eighth Route Army and the New Fourth Army, so as to strengthen the building of our army. The situation that Communists, by sheer weight of numbers, have exclusive control of everything in our army should now also be changed. Of course, the "tripartite system" should not be introduced in our main forces, but so long as the hegemony in the army remains in the hands of our Party (which is completely necessary and inviolable), we should not be afraid of drawing in large numbers of sympathizers to take part in a military or technological capacity in the building of our army. Now that the ideological and organizational foundation of both our Party and our army has been firmly laid, to draw in sympathizers (of course, not disrupters) is an essential policy because it is not only harmless but also indispensable for winning the sympathy of the whole people and expanding our revolutionary forces.

The various tactical principles in the united front mentioned above and the concrete policies formulated in accordance with them should be resolutely carried out by the whole Party. At a time when the Japanese invaders are intensifying their aggression upon China and when the big landlords and the big bourgeoisie at home are carrying out their anti-Communist, anti-popular, high-handed policies and military attacks, it is only by putting into effect the abovementioned tactical principles and concrete policies that we can maintain the resistance to Japan, develop the united front, gain the sympathy of the whole people, and bring about a favorable turn in the situation. In rectifying mistakes, however, we must proceed step by step, and not with such undue haste as to occasion discontent among the cadres, suspicion among the masses, counter-attacks from the landlords, and other undesirable developments.

Notes

Notes

Full authors' names, titles, and publication data for all works cited in the Notes will be found in the Bibliography, pp. 299–311. Titles followed by "CCP" and a number, both in brackets, will be found in the Bibliography under Chung-kuo kung-ch'an-tang (Chinese Communist Party) documents. The abbreviation *SW* refers to the Peking Foreign Language Press edition of Mao Tse-tung's Selected Works, unless the Note indicates otherwise. The following abbreviations are used in the Notes:

CB	*Current Background*
CQ	*China Quarterly*
JMJP	*Jen-min jih-pao*
KMJP	*Kuang-ming jih-pao*
NCNA	*New China News Agency*
PC	*People's China*
PR	*Peking Review*
RHKCP	*Review of the Hong Kong Chinese Press*
SCMP	*Survey of the China Mainland Press*
SW	*Selected Works of Mao Tse-tung*

Introduction

1. "Introducing *The Communist,*" *SW,* II, 288. The original text of the article, very greatly altered in *SW,* is in *Kung-ch'an-tang jen,* No. 1 (Oct. 4, 1939), pp. 1–10.
2. "On the People's Democratic Dictatorship," *SW,* IV, 422.
3. Lin Piao, "Long Live the Victory of the People's War," *Peking Review,* No. 36 (Sept. 3, 1965), pp. 12–14.

Chapter 1

1. For descriptions of the inception of Communism in China, see Schwartz, *Chinese Communism and the Rise of Mao*; Brandt, *Stalin's Failure in China*; Wilbur and How, *Documents on Communism*; and Ch'en Kung-po, *The Communist Movement in China.* Soviet and Comintern policy is covered in Whiting, *Soviet Policies in China*; Degras, *The Communist International*; Eudin and North, *Soviet Russia and the East, 1920–1927*; and Borkenau, *World Communism.*
2. Borkenau, p. 227.

3. Eudin and North, p. 66.
4. *Ibid.*, p. 69.
5. Degras, I, 143–44.
6. Whiting, pp. 81ff.
7. *Ibid.*, p. 83.
8. *Ibid.*, p. 82.
9. Eudin and North, p. 227.
10. Ch'en Kung-po, p. 108.
11. *Ibid.*, p. 106.
12. *Ibid.*, p. 109.
13. *Ibid.*, p. 84.
14. *Ibid.*, pp. 111–39; Brandt, Schwartz, and Fairbank, pp. 54–65. See also Schwartz, pp. 28–36.
15. "The First Manifesto on the Current Situation," in Brandt, Schwartz, and Fairbank, pp. 62–63.
16. Eudin and North, p. 41.
17. Whiting, pp. 88–89.
18. Wilbur and How, p. 89.
19. Eudin and North, p. 151.
20. Isaacs, p. 59n.

Chapter 2

1. Wilbur and How, p. 64.
2. *Ibid.*, p. 71.
3. *Ibid.*, p. 41.
4. *Ibid.*, pp. 64, 90.
5. Mao, "Report of an Investigation into the Peasant Movement in Hunan," *SW*, I, 24.
6. Wilbur and How, pp. 285, 376.
7. Schwartz, p. 53.
8. Stalin, pp. 24–25.
9. Quoted in Wilbur and How, p. 276.
10. *Ibid.*, p. 255. Emphasis mine.
11. *Ibid.*
12. *Ibid.*, p. 381.
13. Further details are contained in Wilbur and How, pp. 396–401.
14. Quoted in North and Eudin, p. 32.
15. Isaacs, p. 117.
16. North and Eudin, p. 138.
17. *Ibid.*, p. 32.

Chapter 3

1. Schwartz, pp. 98–99.
2. Borkenau, pp. 336–37.

3. Details may be found in Helen F. Snow, *The Chinese Labor Movement.*
4. Helen F. Snow, pp. 71, 164.
5. Tyau, p. 196.
6. Degras, III, 66.
7. "Li-san t'ung-chih chi cheng-chih-chü yü ssu-chung ch'uan-hui ti sheng-ming-shu," in Hsiao Tso-liang, p. 124.
8. Quoted in Helen F. Snow, p. 65.
9. Degras, III, 168.
10. *Ibid.,* pp. 172–73.
11. Quoted in Schwartz, p. 169.
12. A-hsiang, *Ju-ho yün-yung hsia-ts'eng t'ung-i chan-hsien ti t'ao-lun.*
13. Pi Ou, "Ch'ih-se kung-hui yü hsia-ts'eng t'ung-i chan-hsien," *Hung Ch'i,* No. 29 (Jan. 25, 1932), pp. 7–9.
14. Israel, *Student Nationalism,* p. 101.
15. Degras, III, 240.
16. *Ibid.,* p. 242.
17. *Ibid.,* pp. 241–42.
18. McLane, p. 269.
19. Hsiao Tso-liang, pp. 224–25. A brief summary, dated January 10, 1943, is included in McLane, p. 269. McLane's text comes from Russian sources. This pronouncement should be distinguished from the ad hoc defections by individuals that occurred in the CCP and the KMT in all periods.
20. The agreement is paraphrased in Hsiao Tso-liang, pp. 248–49, which references the location of the original. The text is also given in Wang Chien-min, II, 601–2. The agreement was signed for the CCP by P'an Hannien, under the alias P'an Chien-hsing.
21. Hsiao Tso-liang, p. 25.
22. Rue, pp. 260–61.
23. Wang Chien-min, II, 600.
24. McLane, p. 65n.
25. Hu Chiao-mu, p. 36.
26. Sheridan, p. 271.
27. Wang Ming [Ch'en Shao-yü] and Kang Sin [K'ang Sheng], *Revolutionary China Today.*
28. Wang and Kang, p. 115.
29. See, for example, Israel, *Student Nationalism,* p. 101.

Chapter 4

1. Quoted in Borkenau, p. 377.
2. See Degras, III, 331–32.
3. *Ibid.,* p. 333.
4. *Ibid.*
5. Borkenau, pp. 404–5.
6. Degras, III, 346.

7. Dimitrov, p. 110. Emphasis in original.
8. *Seventh Congress Proceedings,* p. 16.
9. Dimitrov, p. 47.
10. *Seventh Congress Proceedings,* p. 12.
11. *Ibid.,* p. 17.
12. Dimitrov, p. 69.
13. Wang Ming, *The Revolutionary Movement in the Colonial Countries.* A somewhat abbreviated text appears in *Seventh Congress Proceedings,* pp. 280–313. The Chinese text is contained in Ch'en Shao-yü, *Chiu-kuo yen-lun hsüan-chi,* pp. 1–61. This text has been edited to remove the most unfavorable references to Chiang and the KMT. The first text cited above is the best I have seen; a note inside the front cover indicates that it was set up and ready for printing in October 1935.
14. North, *Moscow and Chinese Communists,* p. 177. This is Thomson's position also.
15. Communist International, Seventh Congress, *Resolutions and Decisions,* pp. 29–30.
16. Dimitrov, p. 69.
17. Wang Ming, p. 13.
18. Manuilsky, "The Work of the Seventh Congress of the Communist International," p. 40; in Communist International, *Report of the Seventh World Congress.*
19. Communist International, *Resolutions and Decisions,* pp. 43–44. This was part of a resolution submitted by the Italian Communist Ercoli (Palmiro Togliatti).
20. Rosinger, *China's Wartime Politics,* p. 67.
21. *Ibid.,* p. 63.
22. *Ibid.,* p. 67.
23. North, *Moscow and Chinese Communists,* pp. 175–77.
24. According to Thomson, p. 145, this was first published as "Ta fan-ti t'ung-i chan-hsien fan-tui-che," *Pa-li chiu-kuo pao* (Paris), Nov. 7, 1935; it was reprinted in *Chiu-kuo wen-hsüan* (Paris, 1935). I have not seen this version, but an undated one: "Po-fu k'ang-Jih t'ung-i chan-hsien ti fan-tui-che," in Ch'en Shao-yü, *Chiu-kuo yen-lun hsüan-chi,* pp. 84–85.
25. *Ibid.*
26. *Ibid.*
27. Quoted in McLane, p. 76.
28. *Inprecor,* 15.70: pp. 1728–29.
29. *SW,* I, 153 (ed. intro.).
30. Yü Ch'i, p. 217.
31. *Ibid.,* pp. 164–65.
32. *Inprecor,* 16.10: p. 377.
33. "Ch'uang-li ch'üan-kuo ko-tang ko-p'ai ti k'ang-Jih jen-min chen-hsien hsüan-yen," April 25, 1936. Text in *I-nien-lai* [CCP 6], pp. 6–9.
34. *Ibid.,* pp. 9–11. English text in *SW,* I, 330–31.
35. Edgar Snow, *Red Star,* pp. 388–89.
36. Chiang, pp. 77–78.

37. *Ibid.,* p. 80.
38. For an account of this campaign, see Gillin, " 'Peasant Nationalism' in Chinese Communism." See also Wan, p. 40.
39. *SW,* I, 279, note 4 to "The Tasks of the Chinese Communist Party in the Period of Resistance to Japan."
40. Original text in *I-nien-lai* [CCP 6], pp. 11–26. Contents summarized and discussed in McLane, p. 273; Thomson, pp. 125–27.
41. *I-nien-lai* [CCP 6], p. 17.
42. Edgar Snow, *Red Star,* p. 387.
43. *Ibid.*
44. McLane, pp. 74–78.
45. *Ibid.,* pp. 74–75.
46. Mao, "To Messrs. Chang Nai-chi, Tao Heng-chih, Chow Tao-fen, and Shen Chun-ju, Members of the All-China National Salvation League" (Aug. 10, 1936), in *March Toward Unity,* p. 71.
47. Dallin, p. 67.
48. *Ibid.*
49. Israel, *Student Nationalism,* p. 155.
50. *Ibid.,* p. 138.
51. *Ibid.,* p. 144.
52. *Ibid.,* p. 149.
53. *Ibid.,* p. 162.
54. Rosinger, *China's Wartime Politics,* p. 14. See also Chang Chih-i, *K'ang-chan chung ti cheng-tang ho p'ai-pieh,* pp. 99–109.
55. Quoted in Rosinger, *China's Wartime Politics,* p. 91.
56. Wales, p. 125.
57. Chung-t'ung-chü, p. 35.
58. Ting Shih-min, ed., *Chiu-wang yen-lun chi.* Pages 74–83 are an article by Ai Ssu-ch'i, "Min-tsu chieh-fang yün-tung ti ching-tsu." The first edition of this collection was published in August 1936. All articles are reprinted from contemporary journals.
59. *Ibid.,* pp. 1–6.
60. *Ibid.,* pp. 45–53.
61. *Ibid.,* pp. 54–73.
62. Bertram, *Sian Mutiny,* pp. 107–8.
63. Edgar Snow, *The Other Side of the River,* p. 466.
64. Kao, p. 426.
65. Bertram, *Sian Mutiny,* pp. 114–15.
66. *Ibid.*

Chapter 5

1. Principally in *Random Notes.*
2. *Ibid.,* Preface, p. 4.
3. Thomson, "Communist Policy and the United Front in China, 1935–1936."

4. *Ti-pa-lu-chün hsing-chün chi* (Hankow: Kuang-ming shu-chü, 1938), 2nd ed., p. 127; quoted in Wang Chien-min, III, 98.

5. See Edgar Snow, *Red Star,* pp. 338–45.

6. Li Chih-kung, p. 75.

7. Wang Chien-min, III, 99.

8. Chiang, p. 84.

9. Donald's account of the Sian Incident, filtered through his biographer, is contained in Selle, pp. 316–38; especially p. 324.

10. Edgar Snow, *Random Notes,* Preface, p. 4.

11. See K'ung, II, 661–62.

12. Chiang and Soong, pp. 70–72.

13. Edgar Snow, *Random Notes,* Preface, p. 4.

14. The telegram was signed by the Chinese Soviet Government and the Central Committee of the CCP. English text in *March Toward Unity,* pp. 122–23. Chinese text in *Chih-nan* [CCP 4], Vol. I.

15. Edgar Snow, *Random Notes,* p. 2.

16. Selle, p. 333. Most other sources maintain that Chou En-lai met with Chiang Kai-shek at least once, on Christmas Eve: Edgar Snow, *Red Star,* p. 475; Bertram, *Sian Mutiny,* p. 133; Edgar Snow, *Random Notes,* p. 12.

17. "A Statement on Chiang Kai-shek's Statement," *SW,* I, 254.

18. Chiang and Soong, p. 107.

19. Chiang, p. 77.

20. Quoted in Edgar Snow, *Random Notes,* p. 12.

21. Selle, pp. 333–34. These two versions are somewhat contradictory, but they agree that the level of explicit agreement was quite low.

22. K'ai-feng, "Lun k'ang-Jih min-tsu t'ung-i chan-hsien chu-wen-t'i," in *Lun k'ang-Jih min-tsu t'ung-i chan-hsien,* p. 21.

23. Edgar Snow, *Random Notes,* p. 3.

24. *SW,* I, 294. Written long after the event, this note is of questionable authority; but such views probably were expressed.

25. Quoted in Wang Chien-min, III, 98.

26. *Pei-fang-chü hsüan-yen* [CCP 10].

27. CCP Southwest Fukien Committee, *K'ou-Chiang yü shih-Chiang* [CCP 8], pp. 36–39.

28. *Ibid.*, p. 1.

29. *Ibid.*, p. 2.

30. Tung, II, 268–69.

31. Kao, p. 429.

32. *SW,* I, 255–58.

33. *I-nien-lai* [CCP 6], p. 28b. English text in *March Toward Unity,* pp. 124–25.

34. Chiang, p. 79. See also Edgar Snow, *Random Notes,* p. 7.

35. Text of the telegram will be found in *SW,* I, 281–82.

36. "Chung-kuo kung-ch'an-tang chung-yang kao ch'üan-tang t'ung-chih shu," *Chih-nan* [CCP 4], I, 43a–53b. This is very similar in content to "The Tasks of the Chinese Communist Party in the Period of Resistance to Japan," *SW,* I, 263–83.

37. "Win the Masses in Their Millions for the Anti-Japanese National United Front," *SW*, I, 285–87. Original in *Chih-nan* [CCP 4], I, App. 4.

Chapter 6

1. *China Handbook*, p. 51. The CCP's Manifesto may have been drafted even before the Marco Polo Bridge Incident. See Brandt, Schwartz, and Fairbank, p. 39.
2. Taylor, p. 97.
3. *White Paper*, p. 52.
4. *Chieh-fang pao*, I:21 (Oct. 31, 1937), pp. 1–2. *Ibid.*, I:24 (Nov. 30, 1937), pp. 3–4.
5. "Democracy vs. One-Party Rule," p. 100.
6. "Unite All Anti-Japanese Forces and Combat the Anti-Communist Die-Hards," *SW*, III, 161–62; and p. 254, note 10.
7. *China Handbook*, p. 51.
8. *White Paper*, p. 88.
9. "The Question of Independence and Initiative within the United Front," *SW*, II, 215.
10. "The Role of the Chinese Communist Party in the National War," *SW*, II, 200.
11. "Conclusions on the Repulse of the Second Anti-Communist Onslaught," *SW*, II, 467.
12. "The Role of the Chinese Communist Party in the National War," *SW*, II, 197. The translation used here is that of the International Publishers ed., *SW*, II, 245.
13. "Introducing *The Communist*," *SW*, II, 287. The translation follows the original, not the *SW* text.
14. *Ibid.*
15. "Urgent Tasks Following the Establishment of Kuomintang-Communist Cooperation," *SW*, II, 39. The translation follows the original, not the *SW* text.
16. "The Situation and Tasks in the Anti-Japanese War after the Fall of Shanghai and Taiyüan," *SW*, II, 69–70.
17. "Introducing *The Communist*," *SW*, II, 288–89.
18. *Ibid*, pp. 290–91. The translation follows the original.
19. "Oppose Capitulationist Activities," *SW*, II, 254.
20. Chung-kung chung-yang tung-nan fen-chü, Question 34.
21. Mao, "Lun 'i-tang chuan-cheng' wen-t'i," in Mao et al., pp. 18ff.
22. As quoted in Brandt, Schwartz, and Fairbank, p. 243.
23. "The Situation and Tasks in the Anti-Japanese War after the Fall of Shanghai and Taiyüan," *SW*, II, 65.
24. *Ibid.*
25. *Ibid*, p. 68.
26. *Ibid.*
27. *Ibid.*

28. "The Question of Independence and Initiative within the United Front," *SW,* II, 215.

29. "Current Problems of Tactics in the Anti-Japanese United Front," *SW,* II, 427. Emphasis added.

30. "Chung-yang kuan-yü shih-chü yü cheng-ts'e ti chih-shih," *Tang ti sheng-huo,* No. 4 (Apr. 1941), pp. 1–2. The directive itself dates from the preceding December.

31. *SW,* II, 421–43.

32. *Ibid.,* p. 421.

33. *Ibid.,* p. 422. My emphasis. This is the language of the 1954 International Publishers edition of *SW,* which more faithfully represents the Chinese version. The Foreign Language Press edition says "roughly as many."

34. *Ibid.,* p. 424.

35. *Ibid.,* pp. 424–25.

36. *Ibid.*

37. *Ibid.,* p. 426.

38. *Ibid.*

39. *SW,* II, 441–50. Unfortunately I have been unable to find an original version for either of these two statements.

40. "Current Problems of Tactics in the Anti-Japanese United Front," *SW,* II, 427.

41. Brandt, Schwartz, and Fairbank, p. 260.

42. Particularly by "The Chinese Revolution and the Chinese Communist Party," *SW,* II, 301–34. Mao is only one of several authors who contributed to this work.

43. Chung-kung chung-yang tung-nan fen-chü, Question 17.

44. *Kuan-yü t'ung-i chan-hsien-pu ti tsu-chih ho kung-tso ti chih-shih,* [CCP 2], pp. 5–6. General statements of the approach to be taken can be found throughout the *cheng-feng* documents, as in Compton, *Mao's China: Party Reform Documents, 1942-1944.* Specific treatment is exemplified by: [Liang] Hua-chih, *Tung-i chan-hsien ti tso-feng,* a collection of 11 essays devoted entirely to the work style of the united front; and Lo Fu, "Lun tai-jen chieh-wu wen-t'i," *Chieh-fang pao,* No. 65 (Feb. 28, 1939), pp. 26–32; a long article on how a CCP member should conduct his individual relations with others, especially those outside the Party.

45. "On Some Important Problems of the Party's Present Policy," *SW,* IV, 188.

46. *SW,* II, 288.

47. "Introducing *The Communist,*" *SW,* II, 295.

48. Chung-kuo kuo-fang-pu hsin-wen-chü, *Chung-kung tsu-chih shih-k'uang,* pp. 19a–21a.

49. *Ibid.*

50. Hsü I-hsin, "Kuan-yü fei-tang kan-pu kung-tso chung ti chi-ko wen-t'i," *Kung-ch'an-tang jen,* No. 3 (Nov. 11, 1939), pp. 32–35.

51. *The Chinese Communist Movement,* p. 2433. The statement is that Ch'en was replaced by "Ssu Ching-ko," which appears to be a mistaken version of K'o's name.

52. *Kuan-yü k'ai-chan t'ung-i chan-hsien kung-tso ti chih-shih* [CCP 5], p. 2. Translated as Appendix 1.

53. *Ibid.*

54. *Kuan-yü t'ung-i chan-hsien-pu ti tsu-chih ho kung-tso ti chih-shih* [CCP 2]. Translated as Appendix 2.

55. *Ibid.*

56. *Ibid.*

57. *Ibid.*

58. *Ibid.*

59. *Ibid.*

60. Kan-su sheng tiao-ch'a shih, II, 93b–95b.

61. Lo Mai (Li Wei-han), "Shen-Kan-Ning pien-ch'ü nei-pu ti t'ung-i chan-hsien, chieh-chi cheng-ts'e yü kung-ch'an-tang," *Kung-ch'an-tang jen,* No. 3 (Dec. 1939), pp. 12–22. See also P'eng Chen's report, discussed below, Chapter 7, n.54.

62. P'eng Chen, pp. 67a ff.

Chapter 7

1. *Chinese Communist Movement,* pp. 2346–63, gives an excellent account of the "friction" between CCP and KMT armies.

2. "Order and Statement on the Southern Anhwei Incident," *SW,* II, 453.

3. Kung-lun ch'u-pan-she, p. 2.

4. "Chung-kung chün-yün kung-tso ti hsin ts'e-lüeh," p. 14. Appended to Kung-lun ch'u-pan-she.

5. *Ibid.*

6. *Ibid.*, p. 12.

7. *Ibid.*, p. 17.

8. Union Research Institute, *Biographical Series,* No. 714 (Oct. 19, 1962).

9. Kung-lun ch'u-pan-she, p. 4.

10. *Ibid.*, p. 5.

11. Union Research Institute, *Biographical Series,* No. 590 (Aug. 11, 1961).

12. *Chinese Communist Movement,* pp. 2337–38.

13. Kung-lun ch'u-pan-she, p. 5.

14. Huai-pei-ch'ü tang-wei, *Kuan-yü chia-ch'iang t'ung-i chan-hsien yü k'uo-ta chiao p'eng-yu kung-tso chih-shih.*

15. *Ibid.*, p. 1b.

16. *Ibid.*, pp. 2a–2b.

17. *Ibid.*, pp. 2b–3b.

18. *Yü-O pien-ch'ü hsien-wei tiao-ch'a tzu-liao.* Section on "united front," Part 3, "Tui yu-chi-tui."

19. *Ibid.*

20. *Ibid.*

21. *Ibid.*

22. *Chen-hsiang*, p. 5a.
23. Gillin, " 'Peasant Nationalism,' " pp. 270–71.
24. *Chen-hsiang*, p. 5b.
25. Gillin, *Warlord*, p. 232.
26. *Ibid.*
27. *Chen-hsiang*, p. 41a. See also Johnson, pp. 99–100.
28. *Chen-hsiang*, p. 41a.
29. Gillin, " 'Peasant Nationalism,' " pp. 280–84.
30. "Po I-po's 7-Man Group and His Dismissal," *RHKCP*, 184/53 (Oct. 6, 1953).
31. *Chen-hsiang*, pp. 6b–7a.
32. Quoted in Hogg, pp. 25–26. Emphasis mine.
33. *Chen-hsiang*, pp. 9b–10a.
34. Lin Piao, "P'ing-hsing-küan chan-tou ti ching-yen," in *Chih-nan* [CCP 4], II, 187–200.
35. Bertram, *Unconquered*, p. 145.
36. Johnson, p. 100.
37. *Chen-hsiang*, pp. 13a–13b.
38. Carlson, p. 92.
39. Belden, p. 52.
40. *Chen-hsiang*, p. 15a.
41. *Ibid.*, p. 16b.
42. *Ibid.*, pp. 16b–17a.
43. Quoted in Johnson, p. 222, note 33.
44. Kan Ssu-ch'i, "K'ang-Jih t'ung-i chan-hsien tsai Shan-hsi," *Chieh-fang pao*, No. 55 (Oct. 31, 1938), pp. 13–16.
45. Taylor, p. 166.
46. "Kuan-yü chien-ch'ih Shan-hsi k'ang-chan k'o-fu wei-hsien ch'ing-hsiang hsüan-yen," *Chieh-fang pao*, No. 87 (Oct. 30, 1939), pp. 2–3.
47. *Chen-hsiang*, p. 24a.
48. Johnson, p. 105.
49. *Chen-hsiang*, pp. 30b–31b.
50. Johnson, p. 106.
51. *Chen-hsiang*, p. 4a.
52. *Ibid.*, pp. 42a–42b.
53. "On the Question of Political Power in the Anti-Japanese Base Areas," *SW*, II, 418.
54. Two documents discuss these problems at some length. (1) Hsiao-Su-T'ung-Ling pan-shih-ch'u, *Ti-ssu-tz'u hsien-cheng hui-i lu yü tang-cheng-chün kung-tso pao-kao ta-kang*, especially the section "Huai-pei Su-Wan Pien-ch'ü kai-tsao cheng-ch'üan ti ching-kuo." (2) P'eng Chen, *Chung-kung "Chin-Ch'a-Chi pien-ch'ü" chih ko-chung cheng-ts'e.* The second, an extremely important document, discusses the background of the Border Region, as well as presenting a detailed and specific analysis of current political, economic, and military conditions. It was circulated by the CCP Central Committee as a model report, to be emulated by others. A copy was obtained by the KMT, and the document was reprinted by

them in a classified edition for intelligence and reference purposes. It is a copy of this edition that has been used here.

55. "On the Question of Political Power in the Anti-Japanese Base Areas," *SW*, II, 418.

56. Hsieh, p. 3b (pagination follows Hoover Institution ms. copy). Hsieh's essay was originally prepared for *Ti-san-tz'u ch'ang-chu hui-i,* April 2 [1942?].

57. "On the Question of Political Power in the Anti-Japanese Base Areas," *SW*, II, 418.

58. Ch'ü-tang-wei, "Kuan-yü jen-chen chih-hsing san-san-chih ho ch'e-ti chin-hsing min-hsüan chüeh-ting (Nov. 20 [1941])," *Tang ti sheng-huo,* No. 14 (n.d.), pp. 1–4.

59. *SW*, II, 419. See also P'eng, p. 18.

60. "Chung-yang kuan-yü shih-chü yü cheng-ts'e ti chih-shih" [Dec. 1940], *Tang ti sheng-huo,* No. 4 (April 1941), p. 5.

61. *SW*, II, 419.

62. Lin Po-ch'ü, *Shen-Kan-Ning pien-ch'ü san-san-chih ti ching-yen chi ch'i ying-kai chiu-cheng ti p'ien-hsiang.*

63. *Ibid.*, p. 1.

64. *Ibid.*

65. *Ibid.*, pp. 2–4.

66. *Ibid.*, p. 4.

67. *Ibid.*, p. 8.

68. *Ibid.*

69. *Ibid.*, pp. 5–6.

70. Hsieh, pp. 5b–6a.

71. *Ibid.*

72. Lin Po-ch'ü, pp. 8–13.

73. As one example among many, see Harrison Forman, *Report from Red China* (New York: Holt, 1945), pp. 56–61.

74. P'eng Chen, pp. 18a–18b.

75. *Ibid.*

76. Hsieh, p. 6b.

77. P'eng Chen, pp. 3a–3b.

78. *Ibid.*

79. *Yü-O pien-ch'ü hsien-wei tiao-ch'a tzu-liao,* section entitled "La-lung shen-shih."

Chapter 8

1. "Chung-kung ko-chung pao-k'an i-lan-piao," in *Chung-kuo kung-ch'an-tang huo-tung kai-k'uang tiao-ch'a pao-kao.* Not paged.

2. *Ibid.*

3. Brandt, Schwartz, and Fairbank, p. 246.

4. One example, among a great many, is Ch'in Po-ku, *Lun k'ang-Jih min-tsu t'ung-i chan-hsien fa-chan, k'un-nan, chi ch'i ch'ien-t'u.*

5. "Current Problems of Tactics in the Anti-Japanese United Front," *SW*, II, 429.
6. *Ibid.*
7. Ch'en Shao-yü, *San-yüeh cheng-chih-chü hui-i ti tsung-chieh,* p. 45.
8. Chinese Communist Party, *Resolutions and Telegrams,* p. 6.
9. See McLane, pp. 87–88n. Chiang, p. 85, treats them as settled fact.
10. Chang Hao, p. 4.
11. Chou En-lai, "Kuan-yü so-wei 'Chung-kuo kung-ch'an-tang ti ts'e-lüeh lu-hsien' i-shu wen-t'i kung-k'ai-hsin," *Chieh-fang Pao,* No. 36 (Apr. 29, 1938), pp. 11–12. Chou, then in Hankow, probably first published this open letter there.
12. *Ibid.*
13. *SW*, II, 454.
14. Lo-fu (Chang Wen-t'ien), *Pai-ch'ü-tang mu-ch'ien chung-hsin jen-wu.* Information on the cover indicates that this document was acquired by the KMT on March 11, 1938.
15. *Ibid.*, p. 6.
16. *Ibid.*, p. 32.
17. Klaus H. Pringsheim, "The Functions of the Chinese Communist Youth Leagues, 1920–1949," *China Quarterly,* No. 12 (Oct.–Dec. 1962), pp. 85–86.
18. *Chinese Communist Movement,* pp. 2343–44.
19. *Min-i chou-k'an,* No. 37 (Aug. 24, 1938), p. 16.
20. Lo-fu, pp. 8–9.
21. "Draft Resolution of the Central Committee of the Chinese Communist Party Concerning the Communist Party's Participation in the Government," *SW*, II, 72–73.
22. *Ibid.*
23. Chinese Communist Party, *Resolutions and Telegrams,* pp. 6–7.
24. *Ibid.*
25. Chiang, p. 88.
26. Liu Shao-ch'i, "Lun kung-k'ai kung-tso yü mi-mi kung-tso," *Kung-ch'an-tang jen,* No. 1 (Oct. 1939).
27. *Ibid.*, p. 2a.
28. *Ibid.*, pp. 4a–4b.
29. "Freely Expand the Anti-Japanese Forces and Resist the Onslaughts of the Anti-Communist Die-Hards," *SW,* II, 434–35.
30. Quoted in Brandt, Schwartz, and Fairbank, p. 346.
31. *Ibid.* The translation used here is that of the International Publishers edition of *SW*, Vol. III, p. 208.
32. "Recruit Large Numbers of Intellectuals," *SW,* II, 303. Original in *Kung-ch'an-tang jen,* No. 3 (n.d.). The directive itself is dated Dec. 1, 1939. Virtually no alterations have been made in the *SW* version.
33. "Freely Expand . . . ," *SW,* II, 435.
34. *Chin-chi t'ung-kao* [CCP 13], pp. 5–6. Although not dated in the original ms., this document appears in a KMT anthology of CCP documents which was published in May 1940.
35. "Chung-kung chung-yang kuan tang-yüan ch'ü-te Kuo-min-tang

t'ung-chih-ch'ü nei hsia-ts'eng chi-kuan kung-wu jen-yüan ti-wei chih-shih" [CCP 11].

36. *Ibid.*, p. 1a.

37. *Ibid.*, pp. 3a–3b.

38. "On Coalition Government," *SW,* III, 309–10. The language is that of the International Publishers edition.

39. "Democracy vs. One-Party Rule," p. 101.

40. *Ibid.*

41. *Ibid.*, pp. 101ff. See also Kennedy, p. 140.

42. Tseng Chao-lun, "The Chinese Democratic League," *Current History,* July 1946, p. 32.

43. *Ibid.*

44. James Shen, "Minority Parties in China," *Asia,* XL:2 (Feb. 1940), p. 83. Ch'ien, p. 352, places membership at a maximum of 30,000.

45. Shen, p. 83.

46. Linebarger, p. 178.

47. Kennedy, p. 117.

48. "Democracy vs. One-Party Rule," p. 117.

49. Shen, "Minority Parties," p. 137.

50. *Kai-k'uang,* pp. 7–8.

51. Quoted in "Democracy vs. One-Party Rule," pp. 104–5.

52. "Democracy vs. One-Party Rule," p. 107.

53. *Ibid.*, p. 108.

54. Rosinger, *China's Crisis,* p. 69.

55. *Kai-k'uang,* p. 29.

56. *Kai-k'uang,* p. 2.

57. Liang Sou-ming, p. 10.

58. Kennedy, p. 160.

59. *Ibid.*, p. 146.

60. Chen Keng, pp. 2–4.

61. *Kai-k'uang,* p. 4.

62. *Ibid.*, p. 5.

63. *Ibid.*

64. *Ibid.*

65. *Chung-kuo ko hsiao-p'ai hsien-k'uang,* pp. 15–16.

66. *Ibid.*

67. *Ibid.*

68. Chang Chih-i, *K'ang-chan chung ti cheng-tang ho p'ai-pieh.*

69. Chou, *Ten Years of Storm,* pp. 48–49. Yü is currently a deputy director of the UFWD.

70. Chen Keng, pp. 2–3. See also *Kai-k'uang,* p. 29.

Chapter 9

1. An account of the earlier negotiation is contained in *White Paper,* pp. 100–110, and relevant annexes. Events surrounding the PCC are covered in pp. 136–70.

2. "The Situation and Our Policy after the Victory in the War of Resistance Against Japan," *SW*, IV, 11–22.

3. Hu Hsi-k'uei, *Shih-chü pien-hua ho wo-men ti fang-chen.* This was a report delivered at a conference called by the North China Bureau of the CCP.

4. *Ibid.*, p. 2.

5. *Ibid.*, p. 3.

6. *Ibid.*

7. Chin-Ch'a-Chi chung-yang-chü hsüan-ch'uan pu, pp. 2–3.

8. *Ibid.*, p. 5.

9. Clubb, p. 267.

10. *Jih-pen t'ou-hsiang hou*, Ch. I, p. 1.

11. *Jen-min shou-ts'e 1955*, pp. 374–76.

12. *Kai-k'uang*, p. 30.

13. Shang-hai-shih tiao-ch'a-ch'u, p. 4b.

14. *Kai-k'uang*, p. 30.

15. Shang-hai-shih tiao-ch'a-ch'u, p. 5a.

16. Kennedy, p. 160.

17. Liang Sou-ming, pp. 28–32.

18. Tseng Chao-lun, "The Chinese Democratic League," *Current History*, July 1946, pp. 34–35.

19. Carsun Chang, p. 184.

20. *White Paper*, p. 183.

21. "Liang Sou-ming hsien-sheng shuo-ming Min-meng tui Chung-kung t'ai-tu," in *Min-chu t'ung-meng wen-hsien*, p. 146.

22. *Kai-k'uang*, p. 31.

23. Chün, p. 2a.

24. *White Paper*, p. 688.

25. *Ibid.*, pp. 839–40. Other information concerning the dissolution of the League (secret police surrounding League headquarters in the days just prior to the 27th, disposition of the property the CCP had turned over to the League, etc.) is covered in Annexes 146, 147, and 148 (pp. 834–40). *Kai-k'uang*, Ch. 4, pp. 3–7, has further data on the alleged activities of Lo, K'ung, and Li.

26. Wang Sze-zee, "Chinese Liberals in Hong Kong," *China Weekly Review*, Oct. 25, 1947, pp. 260–61.

27. Hua-shang jih-pao tzu-liao-shih, Part *Chia*, p. 17.

28. Barnett, p. 86.

29. *Ibid.*, pp. 86ff, and Ch. 18. See also the detailed but unverified material in Chün, pp. 2–10.

30. *Chung-kung chung-yang tsui-chin pan-pu chih "Ti-hsia tou-cheng,"* p. 1b.

31. Barnett, p. 83.

32. Belden, p. 397.

33. Charles J. Canning, "Present Student Movement Held Greatest in History," *China Weekly Review*, June 14, 1947, pp. 48–49.

34. For a description of student attitudes in early 1948 that also contains some background material, see Barnett, pp. 40–51.

35. "Manifesto of the Chinese People's Liberation Army," *SW,* IV, 151.
36. Loh, *Businessmen,* p. 2.
37. *Ibid.,* p. 3.
38. Barnett, p. 318.
39. Quoted in *ibid.,* p. 328.
40. *Ibid.,* pp. 327–28.
41. *Ibid.,* p. 331.
42. *Ibid.,* p. 345.
43. *Ibid.,* p. 356.

Chapter 10

1. "On the People's Democratic Dictatorship," *SW,* IV, 422.
2. *Ibid.,* 415.
3. "Address to the Preparatory Committee of the New People's Consultative Conference," *SW,* IV, 407.
4. "On the People's Democratic Dictatorship," *SW,* IV, 419.
5. *Jen-min shou-ts'e 1950,* Part *Yi,* pp. 18–20.
6. Cole, p. 36.
7. Chou, *Feng-pao shih-nien,* p. 69.
8. George P. Jan, "Minor Parties in Communist China," *Current History,* XLIII:253 (Sept. 1962), p. 175.
9. *SCMP,* 56 (Jan. 25, 1951).
10. "Decision of the Revolutionary Committee of the Kuomintang of China on the Development of Organization," *NCNA,* Jan. 24, 1951; *SCMP,* 56.
11. As given in U.S. Department of State, *Directory of Party and Government Officials of Communist China,* July 1960.
12. "Decision of the China Democratic League on the Development of Organization," *NCNA,* Jan. 24, 1951; *SCMP,* 56.
13. "Decision of the Standing Committee of the Democratic National Construction Association on the Development of Organization," *NCNA,* Feb. 3, 1951; *SCMP,* 62 (Feb. 2–4, 1951).
14. "Decision of the China Association for the Promotion of Democracy on the Development of Organization," *NCNA,* Jan. 24, 1951; *SCMP,* 56.
15. "Decision of the Chinese Peasants' and Workers' Democratic Party on the Development of Organization," *NCNA,* Jan. 24, 1951; *SCMP,* 56.
16. *Ibid.*
17. "Decision of the Chiu-san Society on the Development of Organization," *NCNA,* Jan. 24, 1951; *SCMP,* 56.
18. Seymour, pp. 62ff.
19. "Report on the Question of the Intellectuals," *JMJP,* Jan. 30, 1956.
20. Ch'en Han-po, pp. 4–5.
21. *Ibid.,* pp. 3–4.
22. "The 'United Front' Enterprise in Canton," *RHKCP,* 14/54 (Jan. 21, 1954).
23. Chou, *Feng-pao shih-nien,* p. 69 (English ed., pp. 47–48).

24. "The 'United Front' Enterprise in Canton," *RHKCP*, 14/54 (Jan. 21, 1954).

25. Hsiao and Wang, p. 3.

26. Chou, *Feng-pao shih-nien*, p. 64 (English ed., pp. 45–46).

27. *Chung-kuo min-chu t'ung-meng ti hsing-chih yü jen-wu*, p. 11.

28. *Kung-fei pao-cheng shih-nien*, p. 82.

29. Li Wei-han, "The Chinese Communist Party and the People's Democratic United Front," *PC*, IV:1 (July 1, 1951), p. 38.

30. *Ibid.*

31. Mu, p. 234.

32. *Ibid.*, p. 236.

33. P. C. Yu, "Patriotic Pacts," *PC*, III:8 (Oct. 16, 1951), pp. 31–33.

34. *SCMP*, 94 (Apr. 13–16, 1951).

35. Chou En-lai, "Political Report at the Second Session of the Second National Committee of the CPPCC, January 30, 1956," *PC*, 4/56 (Feb. 16, 1956), supplement.

36. "Shang-hai-shih jen-min cheng-fu ch'eng-li chi-kuan nei-pu t'ung-i chan-hsien kung-tso-tsu," *Shang-hai hsin-wen jih-pao*, Nov. 17, 1952.

37. Hsi Chung-hsün, "Make United Front Work a Success: Raise the Standards of Old Cadres—Train Large Numbers of New Cadres," *CB*, No. 158 (Feb. 15, 1952), p. 9.

38. Li Wei-han, "Chin i-pu chia-ch'iang cheng-fu chi-kuan nei-pu ti t'ung-i chan-hsien," *JMJP*, June 10, 1951. The report was made on April 29.

39. *JMJP*, May 10, 1950.

40. Wei Chin-fei, "Chia-ch'iang jen-min cheng-fu chi-kuan chung ti t'ung-i chan-hsien kung-tso," *Ch'ang-chiang jih-pao*, July 5, 1951.

41. *Ibid.*

42. "GAC Issues Six-Point Concrete Program to Strengthen United Front Work," *NCNA*, June 9, 1951; *SCMP*, 113.

43. "The Present Situation and Our Tasks," *SW*, IV, 164.

44. Chao, *Agrarian Policy*, pp. 74–75.

45. "Different Tactics for Carrying Out the Land Law in Different Areas," *SW*, IV, 193–95. A telegram from Mao to Liu Shao-ch'i, Feb. 3, 1948.

46. "Essential Points in Land Reform in the New Liberated Areas," *SW*, IV, 201.

47. "General Report of the Peking Municipal People's Government on Agrarian Reform in Peking Suburban Areas," *CB*, No. 72 (May 10, 1951), p. 4.

48. Yü Cheng, "The Anti-Feudal United Front in Land Reform," *PC*, III:3 (Feb. 1, 1951), pp. 4–5.

49. *Ibid.*, p. 4.

50. *Ibid.*, p. 6.

51. *Ibid.*

52. *SW*, II, 353.

53. *SW*, III, 281.

54. In Article 26 of the Common Program.

55. Hughes and Luard, pp. 25–26.

56. *Ibid.*, p. 84. For a description of these allocations, see *PC,* III:3 (Feb. 1, 1951), p. 29.

57. C. S. Chu, "Businessmen Oppose U.S. Aggression," *PC,* III:2 (Jan. 16, 1951), p. 27.

58. *Ibid.*

59. "Central-South Military-Administrative Committee Decision on Dealing with Urban-Rural Relations During Agrarian Reform" (Jan. 13, 1951), *SCMP,* 53 (Jan. 21–22, 1951).

60. Loh, *Businessmen,* p. 28.

61. Loh, *Escape,* p. 84.

62. Loh, *Businessmen,* p. 32.

63. Loh, *Escape,* pp. 96–97.

64. *Ch'ang-chiang jih-pao* (Hankow), March 5, 1952.

65. *Ibid.*

66. *SCMP,* 306.

67. *Ibid.*

68. *Ibid.*

69. *Ibid.*

70. Theodore H. E. Ch'en, *Thought Reform of the Chinese Intellectuals* (Hong Kong: Hong Kong University Press, 1960), p. 54.

Chapter 11

1. *CB,* 297 (Oct. 5, 1954), p. 2.

2. Liu Shao-ch'i, "Report on the Draft Constitution of the People's Republic of China," *PC,* No. 19/54 (Oct. 1, 1954), pp. 31–32.

3. *Ibid.*

4. *CB,* 297 (Oct. 5, 1954), p. 4.

5. Chang Chih-i, *Shih-lun,* pp. 22–23.

6. *Ibid.*

7. Liu Shao-ch'i, "Report on the Draft Constitution," *PC,* No. 19/54 (Oct. 1, 1954), pp. 31–32.

8. *CB,* 297 (Oct. 5, 1954), p. 4.

9. Loh, *Escape,* pp. 183–84.

10. Chang Chih-i, *Shih-lun,* pp. 34–35.

11. U.S. State Department, *Directory of Party and Government Officials of Communist China* (1960). The same bureau published similar directories, under the title *Directory of Chinese Communist Officials,* in 1963 and 1966. The listings indicate earliest and latest confirmed information.

12. Li Wei-han, "Continue to Consolidate and Expand the People's Democratic United Front," in *New China Advances to Socialism* (Peking: FLP, 1956), pp. 166–67. Translation of a speech made by Li to the Third Session of the First NPC, June 15–30, 1956.

13. *Ibid.*, pp. 162–63.

14. *Ibid.*, pp. 149ff.

15. Seymour, pp. 62ff.
16. Faure, pp. 62–63.
17. Quoted in Seymour, p. 72.
18. *KMJP,* July 2, 1956. See also Shen, "Lun 'Ch'ang-ch'i kung-ts'un, hu-hsiang chien-tu.' "
19. Wang Hui-min, "Wo tui-yü 'Ch'ang-ch'i kung-ts'un hu-hsiang chien-tu' fang-chen ti t'i-hui."
20. *NCNA,* May 30, 1957.
21. *NCNA,* May 10, 1957.
22. *NCNA,* July 3, 1957.
23. *KMJP,* July 29, 1957; *SCMP,* 1623.
24. *JMJP,* Aug. 19, 1957.
25. *JMJP,* Aug. 29, 1957.
26. Dennis J. Doolin, "Both Red and Expert: The Dilemma of the Chinese Intellectual," *Current Scene,* II:19 (Sept. 1, 1963), p. 3. Also by the same author, "The Revival of the Hundred Flowers Campaign: 1961," *CQ,* No. 8 (Oct.–Dec. 1961), pp. 31–41.
27. *CB,* 639.
28. *SCMP,* 2721.
29. *SCMP,* 3467.
30. See *SCMP,* 3503, 3510, 3515, 3521.
31. *SCMP,* 3521.
32. *China Topics,* YB 322 (Apr. 13, 1965).
33. *Ibid.*
34. *Ibid.*
35. U.S. State Department, *Directory of Chinese Communist Officials* (1966); Union Research Institute, *Who's Who in Communist China* (Hong Kong, 1966).
36. See the various recent works by Chang Chih-i and Li Wei-han listed in the Bibliography.
37. Chang Chih-i, *Shih-lun,* p. 37.
38. Li Wei-han, "The Chinese People's Democratic United Front: Its Special Features," *PR,* 34/61, p. 18. Emphasis mine.
39. *Ibid., PR,* 35/61, p. 12.
40. Li Wei-han, "The United Front—A Magic Weapon," *PR,* 24/61, p. 20.
41. See, for example, A. M. Halpern, "The Foreign Policy Uses of the Chinese Revolutionary Model," *CQ,* No. 7 (July–Sept. 1961), pp. 1–16.

Conclusion

1. Li Wei-han, ". . . Special Features," *PR,* 35–61, p. 12.
2. Edgar Snow, *Red Star,* p. 114.
3. Chou En-lai, "Report on the Work of the Government," *PC,* 14–57 (July 16, 1957), supplement, p. 36.
4. Chou En-lai, "Report on Intellectuals," *JMJP,* Jan. 30, 1956.
5. *PR,* 34/66 (Aug. 19, 1966), pp. 6, 7–8.

Bibliography

This Bibliography is essentially a list of works cited in the Notes. The order is alphabetical by author, issuer, or title, except for official Chinese Communist Party documents, which are listed under Chung-kuo kung-ch'an-tang and numbered in brackets for convenience in citation. An asterisk after a name indicates that the characters for it will be found in the section of Chinese Characters, pp. 313–15.

Aczel, Tamas, and Tibor Meray. The Revolt of the Mind. New York: Praeger, 1959.

A-hsiang. Ju-ho yün-yung hsia-ts'eng t'ung-i chan-hsien ti t'ao-lun (A Discussion on How to Use the United Front from Below). N.p., [1933]. Mimeo.

Barnett, A. Doak. China on the Eve of Communist Takeover. New York: Praeger, 1963.

Belden, Jack. China Shakes the World. London: Gollancz, 1951.

Bertram, James M. First Act in China: The Story of the Sian Mutiny. New York: Viking, 1938.

———. Unconquered: Journal of a Year's Adventures Among the Fighting Peasants of North China. New York: John Day, 1939.

Bodde, Derk. Peking Diary: A Year of Revolution. New York: Henry Schuman, 1950.

Borkenau, Franz. World Communism: A History of the Communist International. Ann Arbor: University of Michigan Press, 1962. First published 1939.

Brandt, Conrad. Stalin's Failure in China, 1924–1927. Cambridge, Mass.: Harvard University Press, 1958.

———, Benjamin I. Schwartz, and John K. Fairbank. A Documentary History of Chinese Communism. London: Allen and Unwin, 1952.

Carlson, Evans F. Twin Stars of China: A Behind-the-Scenes Story of China's Valiant Struggle for Existence by a U.S. Marine Who Lived and Moved with the People. New York: Dodd, Mead, 1940.

CCP documents, *see* Chung-kuo kung-ch'an-tang

Chang, Carsun. The Third Force in China. New York: Bookman Associates, 1952.

Chang Chih-i. K'ang-chan chung ti cheng-tang ho p'ai-pieh (Political Parties and Groups in the War of Resistance). Chungking: Tu-shu sheng-huo ch'u-pan-she, Mar. 1939.

———. Kuan-yü jen-min min-chu t'ung-i chan-hsien ti chi-ko wen-t'i (Some Questions Concerning the People's Democratic United Front). Peking: Chung-kuo ch'ing-nien ch'u-pan-she, 1957.

———. "Kuan-yü tzu-ch'an chieh-chi chih-shih fen-tzu ti chi-ko wen-t'i" ("Some Questions Concerning the Bourgeois Intellectuals"), *Chung-kuo ch'ing-nien,* No. 4/59 (Feb. 16, 1959), pp. 5–8.

———. Shih-lun Chung-kuo jen-min min-chu t'ung-i chan-hsien (Tentative Discussion of the Chinese People's Democratic United Front). Peking: Jen-min ch'u-pan-she, 1958.

———. "Tui-yü 'ch'ang-ch'i kung-ts'un hu-hsiang chien-tu' fang-chen ti jen-shih" ("Recognition of the Line Concerning 'Long-Term Coexistence, Mutual Supervision' "), *Hsüeh-hsi,* No. 2/58 (Jan. 18, 1958), pp. 11–16.

Chang Hao (pseud. of Lin Yü-ying). Chung-kung-tang ti ts'e-lüeh lu-hsien (The Tactical Line of the CCP). N.p.: Kung-lun ch'u-pan-she, Mar. 1941. Appendix: "Chung-kung tsai k'ang-chan ch'i-chien chih cheng-ko yin-mou" ("The Full Scheme of the CCP During the War of Resistance").

[Chang Kuo-t'ao.] K'ang-Jih min-tsu t'ung-i chan-hsien ti fen-hsi yü p'i-p'an (An Analysis and Criticism of the Anti-Japanese National United Front). N.p.: T'ung-i ch'u-pan-she, [1940].

Chang Wen-t'ien, *see* Lo Fu

Chao Kuo-chün. Agrarian Policy of the Chinese Communist Party, 1921–1959. Bombay: Asia Publishing House, 1960.

———. The Mass Organizations in Communist China. Massachusetts Institute of Technology, Center for International Studies, 1953. Ditto.

Chen-hsiang, *see* "Shan-hsi 'Hsin-chün' p'an-pien chen-hsiang"

Chen Keng.* Chung-kuo min-chu t'ung-meng tsu-chih kai-k'uang (The State of Organization of the China Democratic League). N.p., n.d. Mimeo.

Ch'en Han-po.* Chin-jih Pei-p'ing (Peiping Today). Kowloon: Tzu-yu ch'u-pan-she, Apr. 1951.

Ch'en Kung-po. The Communist Movement in China. Edited and with an introduction by C. Martin Wilbur. New York: Columbia University East Asian Institute, 1960.

Ch'en Shao-yü. Ch'en Shao-yü (Wang Ming) chiu-kuo yen-lun hsüan-chi (Selected Addresses of Ch'en Shao-yü (Wang Ming) on National Salvation). Hankow: Chung-kuo ch'u-pan-she, July 1938.

———. San-yüeh cheng-chih-chü hui-i ti tsung-chieh (A Summary of the March Conference of the Politburo). Hankow, May 1938.

———. "Wan-chiu shih-chü ti kuan-chien" ("The Key to Salvation of the Current Situation"), in Mao Tse-tung et al., T'ung-i chan-hsien hsia tang-p'ai wen-t'i.

——— et al. K'ang-Jih min-tsu t'ung-i chan-hsien ti hsin fa-chan (New Developments in the Anti-Japanese National United Front). Hankow, Jan. 20, 1938.

———, *see also under* Wang Ming

Chiang Kai-shek. Soviet Russia in China: A Summing Up at Seventy. New York: Farrar, 1957.

——— and Soong Mei-ling (Mme. Chiang Kai-shek). General Chiang Kai-shek: The Account of the Fortnight in Sian When the Fate of China Hung in the Balance. New York: Doubleday, 1937.

Chieh-fang Pao (*Liberation*). Official organ of the CCP, published in Yenan. Began publication in April 1937 as a weekly; later published irregularly at about 10-day intervals. In July 1941 shifted to daily publication.

Ch'ien Tuan-sheng. The Government and Politics of China. Cambridge, Mass.: Harvard University Press, 1950.

Ch'in Po-ku (Pang-hsien). Lun k'ang-Jih min-tsu t'ung-i chan-hsien ti fa-chan, k'un-nan, chi ch'ien-t'u (On the Development, Difficulties, and Future of the Anti-Japanese National United Front). Chungking, Oct. 1938.

China, Ministry of Information. China Handbook, 1937–1943. New York: Macmillan, 1943.

China: The March toward Unity. New York: Workers' Library, 1937.

Chinese Communist Movement, *see* United States, 82nd Congress

Chinese Communist Party, Central Committee. Resolutions and Telegrams of the Sixth Plenum, Nov. 6, 1938. Hong Kong: New China Information Committee, 1939.

Chiu, S. M. Chinese Communist Revolutionary Strategy, 1945–1950: Extracts from Volume IV of Mao Tse-tung's Selected Works. Woodrow Wilson School of Public and International Affairs, Center for International Studies, Research Monograph No. 13 (Princeton, N.J., 1961).

Chou Ching-wen. Feng-pao shih-nien (Ten Years of Storm). Hong Kong: Shih-tai p'i-p'ing she, 1959.

———. Ten Years of Storm: The True Story of the Communist Regime in China. New York: Holt, 1960.

Chün P'ing.* Chung-kung yü min-meng chih kou-chieh (The Collaboration between the CCP and the DL). N.p., [1947]. Mimeo.

Chung-hua min-kuo Ssu-fa hsing-cheng-pu tiao-ch'a-chü. Kung-fei t'ung-chan kung-tso ti ts'e-lüeh yü yün-yung (The Tactics and Uses of the Communist Bandits' United Front Work). Taipei, Jan. 1960.

Chung-kung chung-yang tsui-chin pan-pu chih "Ti-hsia tou-cheng" ("The Underground Struggle" Recently Published by the CCP Central Committee). N.p.: Chung-lien ch'u-pan-she, Apr. 1947. In the Hoover Institution.

Chung-kuo hsin-min-chu yün-tung chung ti tang-p'ai (Parties and Groups in China's New Democratic Movement). Shanghai: Hsin-Chung-kuo wen-hsien ch'u-pan-she pien-i pu, 1946.

Chung-kuo ko hsiao-p'ai hsien-k'uang (Present Circumstances of China's Minor Parties). N.p., [Aug. 1946]. "Secret."

Chung-kuo kung-ch'an-tang (Chinese Communist Party) documents

[1] Chin-Ch'a-Chi chung-yang-chü hsuan-ch'uan pu. Mu-ch'ien shih-chü jen-wu ho ssu-hsiang wen-t'i ti t'ao-lun t'i-kang (A Discussion Outline on Problems Concerning Our Current Situation, Tasks, and Ideology). Changchiak'ou, Dec. 1, 1945.

[2] Chung-kuo kung-ch'an-tang chung-yang t'ung-chan-pu. Kuan-yü t'ung-i chan-hsien-pu ti tsu-chih ho kung-tso ti chih-shih (Directive Concerning the Operation and Work of United Front Bureaus). N.p., Nov. 2, 1940. Ms. in the Hoover Institution.

[3] ——— chung-yang tung-nan fen-chü, ed. Tang ti hsin cheng-ts'e t'ao-lun ta-kang (A Discussion Outline for the Party's New Policy). N.p., Apr. 7, 1938. Mimeo.

[4] ——— chung-yang wei-yüan-hui, ed. K'ang-Jih min-tsu t'ung-i chan-hsien chih-nan (Guide to the Anti-Japanese National United Front). Yenan, 1937–40. 10 vols.

[5] ———. Kuan-yü k'ai-chan t'ung-i chan-hsien kung-tso ti chih-shih (Directive Concerning Development of United Front Work). N.p., Aug. 5, 1940. Ms. in the Hoover Institution.

[6] ———, ed. Kuan-yü t'ung-i chan-hsien—i-nien-lai wo-men ti k'ang-Jih chiu-wang chu-chang (Concerning the United Front—Our Proposals for Resistance to Japan and National Salvation During the Past Year). N.p., Jan. 1937. Ms. in the Hoover Institution.

[7] ——— cheng-chih-chü. Kuan-yü chun-pei chao-chi tang ti-ch'i-tz'u ch'üan-kuo tai-piao ta-hui ti chüeh-i (Decision Concerning Preparations for Convening the Party's Seventh National Congress). N.p., Dec. 13, 1937. Mimeo.

[8] ——— Min-hsi-nan wei-yüan-hui. K'ou-Chiang yü shih-Chiang (Chiang's Arrest and Chiang's Release). In the Hoover Institution. Extracted from Kuan-yü k'ang-Jih t'ung-i chan-hsien ti chi-ko wen-t'i (Several Questions Concerning the Anti-Japanese United Front). N.p., Apr. 20, 1937, pp. 36–39. Mimeo. A Secret Party document.

[9] ——— nan-fang-chü. Kuan-yü liang-Kuang shih-pien ti chüeh-i (Decision Concerning the Kwangtung-Kwangsi Affair). N.p., July 17, 1936. Ms. in the Hoover Institution.

[10] ——— pei-fang-chü tui Hsi-an shih-pien ho-p'ing chieh-chüeh hsüan-yen. (Declaration of the Northern Bureau of the Chinese Communist Party Concerning the Peaceful Settlement of the Sian Incident). Peking, Dec. 28, 1936. Mimeo.

[11] Chung-kung chung-yang kuan tang-yüan ch'ü-te Kuo-min-tang t'ung-chih-ch'ü nei hsia-ts'eng chi-kuan kung-wu jen-yüan ti-wei chih-shih (Directive of the CCP Central Committee on Party Members' Securing Positions as Public Officials in Lower-level Organs in Kuomintang-controlled Areas), [Yenan, 1940?]. Ms. in the Hoover Institution.

[12] Kuo-min ko-ming-chün ti-shih-pa chi-t'uan-chün cheng-chih-pu, ed. Mo-ts'a ts'ung-ho erh lai? (Where Is the Friction Coming From?). N.p., Apr. 1940.

[13] Nan-fang chü. Tung-chiang kung-ch'an-tang chin-chi t'ung-kao (Urgent Notice of the East River Chinese Communist Party). N.p., n.d., ms.

Chung-kuo kung-ch'an-tang huo-tung kai-k'uang tiao-ch'a pao-kao (Report of Investigations into the Chinese Communist Party's Overall Activities). N.p., June 1940. Not paged, mimeo. Compiled by the Bureau of Investigation and Statistics of the Kuomintang.

Chung-kuo kuo-fang-pu hsin-wen-chü. Kung-fei fan-tung wen-chien hui-pien (Collected Reactionary Documents of the Communist Bandits). N.p., n.d. 4 vols.

——— kuo-min-tang chung-yang wei-yüan-hui tiao-ch'a t'ung-chi chü. Chung-kung tsu-chih shih-k'uang (The True State of Chinese Communist Organization). N.p., [1939]. Mimeo.

Chung-kuo min-chu t'ung-meng kai-k'uang (The General Condition of the China Democratic League). Nanking: T'ung-i ch'u-pan-she, Dec. 1947. "Top secret."

Chung-kuo min-chu t'ung-meng ti hsing-chih yü jen-wu (The Nature and Tasks of the China Democratic League). Canton: Kuang-ming ch'u-pan-she, Nov. 1950.

Chung-lien ch'u-pan-she, ed. Chung-kuo tang-p'ai (Chinese Parties and Groups). Nanking, Jan. 1948.

Chung-t'ung-chü [?], ed. "Jen-min chen-hsien" chih t'ou-shih (An Exposé of the "Popular Front"). N.p., [1937?].

Clubb, O. Edmund. Twentieth Century China. New York: Columbia University Press, 1964.

Cole, Allan B. "The United Front in the New China," in H. A. Steiner, ed. *Report on China,* special issue of *Annals of the American Association of Political and Social Science,* 277 (Sept. 1951), 34–45.

Communist International. Report of the Seventh World Congress of the Communist International. London: Modern Books, 1936. Variously paged.

———, Seventh Congress. Resolutions and Decisions. Moscow-Leningrad: Cooperative Publishing Society of Foreign Workers, 1935.

Compton, Boyd. Mao's China: Party Reform Documents, 1942–1944. Seattle: University of Washington Press, 1952.

Dallin, David J. Soviet Russia and the Far East. New Haven: Yale University Press, 1948.

Degras, Jane, ed. The Communist International, 1919–1943. London: Oxford University Press, 1956–65. 3 vols.

"Democracy vs. One-Party Rule in Kuomintang China: The 'Little Parties' Organize," *Amerasia,* Apr. 25, 1943, pp. 97–117.

Dimitrov, Georgi. The United Front, the Struggle Against Fascism and War. New York: International Publishers, 1938.

Elegant, Robert S. The Dragon's Seed. New York: St. Martin's, 1959.

Eudin, Xenia J., and Robert C. North, eds. Soviet Russia and the East, 1920–1927: A Documentary Survey. Stanford: Stanford University Press, 1957.

Faure, Edgar. The Serpent and the Tortoise. New York: St. Martin's, 1958.

Feis, Herbert. The China Tangle: The American Effort in China from Pearl Harbor to the Marshall Mission. Princeton, N.J.: Princeton University Press, 1953.

Fei-wei jen-shih tzu-liao tiao-ch'a yen-chiu-hui, ed. Fei-wei jen-shih tzu-liao hui-pien: jen-wu chih (Compilation of Personnel Material on Bandits and Collaborators: Biographical Section). Taipei, 1956, with annual supplements. 11 vols., "secret."

Fen-sui Chang Kuo-t'ao fan-ko-ming huo-tung pao-kao ta-kang (Outline of the Report on the Smashing of Chang Kuo-t'ao's Counterrevolutionary Activities). N.p., n.d. Ms. in Hoover Institution.

Gillin, Donald G. " 'Peasant Nationalism' in Chinese Communism," *Journal of Asian Studies,* XXIII (1964), 269–89.

———. Warlord: Yen Hsi-shan in Shansi Province, 1911–1949. Princeton, N.J.: Princeton University Press, 1967.

Hawtin, Elise. "The 'Hundred Flowers Movement' and the Role of the Intellectual in China: Fei Hsiao-t'ung, A Case History," *Papers on China* (Harvard University, ditto) XII (1958), 147–96.

Hinton, Harold C. "The 'Democratic Parties': End of an Experiment?" *Problems of Communism,* No. 7 (1958), pp. 39–46.

Hogg, George. I See a New China. Boston: Little, Brown, 1944.

Hsiao-Su-T'ung-Ling pan-shih-ch'u.* Ti-ssu-tz'u hsien-cheng hui-i lu yü tang-cheng-chün kung-tso pao-kao ta-kang (The Record of the

Fourth Conference on Hsien Government and the Outline of the Report of Party, Government, and Army Work). N.p., Nov. 20, 1943. Ms.

Hsiao Tso-liang. Power Relations Within the Chinese Communist Movement, 1930–1934: A Study of Documents. Seattle: University of Washington Press, 1961.

Hsiao Yeh-na* and Wang Erh-te.* Chung-kung ti min-chu tang-p'ai (The CCP's Democratic Parties). Hong Kong: Tzu-yu ch'u-pan-she, Mar. 1951.

Hsieh Chüeh-tsai. "San-san-chih ti li-lun yü shih-chi" ("The Theory and Practice of the Three-Thirds System"), in Chung-kuo kuo-fang-pu hsin-wen-chü, ed., Kung-fei fan-tung wen-chien hui-pien (A Collection of Reactionary Documents of the Communist Bandits). N.p., n.d., Vol. II. 14 dbl. pp. Ms. in the Hoover Institution.

Hu Chiao-mu. Thirty Years of the Communist Party of China. London: Lawrence and Wishart, 1951.

Hu Hsi-k'uei. "Radio Address," *Foreign Broadcast Information Service* (FBIS), No. 21/60 (Feb. 1, 1960), BBB 8–9.

———. Shih-chü pien-hua ho wo-men ti fang-chen (Changes in the Current Situation and Our Line). N.p., Aug. 30, 1945. Mimeo.

Hua-shang pao tzu-liao-shih,* ed. I-chiu-ssu-chiu nien shou-ts'e (Handbook, 1949). Hong Kong, 1950. Not paged consecutively.

[Huai-pei]-ch'ü tang-wei. Kuan-yü chia-ch'iang t'ung-i chan-hsien yü k'uo-ta chiao p'eng-yu kung-tso ti chih-shih (Directive on the Strengthening of the United Front and Expansion of the Work of Making Friends). N.p., Feb. 26, 1944. 8 dbl. pp. Ms. in the Hoover Institution.

Hughes, T. J., and D. E. T. Luard. The Economic Development of Communist China, 1949–1958. London: Oxford University Press, 1959.

I-nien-lai [CCP 3], *see* Chung-kuo kung-ch'an-tang

International Press Correspondence. This was a semiofficial weekly organ of the Comintern in 1922–41. Published first in Vienna and Berlin, and from 1933 to 1941 in London: renamed *World News and Views* in July 1938. Cited as *Inprecor*.

Isaacs, Harold R. The Tragedy of the Chinese Revolution, rev. ed. Stanford: Stanford University Press, 1951.

Israel, John. The Chinese Student Movement, 1927–1937: A Bibliographic Essay Based on the Resources of the Hoover Institution. Stanford, Calif.: Hoover Institution, 1959.

———. Student Nationalism in China, 1927–1937. Stanford: Stanford University Press, 1966.

Jen-min shou-ts'e 1950 (People's Handbook, 1950). Shanghai: Ta Kung Pao she, 1950. Not paged consecutively.

Jen-min shou-ts'e 1955 (People's Handbook, 1955). Tientsin: Ta Kung Pao she, 1955.

Jih-pen t'ou-hsiang hou ti Chung-kuo kung-ch'an-tang (The Chinese Communist Party since the Surrender of the Japanese). N.p.: T'ung-i ch'u-pan-she, Dec. 31, 1947. "Top secret."

Johnson, Chalmers A. Peasant Nationalism and Communist Power: The Emergence of Revolutionary China, 1937–1945. Stanford: Stanford University Press, 1962.

Kai-k'uang, *see* Chung-kuo min-chu t'ung-meng kai-k'uang

K'ang-Jih chan-cheng shih-ch'i chieh-fang-ch'ü kai-k'uang (A General Account of the Liberated Areas during the Period of the War Against Japan). Peking: Jen-min ch'u-pan-she, 1953.

Kan-su sheng tiao-ch'a shih, ed. Hsien-tang tui Lung-tung chih yin-mou chi wo-fang tui-ts'e chih kai-shu (A General Account of the Schemings of the Illegal Party in Lung-tung, and of Our Methods of Response). N.p., [1940]. 2 vols.

Kao Yin-tsu,* ed. Chung-hua min-kuo ta-shih-chi (A Chronology of the Principal Events of the Chinese Republic). Taipei: Shih-chieh-she, 1957.

Kennedy, Melville T., Jr. "The Chinese Democratic League," *Papers on China* (Harvard University, ditto), VII (1953), 136–75.

K'ung Hsiang-hsi (H. H. Kung). K'ung Yung-chih hsien-sheng yen-chiang chi (The Collected Lectures of Mr. K'ung Yung-chih). Taipei: Chung-yang yin-chih ch'ang, 1960. 2 vols.

Kung-fei pao-cheng shih-nien. (Ten Years of Tyranny by the Communist Bandits). Taipei: Chung-yang wen-wu kung-ying she, 1959.

Kung-lun ch'u-pan-she,* ed. Chung-kung chih mi-mi chün-shih kung-tso (Secret Military Work of the CCP). N.p., Mar. 1941.

Lao Tun. "Hsia-ts'eng t'ung-i chan-hsien" ("The United Front from Below"), in *Lieh-ning ch'ing-nien* (*Leninist Youth*), [Shanghai?], Nov. 1930, pp. 63–66. On the cover and the endpapers, the volume is identified as *Ch'ing-nien pan-yüeh-k'an* (*Youth Fortnightly*), Vol. III, No. 1.

Li Chih-kung.* Chung-kuo kung-ch'an-tang shih-lüeh (An Outline History of the Chinese Communist Party). N.p.: T'ung-i ch'u-pan-she, 1942.

Li Wei-han. "The Chinese Communist Party and the People's Democratic United Front," *People's China,* IV, No. 1 (July 1, 1951), pp. 35–39.

———. "The Chinese People's Democratic United Front: Its Special Features," *Peking Review,* No. 33/61 (Aug. 18, 1961), pp. 11–15;

No. 34/61 (Aug. 24, 1961), pp. 12–18; No. 35/61 (Sept. 1, 1961), pp. 10–14.

———. "The Democratic United Front in China," *Current Background,* No. 402 (July 24, 1956), pp. 1–10.

———. "The Struggle for Proletarian Leadership in the Period of the New-Democratic Revolution in China," *Peking Review,* No. 8/62 (Feb. 23, 1962), pp. 5–13; No. 9/62 (Mar. 2, 1962), pp. 8–14; No. 10/62 (Mar. 9, 1962), pp. 8–14; No. 11/62 (Mar. 16, 1962), pp. 12–17; No. 12/62 (Mar. 23, 1962), pp. 12–18.

———. "The United Front—A Magic Weapon of the Chinese People for Winning Victory," *Peking Review,* No. 23/61 (June 9, 1961), pp. 13–16; No. 24/61 (June 16, 1961), pp. 17–21.

———. "The United Front Work of the Party," *Current Background,* No. 418 (Oct. 11, 1956), pp. 1–9.

[Liang] Hua-chih,* ed. T'ung-i chan-hsien ti tso-feng (The Work Style of the United Front). Taiyüan, Aug. 1939.

Liang Sou-ming and Chou Hsin-min. Li-Wen an tiao-ch'a pao-kao shu (Report on the Investigation of the Cases of Li and Wen). Nanking, Chung-kuo min-chu t'ung-meng tsung-pu, 1946.

Lin Po-ch'ü.* Shen-Kan-Ning pien-ch'ü san-san-chih ti ching-yen chi ch'i ying-kai chiu-cheng ti p'ien-hsiang (Experience with the Three-Thirds System in the Shen-Kan-Ning Border Region, and Tendencies That Should Be Corrected). Yenan, Mar. 1944.

Lin Yü-ying, *see* Chang Hao

Linebarger, Paul M. A. The China of Chiang Kai-shek: A Political Study. Boston: World Peace Foundation, 1941.

Liu Ching-yu. "The Anti-Japanese National United Front," *People's China,* No. 17/57 (Sept. 1, 1957), pp. 32–37; No. 18/57 (Sept. 16, 1957), pp. 27–32.

Liu Shao-ch'i. "Lun kung-k'ai kung-tso yü mi-mi kung-tso" ("On Overt Work and Secret Work"), *Kung-ch'an-tang jen* (*The Communist*), No. 1, Oct. 1939.

Lo Fu (pseud. of Chang Wen-t'ien). Pai-ch'ü-tang mu-ch'ien ti chung-hsin jen-wu (The Central Tasks Currently Facing the Party in White Areas). [Yenan?], 1937. Mimeo., "top secret."

Loh, Robert. Businessmen in China. Hong Kong: China Viewpoints, 1960.

———. Escape from Red China. New York: Coward, McCann, 1962.

Lu Yu-sun. Programs of Communist China for Overseas Chinese. Kowloon: Union Research Institute, 1956. Mimeo.

Lun k'ang-Jih min-tsu t'ung-i chan-hsien (On the Anti-Japanese National United Front). N.p., 1937.

McLane, Charles B. Soviet Policy and the Chinese Communists, 1931–1946. New York: Columbia University Press, 1958.

Mao Tse-tung. "Chung-kuo k'ang-Jih min-tsu t'ung-i chan-hsien tsai mu-ch'ien chieh-tuan ti jen-wu" ("The Tasks of the Chinese Anti-Japanese National United Front in the Present Stage"), *Chieh-fang pao,* Vol. I, No. 2 (May 1937).

———. Mao Tse-tung hsüan-chi. Peking: Jen-min ch'u-pan-she, 1961. 4 vols.

———. The Selected Works of Mao Tse-tung. Peking: Foreign Languages Press, 1961–65. 4 vols.

———. Selected Works. New York: International Publishers, 1954. 4 vols.

———, et al. T'ung-i chan-hsien hsia tang-p'ai wen-t'i (The Question of Parties and Groups under the United Front). Yenan: Shih-shih hsin-wen pien-i-she, Mar. 1938.

March toward Unity, *see* China: The March toward Unity

Min-chu t'ung-meng wen-hsien (Documents on the Democratic League). Nanking: Chung-kuo min-chu t'ung-meng tsung-pu, 1946.

Montell, Sherwin. "The San-fan Wu-fan Movement in Communist China," *Papers on China* (Harvard University, ditto), VIII (1954), 136–96.

Mu Fu-sheng. The Wilting of the Hundred Flowers: The Chinese Intelligentsia under Mao. New York: Praeger, 1962.

Ni Ssu,* ed. Chang Kuo-t'ao t'o-li kung-tang mien-mien kuan (The Different Views on Chang Kuo-t'ao's Leaving the CCP). Canton: Hsin-chung-kuo ch'u-pan-she, June 1938.

North, Robert C. Kuomintang and Chinese Communist Elites. Stanford: Stanford University Press, 1952.

———. Moscow and Chinese Communists. Stanford: Stanford University Press, 1953.

———, and Xenia J. Eudin. M. N. Roy's Mission to China: The Communist-Kuomintang Split of 1927. Berkeley: University of California Press, 1963.

The Overseas United Front of the Chinese Communists. Taipei: Asian People's Anti-Communist League, 1957.

[P'eng Chen.] Chung-kung "Chin-Ch'a-Chi pien-ch'ü" chih ko-chung cheng-ts'e (The Various Policies of the CCP's "Chin-Ch'a-Chi Border Region"). N.p.: T'ung-i ch'u-pan-she, Jan. 28, 1942. Ms. in the Hoover Institution.

P'ing Hsin. Min-tsu t'ung-i chan-hsien lun (Essays on the National United Front). Canton: Chan-shih ch'u-pan-she, May 1938.

Rosinger, Lawrence K. China's Crisis. New York: Knopf, 1945.

———. China's Wartime Politics, 1937–1944. Princeton, N.J.: Princeton University Press, 1944.

Rue, John E. Mao Tse-tung in Opposition, 1927–1935. Stanford: Stanford University Press, 1966.

Schwartz, Benjamin I. Chinese Communism and the Rise of Mao. Cambridge, Mass.: Harvard University Press, 1958.

Selle, Earl Albert. Donald of China. New York: Harper, 1948.

Seventh Congress of the Communist International: Abridged Stenographic Report of the Proceedings. Moscow: Foreign Languages Publishing House, 1939.

Seymour, James D. Communist China's Bourgeois-Democratic Parties. Unpublished M.A. thesis, Columbia University, 1961.

Shang-hai-shih tiao-ch'a-ch'u, ed. Chung-kung yü min-meng kou-chieh chih shih-shih (The Facts about the Collaboration between the CCP and the DL). Shanghai: 1946. Ms. in the Hoover Institution.

"Shan-hsi 'Hsin-chün' p'an-pien chen-hsiang" ("The True Picture of the Shansi 'New Army' Mutiny"), *Tiao-ch'a chuan-pao,* No. 20, Mar. 1940. Chung-yang tiao-ch'a t'ung-chi chü. Cited as *Chen-hsiang.*

Shen Chih-yüan. "Lun 'Ch'ang-ch'i kung-ts'un hu-hsiang chien-tu' " ("On 'Long-term Coexistence, Mutual Supervision' "), *Jen-min jih-pao,* Nov. 20–21, 1956.

Sheridan, James E. Chinese Warlord: The Career of Feng Yü-hsiang. Stanford: Stanford University Press, 1966.

Shih-tai wen-hsien-she, ed. Chiu-kuo wu-tsui: ch'i chün-tzu (National Salvation Is Not a Crime: The Seven Gentlemen). [Shanghai?], Aug. 1937.

Smedley, Agnes. Battle Hymn of China. New York: Knopf, 1943.

Snow, Edgar. The Other Side of the River: Red China Today. New York: Random House, 1961.

———. Random Notes on Red China (1936–1945). Cambridge, Mass.: Harvard University Press, 1957.

———. Red Star Over China. New York: Random House, 1938.

Snow, Helen F. The Chinese Labor Movement. New York: John Day, 1945.

———, *see also under* Wales, Nym

Stalin, Joseph. The Prospects of the Revolution in China (speech delivered to the Chinese Commission of the ECCI, Nov. 30, 1926). Moscow: Foreign Languages Press, 1955.

T'ai-hsien* hsien-wei-hui, ed. T'ai-hsien ch'un-chi kung-tso tsung-chieh (A Summary of Work in T'ai-hsien during the Spring Season). T'ai-hsien, May 1944. Mimeo.

Tang, Peter S. H. Communist China Today. New York: Praeger, 1957. 2 vols.

Tang ti sheng-huo (*Party Life*). This was the organ of the CCP in the New Fourth Army. Began publication in January 1941 as a monthly.

Taylor, George E. The Struggle for North China. New York: Institute of Pacific Relations, 1940.

Thomson, James C., Jr. "Communist Policy and the United Front in China, 1935–1936," *Papers on China* (Harvard University, ditto), XI (1957), 99–148.

Ting Shih-min,* ed. Chiu-wang yen-lun chi (A Collection of Statements on National Salvation), 2d ed. N.p., Jan. 1938.

Tso Shun-sheng. Chin san-shih nien chien-wen tsa-chi (Random Observations during the Past Thirty Years). Hong Kong: Tzu-yu ch'u-pan-she, Mar. 1952.

Tung Hsien-kuang (Hollington K. Tong). Chiang Tsung-t'ung chuan (The Biography of President Chiang). Taipei, 1954. 2 vols.

Tyau, Min-ch'ien T. Z., ed. Two Years of Nationalist China. Shanghai: Kelly and Walsh, 1930.

Union Research Institute. Biographical Service. Hong Kong: Irreg., mimeo.

———, ed. Communist China: 1957. Kowloon, 1958. Mimeo.

United States, Department of State. Foreign Relations of the United States, 1942: China. Washington, D.C., 1956.

———. Foreign Relations of the United States, 1943: China. Washington, D.C., 1957.

———. United States Relations with China: With Special Reference to the Period 1944–1949 (Department of State Publication 3573, Far Eastern Series 30). Washington, D.C., 1949. The "White Paper."

———, Bureau of Intelligence and Research. Directory of Party and Government Officials of Communist China. BD No. 271. Washington, D.C., 1960. 2 vols.

———, Consulate-General, Hong Kong. *Current Background.*

———. *Extracts from China Mainland Magazines.*

———. *Survey of the China Mainland Press.*

———. *Review of the Hong Kong Chinese Press.*

United States, 82nd Congress, Committee on the Judiciary, Subcommittee to Investigate the Administration of the Internal Security Act and Other Internal Security Laws. Institute of Pacific Relations Hearings: Part 7A, Appendix II, "The Chinese Communist Movement, 5 July 1945." Washington, D.C., 1952. Originally compiled by the Military Intelligence Division of the War Department.

Wales, Nym (pseud. of Helen F. Snow). Notes on the Chinese Student Movement, 1935–1936. Notes prepared for the Nym Wales collection on the Far East in the Hoover Institution, Stanford University (1959). Processed.

———, *see also under* Snow, Helen F.

Wan Yah-kang. The Rise of Communism in China, 1920–1950. Hong Kong, 1952.

Wang Chien-min.* Chung-kuo kung-ch'an-tang shih-kao (Draft History of the Chinese Communist Party). Taipei: Hsien-ping yin-shua ch'ang, 1965. 3 vols.

Wang Hui-min. "Wo tui-yü 'Ch'ang-ch'i kung-ts'un hu-hsiang chien-tu' fang-chen ti t'i-hui" ("My Understanding of the Line of 'Long-Term Coexistence, Mutual Supervision' "), *Ta Kung Pao* (Peking), Nov. 18, 1956.

Wang Ming (pseud. of Ch'en Shao-yü). The Revolutionary Movement in the Colonial Countries (Speech, revised and augmented, delivered August 7, 1935). New York: Workers' Library, 1935.

———, and Kang Sin (K'ang Sheng). Revolutionary China Today. Moscow: Cooperative Publishing Society of Foreign Workers in the U.S.S.R., 1934.

———, *see also under* Ch'en Shao-yü

Wang Ta-chung.* Chung-kuo kung-ch'an-tang hsüan-ch'uan kung-tso tsung chien-t'ao (A General Investigation and Discussion of the Chinese Communist Party's Propaganda Work). Ch'ü-chiang: Sheng-li ch'u-pan Kuang-tung fen-she, Mar. 1941.

White Paper, *see* United States, Department of State

Whiting, Allen S. Soviet Policies in China, 1917–1924. New York: Columbia University Press, 1954.

Wilbur, C. Martin, and Julie L. Y. How. Documents on Communism, Nationalism and Soviet Advisers in China, 1918–1927. New York: Columbia University Press, 1956.

Wilson, Edmund. To the Finland Station: A Study in the Writing and Acting of History. New York: Doubleday, 1953. First published in 1940.

Yü Cheng. "The Anti-Feudal United Front in Land Reform," *People's China,* III, No. 3 (Feb. 1, 1951), pp. 4–7.

Yü Ch'i,* ed. Shih-lun hsüan-chi (Essays of the Times). Shanghai: Chih-hsin yin-shu-chü, 1937.

Yü-O pien-ch'ü hsien-wei tiao-ch'a tzu-liao (Materials from an Investigation of Traitors and Puppets in the Honan-Hupei Border Region). N.p., n.d., ms. not paged. Preface indicates that materials were collected by Liang Yüan-p'ing and Hsü Wei-nung. Selected mss. in Hoover Institution.

Chinese Characters

Chang Chih-chung 張治中
Chang Chih-i 張執一
Chang Ching-chiang 張靜江
Chang Ch'ün 張群
Chang Chün-mai (Carsun Chang) 張君勱
Chang Fa-k'uei 張發奎
Ch'ang En-to 常恩多
Chang Hao (pseud. of Lin Yü-ying) 張浩
Chang Hsiao-liang 張效良
Chang Hsüeh-liang 張學良
Chang Kuo-t'ao 張國燾
Chang Lan 張瀾
Chang Nai-ch'i 章乃器
Chang P'ing-hua 張平華
Chang Po-chün 章伯鈞
Chang Shen-fu 張申府
Chang T'ai-lei 張太雷
Chang Tso-lin 張作霖
Chang Tung-sun 張東蓀
Chang Wen-ang 張文昂
Chang Wen-t'ien 張聞天
Chang Yun-ch'uan 張雲川
Chao Ch'eng-shou 趙承綬
Chen Keng 震庚
Ch'en Ch'ang-chieh 陳長捷
Ch'en Ch'eng 陳誠
Ch'en Chi-t'ang 陳濟棠
Ch'en Ch'iung-ming 陳炯明
Ch'en Han-po 陳寒波
Ch'en I 陳毅
Ch'en Kuo-fu 陳果夫
Ch'en Li-fu 陳立夫
Ch'en Ming-ho 陳鳴和
Ch'en Ming-shu 陳銘樞
Ch'en Shao-yü (pseud. Wang Ming) 陳紹禹
Ch'en Tu-hsiu 陳獨秀
Ch'en Yu-jen (Eugene Ch'en) 陳友仁
Cheng Chen-wen 鄭振文
Cheng Tung-kuo 鄭棟國
Ch'eng Ju-huai 程汝懷
Chiang Kai-shek 蔣介石
Chiang Kuang-nai 蔣光乃
Chin Ch'eng 金城
Ch'in Pang-hsien (pseud. Po-ku) 秦邦憲
Chou En-lai 周恩來
Chou Fu-hai 周佛海
Chou Hsin-min 周新民
Chu P'ei-te 朱培德
Chu Te 朱德
Ch'ü Ch'iu-pai 瞿秋白
Chün P'ing 君平
Fang Fang 方方
Feng Yü-hsiang 馮玉祥
Fu Tso-i 傅作義
Han Chün 韓鈞
Han Fu-ch'ü 韓復渠
Ho Chu-kuo 何柱國

Ho Hsiang-ning 何香凝
Ho K'o-ch'üan 何克全
Ho Lung 何龍
Ho Ying-ch'in 何應欽
Hou Chün-yen 侯峻岩
Hsiao Yeh-na 蕭也納
Hsieh Chüeh-tsai 謝學哉
Hsieh Hsüeh-hung 謝雪紅
Hsing Hsi-p'ing (pseud. Hsü Ping) 邢西萍
Hsü Ch'ien 徐謙
Hsü Fan-t'ing 續範亭
Hsü I-hsin 徐以新
Hsü Ming-hung 徐名鴻
Hsü Ping (pseud. of Hsing Hsi-p'ing) 徐冰
Hsü Pin-ju 徐彬如
Hsü Te-heng 徐德珩
Hsü Ti-hsin 許滌新
Hsü Wei-nung 徐慰農
Hsüeh Tzu-cheng 薛子正
Hsüeh Yüeh 薛岳
Hu Tsung-nan 胡宗南
Hua Ch'iang 華強
Huang Ch'i-hsiang 黄琪翔
Huang Yen-p'ei 黄炎培
Jung Wu-sheng 戎武勝
K'ai-feng 凱豐
Kan Nai-kuang 甘乃光
Kan Ssu-ch'i 甘泗淇
Kao Yin-tsu 高蔭祖
K'o Ch'ing-shih 柯慶施
K'ung Hsiang-hsi (H. H. Kung) 孔祥熙
K'ung Ts'ung-chou 孔從周
Kuo Mo-jo 郭沫若
Kuo T'ing-i 郭挺一
Lei Jen-min 雷任民
Li Chih-kung 李致工
Li Chin-te 李金德
Li Chi-shen 李濟琛
Li Hsien-chou 李仙洲
Li Hsien-nien 李先念
Li Huang 李璜
Li K'o-nung 李克農
Li Kung-p'u 李公樸
Li Li-san 李立三
Li Ta-chao 李大釗
Li Tsung-jen 李宗仁
Li Wei-han 李維漢
Li Yin-feng 李蔭楓
Liang Ch'i-ch'ao 梁啟超
Liang Hua-chih 梁化之
Liang Sou-ming 梁漱溟
Liang Tun-hou 梁敦厚
Liang Yuan-p'ing 梁遠平
Liao Ch'eng-chih 廖承志
Liao Chung-k'ai 廖仲愷
Lin Piao 林彪
Lin Po-ch'ü (pseudonym of Lin Tsu-han) 林伯渠
Lin Tsu-han 林祖涵
Lin Yü-ying 林毓英
Liu Chih-tan 劉志丹
Liu Ch'un 劉春
Liu Jen-ching 劉仁靜
Liu Ko-p'ing 劉格平
Liu Shao-ch'i 劉少奇
Liu Shu-chou 劉述周
Liu Ting 劉鼎
Liu Ya-tzu 柳亞子
Lo Fu (pseud. of Chang Wen-t'ien) 洛甫
Lo Lung-chi 羅隆基
Lo Pin-chi 駱賓基
Lung Yun 龍雲
Ma Hsü-lun 馬叙倫
Mao Tse-tung 毛澤東
Miao Chien-ch'iu 苗劍秋
Nan Han-chen 南漢宸

Ni Ssu 尼司
Nieh Jung-chen 聶榮臻
Niu P'ei-tsung 牛佩琮
Pai Ch'ung-hsi 白崇禧
P'an Han-nien 潘漢年
P'an Tzu-nien 潘梓年
P'an Shu 潘菽
P'eng Chen 彭眞
P'eng Te-huai 彭德懷
P'eng Tse-min 彭澤民
P'ing Chieh-san 平杰三
P'ing Hsin 平心
Po I-po 薄一波
Po-ku (pseud. of Ch'in Pang-hsien) 博古
Sha Ch'ien-li 沙千里
Shao Han-ch'i 邵翰啟
Shao Li-tzu 邵力子
Shen Chün-ju 沈鈞儒
Shen Chien 申健
Shih Liang 史良
Su Chao-cheng 蘇兆徵
Sun Ch'i-meng 孫啟孟
Sun Ch'u 孫楚
Sun Fo 孫科
Sun Ming-chiu 孫銘九
Sun Wen (Sun Yat-sen) 孫文
Sun Yat-sen 孫逸仙
Sung (Soong) Ch'ing-ling 宋慶齡
Sung Shao-wen 宋劭文
Sung Tzu-wen (T. V. Soong) 宋子文
T'an P'ing-shan 譚平山
T'ang En-po 唐恩伯
T'ang Sheng-chih 唐生智
T'ao Hsing-chih 陶行志
Teng Ch'u-min 鄧初民
Teng Chung-hsia 鄧中夏
Teng Fa 鄧發
Teng Pi-wu 鄧必武
Teng Yen-ta 鄧演達
Teng Ying-ch'ao 鄧穎超
Ting Shih-min 丁石民
Ts'ai Ho-sen 蔡和森
Ts'ai T'ing-k'ai 蔡廷鍇
Tseng Chao-lun 曾昭倫
Tseng Ch'i 曾琦
Tseng Yang-fu 曾養甫
Tso Shun-sheng 左舜生
Tsou T'ao-fen 鄒韜奮
Wan I 萬毅
Wan Fu-lin 萬福林
Wang Chien-min 王健民
Wang Ching-kuo 王靖國
Wang Ching-wei 汪精衛
Wang Chung-hsü 王仲虛
Wang Erh-te 王爾得
Wang Feng 汪鋒
Wang Jo-fei 王若飛
Wang Ming (pseud. of Ch'en Shao-yü) 王明
Wang Ping-nan 王炳南
Wang Ta-chung 王大中
Wang Tsao-shih 王造時
Wei Li-huang 衛立煌
Wen I-to 聞一多
Wu P'ei-fu 吳佩孚
Wu T'ieh-ch'eng 吳鐵城
Wu Yü-chang 吳玉章
Yang Hu-ch'eng 楊虎城
Yeh Chien-ying 葉劍英
Yen Hsi-shan 閻錫山
Yen Yang-ch'u (James Y. C. Yen) 晏陽初
Yuan Shih-k'ai 袁世凱
Yun Tai-ying 惲代英
Yü Ch'i 于琪
Yü Hsüeh-chung 于學忠
Yü I-fu 于毅夫

Index